ENDING ZERO TOLERANCE

ENDING ZERO TOLERANCE

THE CRISIS OF ABSOLUTE SCHOOL DISCIPLINE

DEREK W. BLACK

NEW YORK UNIVERSITY PRESS

New York

NEW YORK UNIVERSITY PRESS
New York
www.nyupress.org

First published in paperback in 2018

References to Internet websites (URLs) were accurate at the time of writing.
Neither the author nor New York University Press is responsible for URLs
that may have expired or changed since the manuscript was prepared.

ISBN: 978-1-4798-7702-7 [hb]

ISBN: 978-1-4798-8233-5 [pb]

For Library of Congress Cataloging-in-Publication data,
please contact the Library of Congress.

New York University Press books are printed on acid-free paper,
and their binding materials are chosen for strength and durability.
We strive to use environmentally responsible suppliers and materials
to the greatest extent possible in publishing our books.

Manufactured in the United States of America

10 9 8 7 6 5 4 3 2 1

Also available as an ebook

In memory of my grandfather William Franklin Bunch,

who taught me most of what I know of fairness,

forgiveness, understanding, and love

CONTENTS

ACKNOWLEDGMENTS

At its genesis, this book began as no more than an idea for a law-review article. Thomas Crocker and Josie Brown helped me more fully develop the initial logic of that original idea. The net result was a draft rich in detail and thought but one with a scope too broad for a law-review article. Ned Snow, Benjamin Means, and Colin Miller helped me refine it. The refined, shorter article was published as "The Constitutional Limits of Zero Tolerance in Schools," *Minnesota Law Review* 99, no. 3 (2015): 823–904. The members of the law-review staff were impressive in their hard work and conscientiousness. They added several improvements along the way. Another, later article, "Reforming School Discipline," *Northwestern University Law Review* 111 (2016), provided the foundation for chapters 6 and 7 in the book.

The final decision to transform my work to a full-length book was not easy. Wadie Said, Joe Seiner, and Marcia Zug offered meaningful advice and encouragement. Upon deciding to write the book, I pursued new theories and facts, some at the urging of my peer reviewers. Abigail Carson, my research assistant, was particularly helpful in detailing the history of educators' approaches to discipline. Candle Westor, assistant director for faculty services, was also tireless in tracking down documents and lower-court materials that exist only in hardcopy on random shelves in the lower reaches of law schools and courthouses.

Once the book took shape, Inge Lewis pored over the manuscript to ensure it would appeal to readers other than just my academic friends and me. She consistently made sentences and phrases easier to digest. Vanessa Byars then ensured that my writing was not riddled with typographical and formatting errors.

As the date of publication approached, Josie Brown was gracious enough to humor my ideas again, looking both at the logic of my arguments and the overall scope of the book. Both she and an anonymous peer reviewer offered insightful improvements to the book.

I am also grateful to NYU Press, Clara Platter, and Constance Grady, who immediately seized on this project and moved it quickly toward production. I know from the experiences of other authors that the path from proposal to production is often far longer and bumpier than authors expect. That was not the case here.

The book could not have been completed without the forbearance and consideration of the University of South Carolina and my family. Robert Wilcox, my dean, and the University of South Carolina granted me a sabbatical for fall 2015 so that I might concentrate on my writing. My family was supportive without fail, as I knew they would be: Claire in appreciating that my sabbatical was in fact devoted to research; Rohan for excitedly discussing fairness, punishment, and good behavior, even when it meant interrupting his absorption with the latest developments in superhero characters and plots; and Malina for understanding when she had reached the limit on her playful use of daddy's computer while he was working.

Finally, I acknowledge a debt to my grandfather William Franklin Bunch, which I could have never fully repaid. Although his formal education ended with high school, he was a learned man and an avid reader. Our home was littered with historical books, encyclopedias, dictionaries, and crossword puzzles. His love of books and words surely generated my own. I had always hoped that there would be a day when I would place a book of my own in his hands, knowing the joy reading it would bring him. That day never came. He passed away on August 28, 2014. Yet only three weeks before he died, I shared with him that my book had been accepted for publication. He responded with keen interest and deep pride.

INTRODUCTION

Over the past two decades, school discipline has grown increasingly harsh and impersonal. Many schools and states are willing to exclude—temporarily and permanently—students for almost any type of behavior. Even when students' behavior poses no real danger to school and involves the type of immature mischief parents expect of normally developing kids, schools dig in their heels and insist that they must banish students. Local communities and policy advocates have pushed back and managed some important successes in recent years, but the seriousness and scope of the problem demands a systematic long-term check. Relying on basic constitutional rights and fairness concepts, this book proposes strategies for developing those checks and argues that courts must reengage on issues of discipline and enforce students' rights. Courts cannot simply abandon students to school boards and the political process. Too often, both schools and politicians have shown themselves to be irrational and willing to sacrifice students in the expedient pursuit of other goals.

This irrationality and the need for change are best captured through the lives of students who experience discipline. On a Monday morning in October 1999 in the outer suburbs of our nation's capital, an average thirteen-year-old boy named Benjamin Ratner received a note from one of his friends. In the note, Benjamin's friend told him that she had felt suicidal over the weekend and had contemplated slitting her wrists with a knife. Apparently, the feelings persisted. She told Benjamin she brought a knife to school that morning in her bookbinder.

Benjamin took the note seriously. He knew his friend had previously attempted suicide and had even been hospitalized to deal with ongoing issues. Benjamin was worried she would use the knife to hurt herself that morning. Benjamin was smart enough to know that a real solution for her long-term well-being was beyond him. He planned to tell both her family and his own about the incident at the end of the school day and let them determine what to do in the coming days and hours. But in the short term, he was not going to leave her safety—and in his mind possibly her life—to chance. So Benjamin asked his friend if he could take the bookbinder from her locker and put it in his own for safekeeping. She agreed.

Within a few hours, Roberta Griffith, the assistant principal, heard rumors that Benjamin's friend "had brought a knife to school and . . . may have given it to [Benjamin]."[1] Griffith alerted the dean of the school, Fanny Kellogg, who called Benjamin to the office to question him. Benjamin told her that he had the binder in his locker, although it is unclear that he had actually seen or touched the knife inside the binder. What was clear, however, was that Kellogg knew that Benjamin did not pose any real threat to himself or others. Kellogg sent Benjamin by himself to get the binder and bring it back to the office. When Benjamin returned, Kellogg acknowledged that Benjamin "acted in what he saw as the girl's best interest and that at no time did Ratner pose a threat to harm anyone with the knife."[2] But from then on, the school system's thoughtfulness ended, and its disciplinary process took over.

The school's policy approach to weapons was zero tolerance. Regardless of the danger Benjamin's friend faced, his desire to protect her, or any other circumstances, his possession of a knife was deemed a violation of school policy. The assistant principal responded to his admittedly good deed by suspending him for ten days. The principal of the school then escalated the situation and referred Benjamin to the superintendent for potential further punishment. Both the superintendent and two different school district hearing panels decided to increase his punishment. No one questioned Benjamin's story, but they all insisted they must suspend him for the remainder of the semester—approximately three months. Benjamin later asked the court system to reverse his punishment as irrational, but no court ever took his case seriously. The courts all claimed their hands were tied.

The irrationality of Benjamin's punishment is not unique. Not only have states taken a zero-tolerance approach to real weapons or drugs, but they have extended the approach to everyday items that a student might have, like a cough drop or fingernail clippers. In some instances, their rationale has appeared to be that everyday items could be used as weapons or for illegitimate purposes. In other instances, the rationale is simply that students must do what they are told or suffer the consequences. A Pennsylvania statute, for instance, directs schools to expel and refer to law enforcement any student who brings a weapon to school. According to the statute, a weapon includes, "but [is] not . . . limited to, any knife, cutting instrument, cutting tool, nunchaku, firearm, shotgun, rifle and any other tool, instrument or implement capable of inflicting serious bodily injury."[3]

Schools in Pennsylvania and other states have taken the concept of items capable of inflicting serious bodily injury to ridiculous extremes. For instance, according to media reports in 2013, a seven-year-old boy brought an ink pen to Hershey Elementary School. Apparently, the pen buzzed or vibrated when touched a certain way, presumably to startle the unsuspecting user. The boy's principal did not see the novelty in the item. She said it was a weapon and suspended him for four days.

Over the past decade, newspapers have been littered with similar stories of so-called weapons. From the craft scissors of elementary students to the fingernail clippers of the hygienically obsessed student to the butter knife of a culinarily exacting student, schools have concluded that students are carrying weapons, sometimes even when those items turn up accidentally in a student's backpack. Schools have taken similarly broad approaches to the meaning of drugs. According to reports, students have been expelled for various everyday over-the-counter medicines that they had brought to school for legitimate reasons.

Some districts take zero tolerance toward weapons even further. They punish students for just thinking or talking about them. Students have been suspended or expelled for drawing pictures of weapons, chewing their Pop-Tarts into the shape of weapons, making gun gestures with their hands on the playground, having squirt guns in their possession, and simply writing stories that included guns or violence in them.

In all fairness, these behaviors could be early warning signs of a troubled student. But more often, they are signs of a playful and normally developing child. Even in those rare instances when the behavior is a warning sign, summarily suspending a student is not an effective way to respond. Yet many schools and states do not distinguish between the normal and troubled child.

Even when schools can tell the difference between these students—which is not always easy—they refuse to do so. Some believe state law prohibits them from making reasonable distinctions. Others believe that making distinctions and exercising judgment are simply bad ideas. Either way, both groups adopt harsh discipline policies and procedures that remove all judgment and wisdom from official policy.

Dustin Seal's experience at Powell High School in Knox County, Tennessee, offers one of the most obvious examples. One evening after school, Dustin left his friends waiting in his car while he went inside his girlfriend's house. While he was gone, one of his friends put a hunting knife in the glove compartment and left it there. The friend had started carrying it—purportedly for self-defense—following an out-of-school altercation with another boy regarding a former girlfriend. When Dustin dropped his friend off later, the friend left the knife in the car. Dustin did not know his friend had put or left the knife in the car.

The next night, Dustin drove his friends to school for a football game and parked in the school parking lot. They were all members of the band and were to perform that night. At some point before the game, some other students told the band director that they had seen Dustin drinking what they believed to be alcohol with one of his friends. The band director questioned Dustin and his friend but released them because he did not smell any alcohol on them. Fifteen minutes later, the assistant principal decided to question them again. He did not find any evidence of alcohol either but decided he would search Dustin's car. The search did not turn up any hint of drinking. It did, however, turn up the knife that had been left in the glove compartment. As with Benjamin Ratner, at that point, judgment and circumstances were cast aside.

School district officials quickly took steps to expel Dustin. They conducted several hearings at the school and district level. Everyone involved—from principals and the hearing officer to each school board member—agreed that they would expel him. At each point, the evidence was straightforward and uncontroverted. The only thing that mattered was that the knife was in Dustin's car. That he and the others involved testified that he did not know it was there was irrelevant. They simply reasoned that the evidence "place[d] the knife in the glove compartment of the car [Dustin] was driving and which he parked on the campus of Powell High School. Possession of a weapon on school property is a violation of Knox County Policy."[4]

Initially, Dustin could do little more than watch the school system process him toward complete exclusion. But by the time Dustin reached the school board, he had secured an attorney, who pushed harder on the district's simplistic reasoning. The attorney emphasized that the evidence showed that Dustin "had no idea that the knife was in his mother's car [on the day in question], or at any other time that the car was on school property."[5] A school board member then directly questioned Dustin on this point, and Dustin reiterated his ignorance of the knife in his car. The school board member's response indicated that he believed Dustin.

> The problem I see is that we always have to be consistent in sending a clear message to students. Two or three years ago we were dealing with guns, guns, guns. Now, it's down to knives, knives, knives and I don't want to send a confusing message. Justin [sic], you are responsible for what's in your car and that's where I'm torn but I would have to say that you have to be held responsible as a driver for what's in your car. And that's a problem that you're going to have to deal with.[6]

The board then voted unanimously to affirm Dustin's expulsion.

In subsequent litigation, the board's position grew even more interesting. Before the Sixth Circuit Court of Appeals, the board asserted that it could and would expel ignorant, or otherwise innocent, students because intent just does not matter under its rules. Shocked at such a bold assertion, one of the judges pressed the board's attorney. The judge asked "whether the Board was seriously arguing that it could expel a student for unconsciously possessing a dangerous weapon." The judge "pos[ed] a hypothetical example involving a high-school valedictorian who has a knife planted in his backpack without his knowledge by a vindictive student." The judge asked "whether the valedictorian would still be subject to mandatory expulsion under the Board's Zero Tolerance Policy, even if the school administrators and the Board members uniformly believed the valedictorian's explanation that the knife had been planted." The board's attorney still responded yes. "After all, counsel argued, the Board's policy requires 'Zero Tolerance,' and the policy does not explicitly say that the student must know he is carrying a weapon."[7] Dustin ultimately won his appeal, but only by a two-to-one vote. Moreover, his victory stands largely as an outlier among various other courts that have affirmed districts expelling students under similar circumstances.

Zero-tolerance and harsh-discipline responses like these to so-called weapons and drugs reveal a problematic mind-set that undermines rational decision making. The districts and states that adopt these policies never seriously grapple with the goals they are trying to achieve and whether their policies are necessary, much less effective. Rule making and unflinching adherence to rules—regardless of whether the rule and punishment make sense—become ends in and of themselves. States and schools never stop to question whether elementary school students using scissors as real weapons are but remote possibilities or viable threats around which to build a rule. Nor do they stop to seriously examine whether rules for the sake of rules actually make schools safer and improve student behavior instead of simply producing more school exclusions. Most often, these policies are assertions of power that few schools and states have ever seriously questioned. In this respect, they are attempts by states and schools to delude themselves—or the public—into believing they are creating more orderly environments. The truth is that they are often doing the opposite.

If zero tolerance and harsh discipline stopped at drugs and weapons, one might write them off as sensational random acts rather than problems that systematically undermine education. Yet, of all the suspensions and expulsions handed out each year, less than 10 percent are for serious misbehavior like weapons or drugs.[8] It is probably fair to assume that most teachers overlook scissors, send warning notes home to the parent, and do not even appreciate that a buzzing pen is a potential weapon or that a cough drop is a drug of sorts. Thus, the sensational stories that make the news may be random in terms of how often they affect students, but they are, nonetheless, the most poignant examples of how thoughtless and callous overall discipline has become. This overall thoughtlessness is the real problem and leads schools to take harsh approaches, if not zero tolerance, toward typical adolescent behavior.

Many schools do not rationally distinguish between weapons- and drug-related offenses and other simple misbehavior. Once they get comfortable with expelling students for anything that might be drug or weapon related, schools can suspend and expel students for any type of misbehavior. From their perspective, rules are rules. No matter what the rules might be, once the school set them, students are subject to extreme punishment for breaking them.

Until the past two decades, expulsion and suspension were largely reserved for major infractions.[9] Today, schools suspend and expel students for almost anything: truancy, cheating, running in the hall, dress-code violations, foul language, disruption, and disrespect.[10] Just recently, a high school student in Indiana was reportedly expelled for the school year for his adolescent attempt at creative language use on the internet. His goal was to insert "fuck" as many times as possible in a single coherent sentence. His sentence was not directed at anyone, and it was written and published in the middle of the night from his home.[11] While his behavior easily could have warranted a constructive response from his parents and maybe the school, it is hard to fashion a rationale for expelling him, other than that the school had adopted some policy claiming that it could.

Several state statutes encourage this absolutist approach. A South Carolina statute, for instance, provides that, in addition to "crimes and gross misbehavior," a school may expel any student for "persistent disobedience, or for violation of written rules and promulgated regulations established by the district board, county board, or the State Board of Education."[12] In other words, schools can suspend and expel students for anything. A Mississippi statute makes this even clearer, setting a precise low bar for expelling students for routine misbehavior. The statute labels students "habitually disruptive" when they "cause disruption in a classroom, on school property or vehicles or at a school-related activity on more than two (2) occasions during a school year." A habitually disruptive student is "subject to expulsion on the occurrence of the third act of disruptive behavior during a school year."[13] In other words, when kids do the kinds of things that kids do at school, they can be suspended or expelled. Even worse, statutes like Mississippi's all but indicate that this is what school districts should do.

The migration of this harsh mind-set from drugs and weapons toward all student misbehavior threatens the basic functioning of the entire education system. Over the past three decades, suspension and expulsion rates in schools have doubled.[14] As of today, more than 10 percent of middle and high school students are suspended or expelled every year, not because their behavior is worse than their parents but because almost anything they do is misbehavior that can be severely punished. Whether a student's misbehavior is serious, trivial, intentional, or accidental, the response in many districts is the same: exclusion from school.

As a result, suspensions, expulsions, and discipline in general are entirely out of control and threaten the very educational mission of many schools and districts. Some schools suspend one out of every two students over the course of each school year.[15] In our nation's capital in 2011–12, the public middle schools system suspended more than one out of three students at least once that year. Many of these students were suspended multiple times. The total number of suspensions in some schools exceeded the total number of enrolled students. The suspension rates in a few District of Columbia middle schools were so high that they look like errors. Jefferson Middle School, Shaw Middle School, and Johnson Middle School suspended 72 percent, 70 percent, and 67 percent of their students, respectively. Shaw enrolled only 169 students but handed out 397 suspensions. This amounts to 2.35 suspensions per student.[16]

Suspension and expulsion rates, however, tell only part of the story. A single suspension will have reciprocal effects on later exclusions, juvenile justice, academic attainment, and employment for a student. Roughly 40 percent of the student suspensions in any given school year are multiple suspensions.[17] A 2011 study of Texas schools showed that students who were suspended or expelled just once during middle or high school were subsequently suspended or expelled, on median, three more times.[18] One might assume that these are just the troublemakers and that multiple suspensions are the natural result of their personal predisposition. But careful long-term studies show this is not the case. The act of suspending a student, particularly for relatively minor behavior, makes that student more likely to be suspended again. For some students, the very fact that they have been suspended makes them more likely to engage in more troublesome behavior. For others, the suspension labels them in the eyes of peers and school officials. The result is that the school is then more likely to suspend them when it otherwise would have dealt with the behavior constructively or ignored it altogether.

Linda Raffaele Mendez attempted to examine this phenomenon more closely by tracking students who entered kindergarten and following them all the way through the final year of high school. She found that the greatest predictor for being suspended was not a student's socio-economic status, special education status, educational achievement, or even teachers' prior assessment of the student's behavior. The greatest predictor was having been suspended once before. She also found that "frequent use of suspension has no measurable positive deterrent or academic benefit to either the students who are suspended or to non-suspended students. [To the contrary], disciplining elementary and middle school students with out-of-school suspension predicts future suspensions and contributes to students' poor academic performance and failing to graduate on time."[19]

Other studies confirm these findings and further tease out the reciprocal effects of suspension. After suspension, the student sees him- or herself differently, as does the school, but the question is why. The answer lies in psychology, symbolism, and social bonds. To the extent a student's school was once a refuge, it loses that status in the student's mind. To the extent the student was once a member of the community, whom the school felt the need to help, the student loses that status. In effect, both the school and the student experience a psychological break from each other. The student sees the school as hostile toward him or her, and the school abandons the idea of the student as a work in progress in exchange for the belief that the student is an unredeemable bad apple. These changed perceptions predictably lead to additional misbehavior by the student and harsh institutional responses by the school. Of course, this is not the case for all students and schools, but on average, these trends hold true.

These repeat suspensions produce serious academic consequences. A 2012 study of two hundred thousand high school freshmen in Florida found that the dropout rate for students who were not suspended during their freshman year was 16 percent, but a single suspension during their freshman year corresponded with a doubling of the dropout rate to 32 percent. A second suspension drove the dropout rate to 42 percent. Being suspended appeared to have a stronger effect on dropout and graduation rates than actually failing a course, even though the latter presents a formal impediment to graduation. Those who failed a course still graduated at 66 percent, but those who were suspended just once graduated only 52 percent of the time. Those who failed two courses in a single year still had a more than 50 percent chance at graduation, whereas only one out of three students graduated if they were suspended twice.[20]

Dropping out of school then leads to negative employment and criminal justice outcomes. Dropouts have a 40 percent higher unemployment rate than graduates, earn about half the income as those who graduate, and experience poverty at twice the rate as graduates. A significant percentage of dropouts are also subsequently incarcerated.[21] The path from suspension to unemployment and prison is not set in stone, but the odds are significant. An entire body of scholarship and advocacy has arisen around what is called a "school-to-prison pipeline." Various studies document how the school discipline system has morphed from one that dealt with student misbehavior internally to one that funnels students into the criminal justice system.

School exclusion itself makes students more likely to engage in subsequent behavior that will land them in jail, but schools are also pushing students in that direction by formally referring students to the juvenile justice system for relatively minor misbehavior.[22] Secretary of Education Arne Duncan explained of his time leading the Chicago Public Schools, "our schools . . . were calling the police to have our kids arrested and I had no idea." Then he found that "about 7 percent of our schools were producing about 50 percent of the arrests. . . . The school to prison pipeline is real."[23] In some states, more than 10 percent of students will be referred to the juvenile justice system each year.

Decades ago, when scholars were just beginning to understand these trends, the Fifth Circuit Court of Appeals aptly labeled suspensions and expulsions for what they are: educational death penalties. The court wrote, "A sentence of banishment from the local educational system is, insofar as the institution has power to act, the extreme penalty, the ultimate punishment. In our increasingly technological society, getting at least a high school education is almost necessary for survival. Stripping a child of access to educational opportunity is a life sentence to second-rate citizenship."[24] For that reason, no school should ever lightly adopt a policy that mandates or incentivizes school exclusion as a general principal, nor should school officials ever reach the final decision to exclude a particular student without considering all the circumstances and options.

School discipline, however, cannot solely be understood as a function of irrational or shortsighted educational and social policy. Problematic discipline policies intersect with equally problematic racial biases and structural inequalities. African American, Latino, poor, and disabled students are punished at much higher rates than white students are. This inequality starts at the very earliest levels of school and proceeds through high school.

In elementary school, while only 1.6 percent of white students are suspended each year, more than 7 percent of African Americans are suspended. In other words, African American elementary school students are nearly five times as likely to be suspended as whites. In high school, the suspension rates jump for everyone. The suspension rate for whites is 6.7 percent—which ironically still makes an African American student in elementary school more at risk of suspension than a white student in high school. The African American suspension rate is 23.2 percent in high school, more than three times the rate of white high school students. The suspension rate of Latinos, Native Americans, and English-Language Learners are all nearly twice the rate of whites.[25]

These racial disparities in discipline are not new. In the 1970s, when the Office for Civil Rights first began tracking discipline, the data showed that African Americans were suspended at two to three times the rate of whites. The initial theory was that discriminatory discipline became a means by which many schools managed, if not resisted, school desegregation. If white schools could not keep African Americans from entering, they could still try to treat African Americans differently, including kicking out enough to keep the remaining students "in their place."

While outright bias and resistance have significantly dissipated, the passage of time alone has not healed these wounds. Explicit bias has become implicit bias. De jure segregation and inequality, while significantly reduced between 1970 and the late 1980s, have returned as de facto segregation and inequality. Bias, segregation, and inequality now intersect with generally bad ideas about discipline to make matters worse.

Zero tolerance, ironically, was proposed by some advocates as a cure to certain biases and disparities in the discipline system. They would remove discretion from discipline by making certain punishments mandatory. Without discretion, racial bias would lack an obvious entry point into disciplinary decisions, and racial disparities might plummet. In other words, if all students involved in fights are automatically suspended, schools would necessarily treat students equally, even if suspensions went up.

Advocates, however, misjudged where the discriminatory discretion was occurring. It was primarily in the classroom, not the principal's office. Teachers send African Americans to the office at much different rates than they send whites, even when the students engage in similar behavior.[26] Zero tolerance prevents principals from second-guessing teachers and sending students back to class. Even if a principal believes school exclusion is inappropriate in a given case, zero-tolerance policies can require the principal to suspend anyone who lands in his or her office. Thus, the primary effect of zero tolerance has been to amplify discrimination rather than reduce it. Teachers retain the discretion to discriminate, and zero-tolerance policies force principals to perpetuate it. For this reason, it should come as no surprise that racial disparities in suspensions have increased in many places since 1970.

These discipline disparities, in no small part, also contribute to a lingering achievement gap between African Americans and whites. With African Americans disproportionately removed from the learning environment, they are necessarily academically disadvantaged. As the Harvard Civil Rights Project bluntly puts it, "we will close the racial achievement gap only when we also address the school discipline gap."[27] But some reports indicate that the achievement gap may also have reciprocal effects on discipline. In effect, high-stakes testing policies have created an incentive for schools to exclude students on the bottom of the achievement gap. With schools under intense pressure to increase overall student achievement, a low-achieving student who also exhibits mild to moderate levels of misbehavior could be become an immediate target for exclusion.

One researcher found specific evidence that, after the passage of the No Child Left Behind Act, some schools "reduced their suspension penalties for higher-achievers in high-stakes grades (grades four, five, eight, and ten) during the testing window, [and] they raised their suspension penalties for lower-achievers in these same grades at this time."[28] A decade into the high-stakes testing regime of No Child Left Behind, the Advancement Project concluded that "both the use of high-stakes tests and the severity of the consequences attached to them have risen dramatically, leading to a rapidly dwindling set of opportunities for students who do not score well on these exams."[29] In short, the interaction between high-stakes testing and harsh school discipline creates perverse incentives.

Whatever the results for individual students or students in particular demographic groups, however, some educators would say suspensions and expulsions protect other students and ensure their academic opportunities. While unfortunate, high suspension rates, negative life outcomes, and racial disparities are necessary evils. This reasoning has intuitive appeal, which helps explain why harsh discipline persists. The problem is that the facts do not support the argument.

Report after report demonstrates that high suspension rates and harsh discipline do not deter misbehavior, keep the environment orderly, or make schools safer.[30] If they did, student exclusions would have fallen over time. The initial shock and awe of zero tolerance might have caused an initial surge in suspensions, but if zero-tolerance theory were correct, students would have adjusted their behavior accordingly. Instead, school exclusions steadily increased over the past decades. Moreover, by point of comparison, criminal behavior by young people fell during roughly the same period that suspensions and expulsions were rising. Young people were able to control their behavior outside school, where supervision and the chances of repercussions were diminished, but unable to do so in school, where the boundary lines of misbehavior and the assurance of punishment were clear.

The explanation is twofold. First, zero tolerance and harsh discipline treat normal and generally unavoidable student indiscretions as serious misbehavior, while juvenile justice, with all its flaws, makes relevant distinctions in student behavior at least some of the time. Second, harsh discipline actually provokes more misbehavior than would otherwise exist. As noted earlier, for the disciplined student, there is a break from the school that leads to disengagement and increases the likelihood of future misbehavior. But overly harsh discipline toward one student or group of students also negatively affects the rest of the student population.

Studies show that students who attend schools with higher rates of suspension and expulsion perceive their environment to be less safe and more chaotic.[31] This perception is an outgrowth not of higher rates of violence and misbehavior alone but of the harsh response to that behavior. Likewise, when comparing apples to apples, the quality of education in a school tends to go down, not up, with the increased use of suspension and expulsion. Poverty, race, and school type all correlate with school-wide achievement and suspension rates, but after accounting for those demographic and school-level factors, studies still show that "a school's out-of-school suspension rate predict[s] a unique amount of the variance in achievement scores."[32] Moreover, the variance they predict is a "relatively high amount."[33]

Brea Perry and Edward Morris explain that "high levels of out-of-school suspension . . . are associated with declining academic achievement among non-suspended students, even after adjusting for a school's overall level of violence and disorganization[, because] . . . the threat and constancy of punishment permeates highly punitive environments, hindering the academic performance of otherwise well-behaved students."[34] The routine imposition of harsh punishment infects the overall social and cultural makeup of a school. The results are "social psychological outcomes that endure well after the punishment itself, and well beyond the individual who is punished, interacting with behavior to shape meanings, perceptions, and actions."[35] The psychological effects include a destabilization of students' and teachers' sense of community and an increase in the anxiety and distrust that students feel when they are in school. Perry and Morris bluntly characterize such environments as "toxic."

In addition to decreasing the student body's overall academic achievement, these dysfunctional environments also make it more likely that otherwise well-behaved students will misbehave. In examining student surveys and discipline data, Richard Arum found that, while the average student can and does respect discipline and order, when discipline becomes too strict, students perceive the imposition of punishment as random and unfair.[36] When this occurs, Arum indicates that schools lose the moral authority that is key to maintaining a positive learning environment. Perry and Morris similarly find that students fall victim to "legal cynicism." Even students "who hew to rules themselves" come to perceive school authority as "illegitimate."[37] At some point, even good students begin to rebel against harsh discipline. For other students who already face personal and academic challenges, misbehavior becomes all the more likely.[38] In short, routinely suspending so-called bad apples does not, as many schools assume, protect the peers who remain behind. Too often, it makes matters worse because it ignores the underlying shortcomings in the school environment itself.

Over the past decade, social science evidence, like that just cited, has made such an overwhelming case against zero tolerance and harsh discipline that small shifts in discipline policy have begun to occur. A number of major urban school districts have recently taken formal steps to limit zero tolerance and the school-house-to-jail-house pipeline. Suspensions, expulsions, and the educational environment had grown so problematic in these districts that they finally realized they could no longer hope to meet the educational needs of their students and communities without change. Between 2013 and 2014, Chicago, Los Angeles, New York City, and Nashville all joined the Positive and Safe Schools Advancing Greater Equity Initiative, the purpose of which is to help school districts shift their approach to discipline and adopt positive behavioral interventions rather than punitive responses.

Initial reports suggest these voluntary steps are paying immediate dividends. In Chicago, for instance, suspensions for African Americans have already declined, and "students and teachers report feeling safer as harsh discipline practices have eased."[39] In Denver, which was one of the first districts to shift its approach to discipline, suspensions and expulsions were cut in half over the course of several years.[40] And a few select states, like California and Massachusetts, have passed legislation to mitigate the most egregious policies.[41] The most recent data coming out of California indicates a modest but meaningful decline in statewide suspensions.

Spurred, in part, by these local initiatives, the federal government has begun showing leadership on discipline policy. President Obama started the My Brother's Keeper initiative, which incorporated some of these discipline concerns under its broader mission to increase life opportunities for African American males. The initiative has helped highlight and expand existing coalitions to reform school discipline. Most important, however, may be the efforts by the U.S. Departments of Justice and Education to encourage more states and districts to reduce racial disparities and move away from punitive discipline. In January 2014, the departments released official policy guidance on the administration of discipline that lays out the social science justifications for limiting harsh discipline and adopting positive behavioral supports. The guidance also indicated that the departments will intervene and force change when racial disparities in discipline are unjustifiable or reveal racial bias. The

Department of Education, true to its word, has intervened in several districts since then.

This book applauds these efforts but reasons that these policy efforts will not completely resolve the discipline crisis. This is not to suggest that these policies are all inherently flawed. Many are well intentioned and producing real results. These policies, however, remain few and far between in comparison to punitive discipline. They also remain limited in scope. Neither states nor the federal government have taken steps to address the fundamental flaws driving problematic disciplinary practices. And even if more comprehensive policies become more prevalent, serious discipline problems will linger in far too many places and destroy the futures of far too many students. This is to say nothing of the more than three million students whom schools continue to exclude each year right now. The promise of future policy changes will do nothing to salvage their educational careers and life opportunities.

This book's principal argument is that constitutional protections are the only absolute check on abuses in school discipline. Without that check, students are left subject to the political whims of local majorities, which initially took hold, in part, because courts were reluctant to enforce students' rights. This book lays out the case for courts to reengage in school discipline, enforce students' rights, and support broader reforms.

Forty years ago, the U.S. Supreme Court in *Goss v. Lopez*[42] held that students are entitled to due process prior to exclusion from school. While due process requires that schools afford students notice of what they have done wrong, a chance to respond, and rules and punishments that are fundamentally fair, federal and state courts have refused to seriously evaluate or intervene in discipline out of deference to schools. A period of judicial disengagement began shortly after *Goss* and has never been corrected. As a result, irrational and biased discipline policies and practices have been able to flourish, sometimes with the explicit blessing of courts. Benjamin Ratner, for instance, challenged his expulsion before the federal district court, the Fourth Circuit Court of Appeals, and the U.S. Supreme Court. Never once did he get a serious and transparent response from the courts. Each step of the way, the courts summarily indicated that there was nothing they could or would do to help.

Under both federal and state law, these courts are wrong. First, schools' constitutional obligations in discipline reach beyond simply affording procedural due process to students. Most schools have grown adept at providing students with notice of discipline rules, notice of students' violation of a rule, and a chance to tell their side of the story. What schools have not done is justify the rules they are adopting or the punishments they hand out. Substantive due process demands that these rules and punishments be rational. It also places certain administrative shortcuts in discipline off-limits, like presuming guilt, ignoring the circumstances surrounding misbehavior, and exacting enormous consequences for relatively innocent behavior. Yet, with the exception of just a few, federal courts have not considered these substantive due process principles. If they did, courts would be compelled to place limits on the most egregious applications of zero tolerance and harsh discipline.

Second, during the same period that federal courts were disengaging on issues of discipline, state supreme courts in most states were developing a rich body of precedent that recognizes education as a constitutional or fundamental right under state law. Those cases obligate states to deliver adequate and equal education opportunities. These holdings are doctrinal game changers. In states with positive holdings on these points, suspensions and expulsions raise serious questions regarding states' authority and responsibilities in discipline. For the individual student, the existence of a constitutional right to education would presumptively trigger heightened judicial scrutiny of suspension and expulsion. Under heightened scrutiny, schools could not justify much of the discipline they mete out for minor misbehavior.

For the student body as a whole, this precedent also implicates the negative effect that harsh discipline has on the educational environment and overall academic achievement in a school. In those schools that researchers would characterize as having toxic environments, flawed discipline policies and practices are a substantial cause of the unequal and inadequate educational opportunities that students in these schools receive. As such, the state is obligated to intervene and reform discipline in these schools. No state court, however, has directly considered the connections between a state's constitutional duty in education, discipline policy, and school-wide educational opportunity. Only a few have considered the implications for individual students who are deprived of education altogether. The time is now to pursue both issues.

Yet, whatever the merits of these claims, civil rights advocates might question placing faith in courts to help reform discipline. As Erwin Chemerinsky wrote in his recent critique of the U.S. Supreme Court, "The Court has frequently failed, throughout American history, at its most important task, at its most important moments. . . . The Supreme Court is not the institution that I once revered. It has rarely lived up to these lofty expectations and far more often has upheld discrimination and even egregious violations of basic liberties."[43] As others have also emphasized, even when courts get it "right," history has shown the limits of courts to reform society. Given these hard truths, why then should we expect anything different with school discipline? The short answer is that discipline is different.

Harsh discipline policies, while currently entrenched as a matter of practice, are not embedded in our social fabric. In fact, they are contrary to many of our basic values, both legal and social. The public is often shocked when it learns of the types of punishment some schools hand out. In this respect, judicial limitations on suspensions and expulsions do not call for a cultural and political revolution in the same way that desegregation and other civil rights movements have. Thus, broad emotional resistance or dismay with judicial intervention is far less likely.

Harsh discipline is not embedded in our constitutional fabric either. Discipline reform does not necessarily require new sweeping opinions by the U.S. Supreme Court that lay out a new theory of discipline. Serious consideration and application of existing legal principles by lower federal courts would be enough to address most problems. State-level strategies, in contrast, would likely require state supreme courts to recognize new approaches to discipline. But over the past four decades, state courts have been far more receptive to education claims. There, the concept of fair and rational education policy is affirmatively embedded in our constitutional fabric. Plaintiffs simply have not asked much of state courts in discipline.

Finally, discipline claims, for the most part, ask relatively little of courts. They do not ask courts to force states to take on vast new obligations, like integrating schools or raising substantial additional revenues. Rather, they principally ask the state to stop doing something: irrationally casting students out of the education system. This is a far easier task for courts and one to which they have historically proven well suited.

The biggest pushback would be from educators, individual judges, and scholars who simply recoil at the notion of judicial involvement as a general principle. They rightfully charge that courts are not the arbiters of good education policy. For them, the answer that courts would be enforcing constitutional rights, not policy, may be unsatisfying. Their policy concerns may never be alleviated, nor need they be in all cases. Courts are the last line of defense for the marginalized. They are also the only institution whose sole mission is the protection and vindication of constitutional rights. If courts will not defend students' rights, no one will. Courts have run from this responsibility for decades in discipline. But when states and schools willingly and consistently cross the boundaries of students' rights, the responsibility for the rule of law—and interventions that accompany it—fall on courts.

Without judicial intervention, irrational and biased school discipline is unlikely to ever fully disappear, whatever policy developments may come in the future. The Supreme Court's holding in 1977 in *Ingraham v. Wright*[44] serves as a sad reminder of this likelihood. In *Ingraham*, the Court held that schools were free to corporally punish students and that schools need not even afford students with any due process prior to paddling them. The Court reached this conclusion notwithstanding the unsettling facts of the case. Speaking of the lead plaintiff, the Court wrote, "Because he was slow to respond to his teacher's instructions, Ingraham was subjected to more than 20 licks with a paddle while being held over a table in the principal's office. The paddling was so severe that he suffered a hematoma requiring medical attention and keeping him out of school for several days."[45] Ingraham's classmate was regularly paddled for "minor infractions. On two occasions he was struck on his arms, once depriving him of the full use of his arm for a week."[46]

The Court offered up the possibility that students could sue the teacher or school under state tort law as the reason why it need not intervene. A close examination of the case, however, reveals that the Court simply thought it unwise for courts to become further involved with discipline—better to let schools and society work it out. In one respect, the Court's faith in schools and society was not misplaced. In the ensuing years, much of society and the education system came to see corporal punishment as barbaric, renaming it as "beating" rather than "paddling." With this changed perspective, the number of districts and states that authorized corporal punishment sharply declined. By 2014, over half of the states prohibited corporal punishment in schools.[47] In those states that still permit corporal punishment, many school districts or schools prohibit the practice of their own accord. But in another respect, the Court's faith in society and schools was sadly misplaced.

The reality for actual students in many communities remains relatively unchanged since 1977. Twenty-one states still permit corporal punishment, notwithstanding the social science and national consensus against it. The practice holds on the strongest in those places where it has always been the most troubling. Today, every state in the Southeast permits corporal punishment, and many schools there frequently impose it. Alabama, Mississippi, and Texas all paddled more than thirty thousand students in the 2006–7 school year. In Mississippi, 7.5 percent of the student population was paddled each year.[48]

The lesson for school suspensions is simple. Even if a national consensus turns against zero tolerance and harsh discipline, the shift will have little effect on the lives of students in many communities. Only judicially enforced rights can bring justice and fairness to these communities. Even if policy could eventually resolve the problem, courts should not ask students to wait on states and schools to respect their rights. Constitutional rights exist to protect citizens against the whims of local, state, and federal majorities. Each unjustifiably imposed suspension or expulsion is a deprivation of a right that demands a response. Each suspension or expulsion represents a potential educational death sentence and second-class citizenship.

This book lays out its argument for judicial engagement in discipline in two parts across the next seven chapters. Part 1, "The Making of an Educational Crisis," explains how our discipline system reached its current point of crisis and why judicial intervention is necessary. Part 1 includes chapters 1, 2, and 3.

Chapter 1, "From Friends to Enemies," explores schools' historical posture toward discipline, beginning with the traditional notion that schools act as substitute parents during the day and, thus, presumptively in the best interests of students. While that legal concept persists today, the chapter explains how it has become no more than a fiction. Starting in the 1970s, schools' authority as disciplinarians became a vehicle through which to resist desegregation and, even today, continues as a major source of racial bias. The second major triggering events for harsh discipline were the dramatic acts of violence during the 1990s and the societal criminalization of youth. These events led to a zero-tolerance approach to discipline that conceptualized students as threats and adversaries. Only with this shift in mentality can states and schools rationalize their current punitive approach in discipline.

Chapter 2, "Judicial Disengagement," details courts' past involvement in school discipline, beginning with an analysis of *Goss v. Lopez*'s reasoning for why schools must provide students with due process. The opinion in *Goss*, however, left several important questions open—questions that the Court failed to ever revisit in subsequent decisions. This left lower courts with relatively little guidance. Their response was to disengage from serious adjudication of discipline cases. Over time, the problem has become so pronounced that courts today offer almost no reasoning in dismissing student claims. They simply state that it is not their role to evaluate school discipline. The message to schools is clear: they can punish students however they wish and under any circumstances, so long as they go through the motions of holding some minimal hearing.

Chapter 3, "The Insufficiency of Policy Reform: New Research, New Reforms, Same Old Problems," offers an overview of the most important recent developments in social science and policy, pointing out meaningful lessons and progress in each. But the chapter turns to the limits of current policy and details the extent to which these policies fail to alter the status quo. The school-to-prison pipeline remains alive and well in most places. The chapter closes with a discussion of why courts must intervene.

Part 2 of the book, "Courts' Role in Ending the Crisis," identifies the constitutional rights at stake in school discipline and the legal theories by which to protect them. Part 2 includes chapters 4, 5, 6, and 7. Chapter 4, "Making Discipline Rational," puts forward the affirmative argument for applying substantive due process concepts to school discipline. It begins by debunking the pervasive notion that courts' review of discipline is limited to whether the school offered a student a due process hearing. It then identifies the substantive due process principles that give courts the authority to act as a substantive check on discipline. In particular, basic rationality demands that schools make certain distinctions between students and take certain circumstances into account. Otherwise, schools breach foundational concepts of due process by handing out arbitrary punishments, punishing normatively innocent students, and presuming facts that may not exist.

Chapter 5, "Individualizing Discipline," articulates the specific individualized factors schools must consider to make rational discipline rules and decisions. First, schools must consider intent. While exceptions to intent requirements exist in a few contexts, those exceptions are narrow and school discipline does not fit within them. Second, schools must consider students' culpability and the harm their conduct poses. Both the seriousness of the conduct and blameworthiness of the individual are predicate justifications for imposing punishment. For instance, in criminal cases, the Supreme Court has consistently recognized that minors, as a class, have diminished capacity and culpability. This makes extreme punishments for minors inappropriate even for serious crimes. Outside the criminal context, the Court has also limited harsh civil consequences for otherwise minor transgressions. Those same principles apply with added force to school discipline. The behavior for which students are most often suspended is minor in terms of harm. Likewise, students' blameworthiness and culpability are minimal, as they are often engaging in normal adolescent behavior that schools should expect. In fact, it is beyond many students' capacity to comply with certain rules every minute of the day.

Chapter 6, "The Constitutional Right to Education: Can the State Justify Taking It Away?," examines whether the rights and principles established through school finance and quality litigation place limits on school discipline. The most obvious limitation would be based on the notion that those cases establish a constitutional or fundamental right to education. If so, taking that right away through suspension or expulsion triggers heightened scrutiny. Only a few state supreme courts have considered this theory, and they appeared uncertain of how to resolve the tension between the right to education and schools' discretion in imposing discipline. Thus, most of the few courts to take up the issue have decided the cases on alternative grounds. This chapter evaluates those cases and provides the framework for deciding the central questions they avoided. Under the appropriate framework, schools would not be able to justify long-term suspension for relatively minor misbehavior.

Chapter 7, "Ensuring Quality Education through Discipline: Fixing Dysfunctional School Environments," also draws on school finance and quality litigation. But rather than focusing on an individual student's right to education, the chapter focuses on the key doctrine from past litigation: states have a duty to ensure adequate and equal educational opportunities. Cutting-edge social science studies demonstrate that discipline and the educational climate in schools play enormous roles in academic outcomes not just for the disciplined student but for the entire school. Thus, like inadequate funding or teacher quality, dysfunctional discipline policy prevents students from receiving adequate and equal educational opportunities. On this basis, states should be obligated to closely monitor discipline practices and, when necessary, intervene with remedies in dysfunctional schools.

The book concludes with a chapter that offers a holistic evaluation of the claims raised in chapters 4 through 7 and proposes a strategic approach for litigating them. It then explains how these litigation strategies might be integrated with research and policy agendas to finally end zero tolerance and harsh discipline.

PART I

THE MAKING OF AN EDUCATIONAL CRISIS

FROM FRIENDS TO ENEMIES

Today, courts and society continue to repeat the mantra that schools are owed deference in administering discipline. This idea is grounded in the notion that discipline is a teaching tool and schools act in students' best interests in administering it. While these notions may have been accurate for much of our nation's history, in many instances, they no longer are. The past half century has produced a complete transformation of the relationship between students and their schools. This transformation explains why we have arrived at the current crisis in discipline. Courts' failure to acknowledge this transformation, likewise, helps explain why courts have refused to intervene as the crisis unfolded right before them. The following sections briefly trace this historical transformation.

Benevolent Disciplinarians

Traditionally, parents' right to discipline and control their children without the interference of the state and judiciary has gone without question. Schools' disciplinary authority and courts' deference toward schools in the exercise of discipline stem from the idea that schools act in the place of parents during the day. In other words, they are substitute or quasi-parents. As such, the law and society presume that schools act with the best interests of students in mind. In addition, discipline itself is a form of education that schools are particularly well suited to deliver.

This theory of school disciplinary authority also has deep historical roots, dating back to English common law. Tort law in England first articulated the concept as "in loco parentis," which in Latin means "in the place of a parent." When parents turn their children over to schools, principals and teachers become the temporary guardians and caretakers of the children. This legal relationship creates both duties and discretion for school officials. In terms of duties, schools, like parents, should supervise, care for, and educate students during the day. But with these soft duties come the far more legally important discretion and immunity that a parent would enjoy in carrying out these duties.

Unlike any other state or private actor who might interact with children, the concept of in loco parentis shields schools from almost all legal liability. Citing the concept, courts have traditionally refused to second-guess how schools supervise and discipline students, even when parents themselves seek to challenge how their children were treated during the school day. Because parents are said to have delegated their authority to schools during the day, they cannot complain about the exercise of that authority, save for the most egregious circumstances imaginable. Gordon Gee and David Sperry offer a less technical explanation: "This legal fiction was initially necessary to protect teachers in their relationship with students, and to give parameters and certainty to the powers that teachers could wield over students."[1]

One of the most notable early applications of in loco parentis in the United States was in *State v. Pendergrass*[2] in 1837. The case involved a North Carolina schoolmaster who had whipped a six- or seven-year-old girl with a switch and left marks on her body. The schoolmaster also hit the girl with what the court characterized as a "larger instrument." That larger instrument left marks and bruises on her arm and her neck. The state brought criminal charges against the schoolmaster, and a jury convicted him of assault and battery.

The North Carolina Supreme Court, however, reversed on appeal. It held that the law grants schoolmasters and teachers a power to correct students "analogous to that which belongs to parents, and the authority of the teacher is regarded as a delegation of parental authority."[3] The court emphasized that the discharge of this authority is a "sacred dut[y]" necessary to ensure that children become "useful and virtuous members of society." Moreover, "this duty cannot be effectually performed without the ability to command obedience, to control stubbornness, to quicken diligence, and to reform bad habits; and to enable him to exercise this salutary sway, he is armed with the power to administer moderate correction, when he shall believe it to be just and necessary."[4] Only immoderate punishment—which the court defined as disfigurement or serious permanent injury to life, limbs, or health—might go beyond the school's authority.[5] And the court expressed no interest in closely policing the line between moderate and immoderate punishment, writing that punishment, in its various forms, is "necessary for the reformation of the child" and benefits the student in the long run.[6]

Conceptualizing discipline as beneficial to the child, the court reasoned that schools, not judges, are best suited to determine appropriate punishment. The schoolmaster "is the judge when correction is required, and of the degree of correction necessary; and like all others intrusted with a discretion, he cannot be made penally responsible for error of judgment, but only for wickedness of purpose.... His judgment must be *presumed* correct, because he is the judge."[7] Only the schoolmaster knows the details of the student's past and present behavior and character and whether prior milder correction has been effective.[8] No matter "how[] severe the pain inflicted" or how "disproportionate to the alleged negligence or offence of so young and tender a child" the punishment might seem,[9] the court held that school officials were immune from suit, save those instances when they "grossly abuse" their powers and act with malice to cause lasting injury.

This concept of school authority and presumptive benevolence dominated both state and federal law for the next century and a half. The Supreme Court summarized that history in upholding schools' authority to corporally punish students in 1977. It wrote,

At common law a single principle has governed the use of corporal punishment since before the American Revolution: Teachers may impose reasonable but not excessive force to discipline a child. Blackstone[, for instance,] . . . did not regard it a "corporal insult" for a teacher to inflict "moderate correction" on a child in his care. To the extent that force was "necessary to answer the purposes for which (the teacher) is employed," Blackstone viewed it as "justifiable or lawful." The basic doctrine has not changed. The prevalent rule in this country today privileges such force as a teacher or administrator "reasonably believes to be necessary for (the child's) proper control, training, or education." To the extent that the force is excessive or unreasonable, the educator in virtually all States is subject to possible civil and criminal liability.[10]

Starting in the 1970s, however, historical events began to prove false the theory of schools as benevolent parental figures acting in the best interests of students, even when they punish them. The first series of events related to school desegregation and the high rates of discipline that followed for African American students in integrated schools. Data, reports, and personal stories all suggested that some school officials were misusing their discretion, sometimes for ulterior purposes. Some were summarily suspending and expelling students with little or no thought. Others were doing so for discriminatory reasons.

Discipline as Resistance to Desegregation

In 1954, in *Brown v. Board of Education*, the Supreme Court declared school segregation unconstitutional. The political resistance to the holding was swift and fierce. For the next ten years, the resistance was sufficiently powerful to prevent school integration in all but the rarest of circumstances. By 1964, only about 1 percent of African American students had enrolled in integrated schools. Not until the late 1960s and early 1970s did school desegregation begin in earnest in most places. By then, Congress had passed the Civil Rights Act of 1964, prohibiting discrimination in federally funded programs. And, in 1968, in *Green v. County School Board of New Kent*, the Court held that the time for "all deliberate speed" in desegregating schools had come to an end.

Together, the Court and Congress made it clear that integration could not be stopped. As the Court ordered in *Green*, the time had come for districts to implement integration plans that "promise[] realistically to work and promise[] realistically to work now" to eliminate the "vestiges" of discrimination "root and branch."[11] The most pertinent vestiges to eliminate were racial disparities in student assignment to schools, faculty, staff, facilities, transportation, and extracurricular activities. Beyond those high-level issues, the Court did not spell out what would happen within those integrated school buildings. This gave opponents of integration an opening. If they could not prevent the physical integration of schools, they could resist integration indirectly within the schools.

One of the primary means of indirectly resisting or coping with integration was to treat African American students differently. The biggest concern for many whites was simply that their children would have to interact with African American students socially and in the classroom. They feared African Americans would disrupt the classroom learning environment by misbehaving, act violently toward whites, or simply slow others' learning down because they were not smart enough to keep up. Thus, many whites demanded that schools keep African American students "in line." As a practical matter, this meant excluding those who were perceived to be problems and scaring the rest straight. Many schools responded accordingly with unflinching stances toward African American students and their perceived behavioral problems. As a result, many individual African American children bore the brunt of society's larger racial tensions on a daily basis through school discipline.

Douglass Reed explored these dynamics and the roots of harsh disciplinary stances toward African American students during the initial period of desegregation in a case study of Alexandria, Virginia. In 1970, the Alexandria School District was on the cutting-edge of integration. Armed with the Civil Rights Act of 1964, the Court's decision in *Green*, and the demands of the local African American community, the U.S. Department of Health, Education, and Welfare demanded that the district take more aggressive steps to desegregate. District officials believed that they were already taking the appropriate steps toward desegregation. The white community believed anything more would be too much too quick. Rather than explicitly oppose integration, the district and the white community adopted the "politics of order."[12]

The district and white community articulated African American students' discipline, or the lack thereof, as the reason why desegregation needed to slow. Integrating African American students into white schools too quickly would lead to the loss of educational quality and order. As one white community leader asserted, "What the whole thing boils down to . . . is that they do not have enough discipline. . . . Everything will fall into place if we could get discipline back into the schools."[13] This issue of discipline, Reed found, "frequently devolved into arguments about how best to control black children."[14] This then produced negative reactions from African American students, who rightly felt disrespected and discriminated against. Some pushed back and confronted whites who sought to control and denigrate them.

Teachers feared that they were unprepared to deal with integrated classrooms and that the racial unrest could spiral out of control, so they bargained "for greater powers to exclude disruptive students from their classes."[15] Early in 1971, the district's superintendent announced that the district had reached a new labor contract with teachers that granted them "the unilateral right to expel a student from his or her classroom, permanently."[16] Local reporting at the time claimed that such a power was unprecedented,[17] although it is unclear whether Alexandria teachers actually excluded large numbers of students. In comparison to other districts across the state and country, however, the transition to integrated schools was relatively smooth in Alexandria. The opposition to desegregation and the politics of order eased over the next two years, and in 1973, the school board voted to adopt a plan that largely conceded to demands from the local NAACP and the federal court.

The transition in other districts was far more difficult and placed more extended pressure on school discipline practices. In those districts, the disciplinary consequences for African American students were systematic. For instance, in *Hawkins v. Coleman*, a school-desegregation case in Dallas, Texas, from the early 1970s, the court detailed significant disparities in discipline. Explaining why these disparities were occurring, plaintiffs' lead expert witnesses testified that the discipline rules were facially neutral, but school personnel applied them in a racially biased way. In particular, "there was a substantial reliance upon non-violent 'offenses' as a justification for suspension."[18] These offenses were "highly susceptible [to] selective perception [and] had selective prosecution."[19]

A second expert testified that the district's disparate discipline practices "fit into an existing national pattern of race discrimination in that the [Dallas Independent School District] is a 'white controlled institution' with 'institutional racism' existing in the operation of its discipline procedures."[20] The standard operating procedures of these institutions "are prejudiced against, derogatory to, or unresponsive to the needs of" African Americans.[21] "Conduct by black students that would not be 'unusual' or 'offensive' in a black environment becomes to many teachers 'disruptive' or 'suspendable conduct.' To teachers unfamiliar with Blacks, this conduct, that is non-violent and characteristic of the black race, stands out and becomes thereby subject to selective prosecution."[22] Even the school district's superintendent, when asked for his explanation of why African Americans were suspended at higher rates than whites, bluntly testified, "Well, we are a White controlled institution, institutional racism, racism among individuals."[23]

The district court agreed with the foregoing assessments. "If there is to be progress in Dallas towards removing institutional racism there must be a change in attitude of both the School Board and the officials." The court chided local officials for their extensive efforts to subvert desegregation at every turn and to incite public opinion to support this subversion. The remedy was not just to adopt new policies. An effective remedy must be directed at "materially lessening 'white institutional racism' in the [district]."[24]

Dallas was not unique. National studies found that, during this period of initial desegregation, suspension rates for African Americans rose to two to three times the rate for whites.[25] African American students were also more likely to receive multiple, longer, and harsher suspensions, as well as to be suspended at a younger age.[26] Researchers found that these disparities stemmed from a variety of factors, including ambiguous rules affording teachers significant discretion, bias in carrying out discretion, cultural misunderstandings and misinterpretations of behavior, and highly stressful environments that led to overreactions. Among these causes, however, racial bias and cultural insensitivity stood out as the most significant. Researchers found that white teachers lacked "the capacity to interact effectively and respectfully with people from different racial, ethnic, and economic backgrounds."[27] As a result, they prejudged many African American students as troublemakers and sought to strictly control their behavior through harsher disciplinary responses.

Courts, however, never fully tackled or resolved this problem. The court in *Hawkins*, for instance, was the most forward thinking in indicating that real solutions demanded a change in institutional culture, but even it refused to mandate any specific remedy, leaving the remedy to the district's discretion. Other lower courts often did not even recognize the problem. Instead, they sought to rationalize discriminatory discipline. For instance, *Tillman v. Dade County School Board*[28] involved a large-scale fight between several white and black high school students that resulted in forty-eight long-term suspensions. But only one of the suspended students was white. The school officials' explanation was that they did not know who the white students involved in the fight were because the officials had ushered the whites off campus to break up the fight while detaining African Americans on campus. The court accepted this explanation as a "fortuitous circumstance" and upheld the suspensions.[29]

Similarly, in *Rhyne v. Childs*,[30] fights arising out of racial tensions had been occurring on and around campus. In one particular instance, a group of African American students had been expelled, but no whites were. The African American students charged that the school had an overall pattern of racial discrimination in discipline and that their expulsions were but another example of the school singling out students for discriminatory discipline. The court, however, soundly rejected their claim, reasoning that the students had been expelled for disrespect and aggression toward school officials following the fight, not for the fight itself. White students had not been disrespectful or aggressive following the fight—although one might question whether they had received friendlier treatment from school officials and had no reason to respond negatively.

Even if the court's conclusion regarding those particular instances were correct, its reasoning in regard to the overall disparities was entirely unpersuasive. "In the absence of substantial factual showing to the contrary," the court indicated it would presume that school officials had done no more than exercise the "discretion vested in them as regards school discipline." The court reasoned that this presumption, along with the fact that African American students purportedly "preferred suspension from school to the other form of punishment, viz., corporal punishment," accounted for and explained away the larger systemic racial disparities in discipline. Thus, the court concluded that the disparities, like those in *Tillman*, were but a "fortuitous circumstance," not evidence of discrimination.[31]

While a number of other district courts did force schools to address discipline disparities in the context of integration, discipline was almost always relegated to a secondary issue. Issues of bias in discipline never made it to the Supreme Court and rarely surfaced in appellate courts. Nonetheless, these issues loomed large in the background when the Supreme Court took its first school-discipline case in *Goss v. Lopez* in 1975. The issues in *Goss* were solely in regard to the basic right to process prior to suspension. But J. Harvie Wilkinson explained that "*Goss* ultimately represents more of a sequel to *Brown v. Board of Education* than to the free speech cases. If in *Brown* the racial question was very much on the surface, in *Goss* it lay not very far below."[32] The underlying purpose of *Goss* was to "vindicate the promise of *Brown* . . . [and, through hearings,] help relieve racial tensions by enhancing the appearance of evenhanded discipline."[33]

The Court in *Goss*, unlike in *Brown*, was sharply divided, as it sought not to apply equal protection but to set new due process precedent. To do so, the majority had to justify breaching the long-standing tradition of near-absolute deference to schools in discipline. This was no small task. Implicit in the Court's holding in *Goss* that schools comply with certain processes prior to suspension was the notion that schools could not be entirely trusted to be fair if left to their own devices. Yet the Court was loath to explicitly voice this sentiment and, on the surface of its opinion, remained wedded to the concept of benevolent school officials who needed latitude.

This difficult balance produced a majority opinion built on four distinct, and sometimes contradictory, ideas that belied the ongoing transition in the student-school relationship. The Court's first three ideas were consistent with tradition. First, to maintain order, schools must be able to take "immediate, effective action" in response to the frequent disciplinary issues that arise throughout the day. In other words, discipline is a management tool. Second, discipline is a "valuable educational device" or teaching tool. As such, schools must remain largely free to teach those lessons as they see fit. Third, the intervention of courts into school discipline has the potential to impede both the management and teaching functions of discipline. And demanding too much formality in discipline would only make it adversarial and costly and "destroy its effectiveness as part of the teaching process." But juxtaposed against these traditional theories was the Court's final conclusive point: courts also know much about justice, punishment, and the lessons they teach. Thus, the Court offered its own version of how discipline should operate and the lessons it should teach students:

It would be a strange disciplinary system in an educational institution if no communication was sought by the disciplinarian with the student in an effort to inform him of his dereliction and to let him tell his side of the story in order to make sure that an injustice is not done. "(F)airness can rarely be obtained by secret, one-sided determination of facts decisive of rights. . . ." "Secrecy is not congenial to truth-seeking and self-righteousness gives too slender an assurance of rightness. No better instrument has been devised for arriving at truth than to give a person in jeopardy of serious loss notice of the case against him and opportunity to meet it."[34]

The Court, however, refused to commit entirely to the traditional approach to discipline or an entirely new one in which students' constitutional rights reigned supreme. Instead, it sought to strike a balance between the two, requiring only minimal notice and a quick chance to respond. The Court reasoned that minimalistic process would fit easily within the classroom setting and demand no more "than a fair-minded school principal would impose upon himself in order to avoid unfair suspensions."[35]

This measured balancing of interests was, nonetheless, a significant shift in the student-school relationship. The dissent made this point clear in lashing out against the majority. It maintained that the real point of school discipline was to teach students good behavior, good citizenship, consequences, and personal responsibility.

The State's generalized interest in maintaining an orderly school system is not incompatible with the individual interest of the student. Education in any meaningful sense includes the inculcation of an understanding in each pupil of the necessity of rules and obedience thereto. This understanding is no less important than learning to read and write. One who does not comprehend the meaning and necessity of discipline is handicapped not merely in his education but throughout his subsequent life. . . . When an immature student merits censure for his conduct, he is rendered a disservice if appropriate sanctions are not applied or if procedures for their application are so formalized as to invite a challenge to the teacher's authority—an invitation which rebellious or even merely spirited teenagers are likely to accept.[36]

According to the dissent, courts and legal rules serve no legitimate purpose in that process. To the contrary, in a benevolent and pedagogical system of discipline, judicial interference under the auspices of due process is both nonsensical and harmful, undermining the educational aspects of discipline.

Mandating due process would simply erode the relationship between students and teachers. "There is an ongoing relationship, one in which the teacher must occupy many roles—educator, adviser, friend, and, at times, parent-substitute. It is rarely adversary in nature except with respect to the chronically disruptive or insubordinate pupil whom the teacher must be free to discipline without frustrating formalities."[37] But imputing due process would make discipline adversarial and, thus, ineffective. The dissenters argued that the risk of undermining discipline simply outweighed the possibility that students would be erroneously disciplined from time to time. Equally problematic, for the dissenters, was the notion that "subjecting routine discipline to the formalities and judicial oversight of due process" would undermine "the daily functioning of schools" more than almost any other remedy a court might devise.[38] "If hearings were required for a substantial percentage of short-term suspensions, school authorities would have time to do little else."[39]

The dissent's perception of the holding in *Goss*, however misguided or overstated in practical terms, clearly revealed that ideological change was occurring. That ideological change, unfortunately, may have resonated most disturbingly with many school officials. Even if the due process burdens of *Goss* were minimal, the practical burden fell solely on teachers and administrators. With the practical burden came a psychological burden and shift—the very thing the majority had sought to avoid.

Administrators and teachers felt that someone was watching them and that they would be accountable in court for carrying out due process. The deference they once had was gone, at least psychologically.[40] Surveys showed that a large percentage of teachers believed that the Court was taking away their power and authority to discipline students, even though *Goss* asserted otherwise.[41] Teachers and administrators were either unsure of what they were allowed to do or upset about what they now could not do in certain instances. Either way, teachers and schools felt threatened by the idea that they might be sued for trying to do the right thing in disciplining a student. As a result, some claimed they just stopped acting, which then robbed students of the valuable lesson of discipline and incentivized misbehavior.[42]

Even more problematic was schools' perception that due process requirements had pitted them against students. Those schools that were discriminating against minority students brought this problem on themselves. That they would complain is disingenuous. Many minority students needed legal protection against schools that had already chosen to be adversarial. But in other instances, perception increasingly became reality among well-meaning administrators and teachers in the following years.

Today, school officials' and teachers' overall perception of the disciplinary process is solidly adversarial.[43] This fact, as much as any legal dictate, has altered schools' entire approach to discipline. A study by Youssef Chouhoud and Perry Zirkel found that school personnel believe *Goss* constrains their discretion, imposes unnecessary procedural and operational burdens,[44] and this places them at odds with students.[45] Other scholars find that both the process and the students have become the enemy.[46]

Schools now cope with this tension by routinizing the process to produce the favored result.[47] Rather than a deliberative or collaborative process aimed at accuracy, justice, or educational lessons, due process is the routine through which a school must run.[48] Although Richard Arum would blame courts rather than schools, he reaches the same general conclusions. He argues that by granting students legal recourse for deprivations of process, *Goss* did, in fact, place students and schools in adversarial positions. These adversarial positions undermine the moral authority of schools.[49] Regardless of who is to blame, the end result is the same: a transition from friends to enemies. That transition fully concluded with events that followed in the 1980s and 1990s.

Criminalizing Youth and Eliminating Discretion

The adversarial nature of discipline became a full-scale, hardened reality during the 1980s and 1990s. An overall national movement to get tough on crime and breaches of the social order paved the way. High-profile shootings in schools shocked the nation and sped our schools along the path. During the 1980s, federal and state officials declared a war on drugs, enacted mandatory sentencing schemes for various crimes, and imposed longer jail sentences. The "broken windows" theory of policing also took hold in places like New York City that were determined to lower crime rates and improve the overall quality of life in the city. The thought was that by aggressively policing all problematic behavior, even the most minor, with a zero-tolerance approach, overall crime would decrease. Clear lines of acceptable behavior accompanied by harsh punishment would both scare the bad actors straight and create new social norms by which average citizens would become less tolerant of aberrant behavior. The social norms that average citizens adopted would further help prevent aberrant behavior. This shift in policing policy at all levels of government resulted in a tripling of the nation's prison population over the next two decades.[50]

Juveniles eventually got swept up in the movement as well. The zero-tolerance approach to aberrant behavior meant that no one—not even kids—would be exempted from harsh policing. Harsh policing of juveniles was spurred along by the popular narrative of the "superpredator" juveniles that developed during the 1990s. These juveniles were purportedly as dangerous as adults and must be stopped early before they wreaked even more havoc. John DiIulio, the professor who coined the concept, predicted that the number of juvenile criminals would rise dramatically in coming years and remain on the streets unless the nation took action quickly.[51] In the same vein, the criminologist James Fox said, "Unless we act today, we're going to have a bloodbath when these kids grow up."[52] This rhetoric was laced with racial imagery of "elementary school youngsters who pack guns instead of lunches."[53]

The result was a crackdown on juvenile behavior that was nearly as harsh as the crackdown on adults. Juveniles were increasingly arrested and jailed for relatively minor behavior. Whereas in the past, minors would have been tried in juvenile court, they were increasingly tried as adults. In just a five-year span in the mid-1990s, forty-four states and the District of Columbia passed laws making it easier to try juveniles as adults. This shift signaled an abandonment of the notion that minors were children, works in progress, and individuals who could be rehabilitated. Studies showed that criminalizing youth just made matters worse. As a study in Florida showed, minors held in adult prisons had far higher rates of recidivism than did those tried and held as juveniles.[54]

The Gun Free Schools Act of 1994 officially brought this zero-tolerance approach to schools. The federal statute required states receiving federal education funds to mandate that school districts expel students who bring weapons to school. Schools were also required to refer these students to the criminal or juvenile justice system for further punishment. All fifty states acted accordingly, passing zero-tolerance legislation for weapons in school.

Given the relatively small number of students who bring weapons to school, the school discipline system probably could have weathered the get-tough storm had it stopped with weapons. But many states took the occasion to adopt zero tolerance as a general operating principle in discipline. States and local districts began mandating suspension and expulsion for any number of student misbehaviors, ranging from drug possession to general disorderly conduct. Some even mandated punishment for off-campus behavior. According to a U.S. Department of Education study, by 1999, 79 percent of public schools had zero-tolerance policies for tobacco, and nearly 90 percent had zero-tolerance policies for alcohol and drugs.[55] The numbers are harder to pinpoint for behavior not related to weapons or drugs, but numerous state statutes authorized schools to expel students for disrespect, defiance, disorderly conduct, and breaches of the school behavioral code, whatever it might prohibit.

Highly publicized acts of school violence during this period further created a sense of urgency among states and schools in stamping out so-called troubled students. Most notably, in 1999, two high school students entered Columbine High School in Colorado and shot and killed twelve students and one teacher. They injured another twenty-one people. The massacre was highly calculated. The students had acquired multiple handguns and shotguns in advance, including a semiautomatic handgun. Collectively, they fired about two hundred shots and detonated numerous explosive devices to create confusion and chaos. They ended their attack by committing suicide.

The shooting was not the first and surely not the last, but the media coverage was intense. It prompted President Clinton to address the nation on the day of the event and travel to Columbine a month later to address the community directly. The shootings dominated a national conversation about school safety and dangerous students that persisted for years. They also prompted increased attention and scrutiny of several other acts of gun violence in schools that followed. As the Advancement Project's report *Test, Punish, and Push Out* concluded, Columbine and the other shootings that followed it "effectively opened the floodgates to the increased use of zero-tolerance approaches."[56]

The Complete Transformation of the School-Student Relationship

This period of criminalizing youth, adopting zero-tolerance discipline policies, and conceptualizing young people as threats finalized the complete transformation of school discipline that had begun in the 1970s. For the century preceding the 1970s, schools had operated, conceptually and practically, as the friends and daytime parents of students. Society and the law trusted them to act in the best interests of students. This is not to suggest that discipline during this time was soft. Both at home and at school, students were regularly struck with rulers, switches, and other instruments intended to inflict pain. But this discipline, nonetheless, was widely understood as a means to teach individual students important lessons in behavior and character. The occasional sadistic schoolmaster was, in effect, tolerated for the greater good that discretion in school discipline could serve.

Prior to the late 1960s, however, our nation's schools remained completely segregated. School officials were of the same race as the students they punished, and the possibility that school officials would abuse their authority and act with bias toward children was less obvious. The advent of school desegregation brought these concerns to the forefront. White community members, school officials, and classroom teachers all began to call for stricter versions of discipline, not just to teach students lessons but to subjugate African Americans and ease whites' racial fears. No longer was everyone on the "same team." Battle lines had been drawn during desegregation, with much of the white establishment making clear that it did not want African Americans in its schools and that it would resist in any way it could. When African Americans finally arrived in formerly white schools against the will of the white community, racially discriminatory discipline followed.

This new form of discipline presented a problem for the courts. How could they retain benevolent disciplinary discretion while restraining discriminatory discretion? The Supreme Court's solution was to adopt new facially neutral discipline processes that promised fairness for all students. The Court presumed that schools' historical good faith in discipline, combined with basic process, would be enough. It was wrong. Fair process did not eliminate underlying bias. Even worse, the demand of process itself unsettled many school officials, who believed that the Court had officially pitted schools as students' adversaries.

Schools' perception of due process may very well have been flawed, but societal developments reinforced that perception nonetheless.

Society and state legislatures soon enough labeled all students as potential threats and enemies. The idea of discipline as a give-and-take between students and teachers through which schools could mold better behavior, teach pedagogical lessons, and shape punishments to "fit the crime" came to a screeching halt with the rapid adoption of zero-tolerance policies. Due process hearings developed into nothing more than a few very simple questions. Did the student do X? If so, the school automatically suspended or expelled the student, with no thought of the wisdom or consequences of doing so.

In this context, students and schools could not be friends. They became enemies. Students became threats that schools must automatically exclude. Discipline was no longer a tool through which to teach students but the process through which to exclude undesirables. Moreover, the number of students treated as undesirable had grown extensively, including everyone from the student who does not sit still to the one who places his peers' safety in peril. Schools' position against students grew so rigid that they even saw fit to have students arrested for behavior that previously would not have even warranted punishment.

This shift in relationships is important background to all the data and arguments that follow. How else could an education system rationalize the extreme punishment that has persisted in recent decades? How else could the education system ignore a students' age, the long-term effects for both the student and school as a whole, and various other crucial circumstances surrounding a student's behavior? How else could schools prove so recalcitrant to common sense when it is put before them? Equally important, how else could courts permit schools to persist in irrational, ineffective, and unjustified discipline other than to retain the myth of benevolent school officials?

[2]

JUDICIAL DISENGAGEMENT

The role of courts is to vindicate constitutional rights. The role of schools is to educate students and move them on to be productive members of society. The role of state and local government is to come up with policies that make sense and fix problems. Yet none of these institutions have done much to make the dominant discipline regime any better. In fact, in many instances, each of them has made things worse over the past few decades. The most disappointing, however, has been the courts.

On any number of occasions, students have raised serious constitutional challenges to zero tolerance and harsh discipline, but courts have refused to carefully consider the claims, much less intervene. In some instances, federal courts have been downright hostile toward litigants who sought their refuge. Time and time again, courts have told students that they must instead seek change from the very people abusing their rights: the school boards. The only thing that courts have required of schools is a very basic form of process prior to the removal of students from school. The substance of the school rules and the severity of the punishments they hand out have drawn almost no attention from courts.

Schools, or their attorneys, have gotten the message that the courts will not second-guess decisions to exclude students so long as schools jump through a few hoops in advance. This raises the question, however, of why schools need to jump through those hoops in the first place if they can do whatever they want at the end. If schools are completely free to do what they want, courts have managed to impose burdens on schools without ensuring any benefit for students. The result is a harsher and more thoughtless discipline process than the one the Supreme Court initially attempted to reform in the 1970s.

The Supreme Court's Incomplete Intervention in Discipline

In 1969, in *Tinker v. Des Moines*,[1] the Supreme Court blocked a school's attempt to punish students for protesting the Vietnam War. The Court's holding, however, was based solely on the students' free speech rights. The Court's first general non-free-speech intervention into school discipline principles was in 1975 in *Goss v. Lopez*.[2] In *Goss*, the Court held that due process protections apply to student suspensions and expulsions, regardless of the grounds for the removal. Before a school can deprive students of their right to attend school, it must afford students notice of why they are to be punished and an opportunity to respond. Today, this holding appears so obvious and unobtrusive that *Goss* appears mundane in retrospect. But as explored in chapter 1, school desegregation tensions were straining discipline policy and transforming the relationship between schools and their students.

The decision in *Goss* was far closer than one might have expected. Prior to *Goss*, many lower courts had already held that students were entitled to due process. Yet the Supreme Court recognized students' right to due process prior to suspension by a mere five-to-four vote. The five justices in the majority believed they were delivering a monumental victory for discipline fairness and reform; the four dissenters characterized it as a monumental mistake. The disagreement revolved around competing theories of education and discipline discussed in chapter 1. The struggle to moderate these internal debates resulted in a decision that could not achieve its stated goals.

The flaw in *Goss* is not that it intervened in discipline but that its intervention was too modest. The Court relied on assumptions that later proved false and failed to articulate due process standards that were rigorous enough to stand the test of practical reality. The Court surely knew its due process standards would require revisiting later. The Court may very well have intended to issue more forceful subsequent opinions, rolling out progressive doctrine over time. Or the Court may have hoped courts of appeals, based on the facts of individual cases, would add nuance to the broadly stated principles of *Goss*. Either way, solutions in subsequent opinions never came from the Supreme Court. Even worse, lower courts interpreted the Court's dicta from other cases as precluding them from devising their own solutions.

The other possibility is that the Court never intended to impose any standards beyond the vague ones articulated in *Goss*. If so, history has proven the *Goss* dissenters correct in certain respects. The majority's half-measure solution for discipline may be worse than no solution at all. Today, students lack any meaningful protection against unfair discipline. The procedural hoops of discipline have done little more than make the process adversarial. And many schools no longer use discipline as a pedagogical tool. This is a critique not of due process in discipline but of the Court's assumptions about discipline and its failure to ensure meaningful due process protections.

The Court's primary assumption was that nonadversarial discipline could persist naturally, notwithstanding the Court's intervention. The Court may have wanted to have its cake and eat it too on this score. The notion that most schools would interpret *Goss* as practically inconsequential is inconsistent with the Court's notion that *Goss* was monumental. Right or wrong, schools responded negatively to this intervention. This negative reaction later interacted with the zero-tolerance movement to disastrous effect. The Court could not have seen harsh discipline or zero tolerance coming, but it should have anticipated that its assumption of benevolent administrators, even if true in general, would not be uniform in practice then or in the future. This inevitable reality called for more definite and substantive due process standards.

Indefinite and Substanceless Standards

Regardless of the Court's motivations—stated or otherwise—the four corners of its opinion in *Goss* are devoid of meaningfully enforceable substance. To protect both students' rights and the educational value of discipline, the Court in *Goss* needed to do more than announce grand theories and principles. The Court announced the basic idea of affording notice and response, but it ignored several key issues and intentionally left others obviously open.

The Court articulated due process in discipline as an investigation into whether discipline is warranted, with the goal being to reach the correct result. If by "warranted" or "correct" the Court meant that a student had engaged in prohibited behavior, the broad dictates of *Goss* are theoretically sufficient to achieve that end. Tell the student what he or she has done, give him or her a chance to object or provide counterevidence, and then let the school make a final decision of whether the student did the thing of which he or she is accused. The Court's language in *Goss*—"determin[ing] whether the misconduct has occurred"[3]—is certainly susceptible to this narrow meaning of whether discipline is warranted.

Determining that an individual has engaged in some particular act, however, does not answer the question of whether a particular punishment is normatively or constitutionally warranted. These latter questions would also require a substantive evaluation of a student's behavior and the range of available punishments. In other words, even if a student did the thing, how bad was his or her behavior and what is the school going to do about it? Surely, for instance, expulsion is not warranted for talking out of turn in class.

The Court in *Goss* makes no mention of a student's culpability as an inquiry of due process. Nor does the Court indicate that a school might need to justify some punishments, particularly harsh ones, with an important interest. Does this mean, then, that a school could expel a student for talking out of turn? The lack of specificity on this point is not necessarily problematic. The Court's "fair-minded" administrator would presumably consider a student's culpability and the punishment that it warranted. Thus, expulsion for talking out of turn is probably not a routine concern. But when the administrator is not "fair-minded" or is unconcerned with pedagogically appropriate discipline, the answers to the questions the Court left open are essential. The answers to these questions would be the only thing left to protect a student from the unfair principal or ill-conceived disciplinary rule.

Even the "fair-minded" administrator may not be immune from the problem of imposing unwarranted discipline when a student's notice and opportunity to respond becomes nothing more than a routinized process offered primarily for the sake of process. If culpability and necessity are not mandated considerations, they can easily go unaddressed. The focus in discipline hearings becomes whether a student did something wrong, which is often the easiest thing to figure out, not the far more complex questions of whether the student deserves to be punished and how.

The Court's failure to articulate substantive limits or standards regarding these questions risks the possibility that the Court's broad goals and principles about fair discipline will ring completely hollow in those instances when they are needed most. At best, the issues of culpability and appropriate discipline are left open by *Goss*. At worst, they are irrelevant because the only objective of the process is to assess whether a particular behavior occurred. The latter would leave schools free to turn discipline policies into strict liability codes, in which intent and culpability are irrelevant.

The one potential exception may be regarding long-term suspensions. By distinguishing between long- and short-term suspensions, the Court in *Goss* hinted at some underlying substantive limits. With the most severe penalties, the Court indicated schools should be more careful, writing that "longer suspensions or expulsions for the remainder of the school term, or permanently, may require more formal procedures."[4] But again, the Court did not explore what these more formal procedures might look like or suggest a standard by which to gauge them. The Court simply recognized that these circumstances warrant more formal procedures without specifying those procedures. As a practical matter, this has meant that students do not have a right to anything in particular. Without specific rights, students are left to the whims of a system arrayed against them.

However far one might attempt to stretch the notion of the benevolent administrator doing what is best for a student, the notion does not fit well in the context of long-term suspensions and expulsions. Once long-term punishment is at issue, the benevolent administrator is a contradiction of terms. The school's purpose at that point is to exclude a perceived threat or problem, not to use discipline as a teaching tool. As Brooke Grona has written, "Perhaps it is as disciplinarian that the school most delicately balances its roles: as state, as quasi-parent, as police, and as educator. But in its goal to achieve safety on the campus, the school loses its concern for educating the student."[5] In these very instances when students are most vulnerable, they have nothing more than the Court's vague, substanceless standards to protect them. Thus, while the notion of heightened process for longer suspensions hints at substantive limits on discipline, the Court's opinion is not even sufficient to protect procedural rights, much less substantive ones.

Goss's Unfinished Business

That the Court would announce important constitutional doctrine in *Goss*, leave it intentionally vague, and never refine it later is problematic. The Court was either naively optimistic about what *Goss* would achieve or intended it to be but the first in a series of progressively evolving discipline decisions. A progressive approach could have made sense. The Court in *Brown v. Board of Education*, for instance, took this approach, initially saying nothing as to the meaning of desegregation or when and how schools would achieve it. The Court sensed that moving too far too fast would have overstretched the Court's institutional capacities, undermining both effective desegregation and the Court's authority. Thus, the Court waited over a decade to issue the decisions that offered the substantive specifics of desegregation.[6] The contentiousness of disciplinary due process pales in comparison to desegregation, but a similar approach in *Goss* would have made sense given that the Court was reforming a major aspect of education that was intertwined with school culture and bias.

That approach, however, required subsequent action by the Court. For instance, without later desegregation decisions like *Green v. County School Board of New Kent*[7] to impose affirmative duties and identify specific criteria to measure compliance, *Brown* would have had very little effect on the education of students. As noted in chapter 1, during the decade between *Brown* and *Green*, actual desegregation was nonexistent. Just over 1 percent of African American children in the South attended desegregated schools.[8]

The same principle applies to *Goss*. The broad concept of due process embedded in *Goss* risked irrelevance unless it was followed by another substantive decision. That substantive decision never came because the Court either naively thought benevolent administrators eliminated the need or misjudged the times, assuming that the justices who supported liberal school ideology would remain the majority on the Court. Regardless, in retrospect, *Goss* is seriously flawed in its lack of detailed and contextualized due process standards.

This lack of specificity left *Goss*'s broad principles subject to retraction. The basic holding of *Goss*—that due process applies to educational deprivations and requires notice and an opportunity to respond—has never been questioned, but tangentially related cases have undermined and curtailed its impact. The four *Goss* dissenters would eventually become the controlling majority in cases that practically and ideologically vindicated their dissent in *Goss*.

Just one month after *Goss*, the Court issued its decision in *Wood v. Strickland*.[9] The primary issue in *Wood* was whether school board members were immune from damages for due process violations. The majority held that school board members who knew or should have known they were violating due process were subject to monetary damages. To reach this holding, however, the Court first needed to address whether, as a factual matter, a due process violation had occurred.

The court of appeals had reversed the suspension of students who spiked the punch bowl at a school meeting on the rationale that the school had not established that there was enough alcohol in the punch for the punch to qualify as an "intoxicating beverage" under state law. The Supreme Court reinstated the punishment, reasoning the school had the authority to adopt its own definition of alcoholic beverage, which it had done. Thus, the Court held that although students are entitled to damages for deprivations of due process, the school in *Wood* had not denied the students due process.

On these points, *Wood* is rather unremarkable. The case simply held that school officials, like other state officials, are subject to suit but endowed with discretion in adopting and administering their own regulatory code. What was striking was the Court's hostility to the lower court's review of the case. This hostility, more than any other aspect of the case, has dominated due process analysis in discipline cases ever since. The Court wrote,

> It is not the role of the federal courts to set aside decisions of school administrators which the court may view as lacking a basis in wisdom or compassion. Public high school students do have substantive and procedural rights while at school. But § 1983 does not extend the right to relitigate in federal court evidentiary questions arising in school disciplinary proceedings or the proper construction of school regulations. . . . Public education . . . relies necessarily upon the discretion and judgment of school administrators and school board members, and § 1983 was not intended to be a vehicle for federal-court corrections of errors in the exercise of that discretion which do not rise to the level of violations of specific constitutional guarantees.[10]

The tone of this quote is hard to reconcile with the holding in *Goss*, particularly given that the two cases were decided a month apart. One explanation is that *Goss* was intended as a minimalist decision, not to reform discipline or offer meaningful protections. The hostile quote in

Wood would support that idea. It is also consistent with the weak and flexible nature of *Goss*'s due process mandate and a conscious decision of the Court to go no further.

This explanation, however, does not fit with the actual holding in *Goss* and its historical significance. J. Harvie Wilkinson's exploration of the overall historical record compellingly demonstrates that the Court in *Goss* was responding to underlying evidence of racially disparate practices and intentionally breaking important new doctrinal ground.[11] Wading into this contested area just to offer an advisory opinion—one that was not internally defended against subsequent retraction by the harsh dissent—would have been a fool's errand that stood the chance of doing more harm than good. More important, *Goss* extended new rights to students, and *Wood* made them enforceable with monetary damages. Thus, practical flaws and rhetoric aside, *Goss* and *Wood* represent concrete doctrinal expansion. Read this way, *Wood* does not vindicate a minimalist *Goss* but is still part of a measured and progressive rollout of *Goss*. And for that reason, it drew the same vigorous dissenters from *Goss*, who reiterated their objection to any judicial intervention that might alter the delivery of discipline. This time the dissenters added that "in view of today's decision significantly enhancing the possibility of personal liability, one must wonder whether qualified persons will continue in the desired numbers to volunteer for service in public education."[12] In short, from the perspective of the Court at the time, *Wood* was a continued enforcement of the principles in *Goss*, not a retraction.

With that said, *Wood* did not answer any of the questions left open in *Goss* regarding the details of process, the inquiries to be examined, or the permissible punishments to impose. The only thing even approaching those questions was the dicta admonishing the lower court for second-guessing school officials and permitting students to relitigate their punishments in court. This dicta later became the most significant barrier to enforcing due process of anything the Court has written. For that reason, it warrants extended discussion, which I undertake in chapter 4. For now, it suffices to say that the Court in *Wood* did not intend due process to serve as a mechanism whereby courts would permit misbehaving students to escape punishment or seek de novo reviews of evidence and school rules. In fact, intervention on that basis would be inconsistent with the *Goss* theory of benevolent administrators acting in students' best interests. Intervention would have also been a move toward an inherently adversarial and legalized disciplinary process, in which courts stood on the side of students seeking to use technicalities to out-argue well-intentioned school officials.

Retracting Due Process Protections from Discipline

While *Wood* did not retract *Goss*, the sharp division between the majorities and the dissents in *Goss* and *Wood*, combined with the fact that the majority was less certain in its position, signaled that a majority to enforce students' rights might not hold. That signal became reality in 1977 in *Ingraham v. Wright*,[13] a corporal punishment case. *Ingraham* marked a formal shift on the Court toward the *Goss* and *Wood* dissenters. The Court in *Ingraham* held that students are not entitled to any process prior to being corporally punished. The state already offered a postpunishment remedy to students in the form of a civil cause of action for malicious punishments, and according to the Court, this was sufficient to protect students' rights. Of course, *Goss* had required process prior to suspension or expulsion, regardless of the school's intent. The Court in *Ingraham* made no attempt to overrule *Goss* but simply dismissed *Goss* as irrelevant because corporal punishment and suspension are different forms of punishment. This factual distinction, however, cannot hide the logical inconsistency between the Court's opinions in the cases.

If a one-day suspension is a sufficient loss of property to trigger due process prior to punishment in *Goss*, it is difficult to reason that the deprivation of physical liberty in *Ingraham* does not require the same. Arguments that the corporal punishment analysis is different from the suspension analysis are no more than window dressing. The cases are intellectually inseparable because both raise the exact same questions of educational pedagogy and disciplinary procedures. The real-world explanation is that the Court in *Ingraham* went through the same balancing of burdens as *Goss*, but this time, the dissenters from *Goss* were the ones whose balancing analysis mattered. When this new majority in *Ingraham* found that a prepunishment process is burdensome and undermines the educational effectiveness of the punishment, it marked a post facto practical limitation on *Goss*'s doctrine and rationale, even though the *Goss* holding remained intact.

This ascendancy of the *Goss* dissenters and the pattern of indirectly undermining *Goss* repeated itself again in *New Jersey v. T.L.O.* in 1985.[14] Because *T.L.O.* was a Fourth Amendment search case, its specific doctrine is not directly related to *Goss*. But as a practical matter, searches are often the starting point of school discipline. When those searches uncover the contraband that proves a student has broken some school rule, the due process rules that precede the punishment for that rule violation become immediately applicable. *T.L.O.* is also ideologically connected to *Goss* because both due process and searches raise the same concerns regarding schools' need to maintain administrative flexibility to regulate student behavior.

The Court in *T.L.O.* cast aside *Goss*'s idealistic notion that constitutional protections facilitate life lessons for students and help fair-minded principals do their jobs. The Court in *T.L.O.* reinforced the *Ingraham* approach, making clear that any progressive agenda that *Goss* might have contemplated was foreclosed. First, the Court in *T.L.O.* held that schools need not meet the generally applicable probable cause standard to search students. In place of probable cause, the Court adopted the far more permissive and malleable "reasonable suspicion" test for school searches. In the past, such exemptions from probable cause were rare and required a detailed and precise doctrinal justification, which the dissent argued the majority did not even bother to offer.

Second, and more problematic for disciplinary pedagogy and doctrine, the Court in *T.L.O.* treated violations of all school rules as equivalent in terms of their ability to justify a search. In other words, schools have just as much power and leeway to search students whom they suspect of having written dirty notes as they do to search students whom they suspect of having brought cocaine to school. The Court in *Goss*, in contrast, clearly distinguished between long- and short-term punishments and, by implication, certain types of behavior. The Court held that each warranted a different due process response. *T.L.O.* left that due process principle untouched but gave schools free reign in the investigation that precedes the process. Minor misbehavior could subject students to the same level of privacy invasion as criminal behavior. Thus, *T.L.O.*, unlike *Goss*, is not premised as a meaningful check on discipline but is a validation of nearly unfettered investigatory authority by schools.

After *T.L.O.*, the Court's commentary and analysis of school discipline abruptly ended. The Court did not issue another individualized student search or investigation case until 2009[15] and has still not issued another due process case to flesh out the principles initially announced in *Goss*. Thus, *Goss* remains an unreinforced decision, insufficient to meaningfully protect against arbitrary or harsh discipline. The only thing to fill this precedential vacuum has been the line of related cases dealing with corporal punishment and student searches, each of which revisited *Goss*'s underlying premises. While they left *Goss*'s holding intact, they actively cabined and circumscribed its impact.

As a result, *Goss*'s final legacy has fallen short of its initial promise. Students may have the right to some process before suspension, but the process is vague and not susceptible to strict enforcement. Nor do these vague principles apply to discipline across the board. Punishment as severe as "beating" is exempted. And schools are entitled to extensive deference in terms of the behavioral rules they set and how they investigate them. These approaches may prevent courts from interfering with the proper functioning of schools, but they also impede the protection of rights that *Goss* indicated students have.

Going through the Motions: Due Process Hearings as a Sham

The internal flaws of *Goss* and the subsequent cabining of its doctrine have resulted in due process practices and hearings that do not serve the interests of students or schools. The hearings do not involve meaningful exchanges between schools and students or earnest attempts to arrive at the truth of what happened or the best punishment to impose. Rather, these hearings and other disciplinary practices are primarily motions through which schools go. As a result, due process is reduced to a sham.

J. Harvie Wilkinson, to his credit, predicted this would occur right after the Court's decision in *Goss*. He reasoned that the "skeletal" and "threadbare" process guaranteed by *Goss* is "anything but searching"[16] and "hardly . . . sufficient to protect . . . against deprivation by pretext."[17] Absent the benevolent administrator that *Goss* assumed, due process would not be "an exercise in democracy, but more a charade which authorities play as quickly as possible in order to reach the predetermined res[u]lt."[18] David Kirp joined Wilkinson, concluding that, in absence of substantive protections, *Goss* hearings could be reduced to "prepunishment ceremonies."[19]

History has proven these predictions sadly true. In 1992, Donald Stone surveyed schools across the nation about their school discipline practices. The results were startling. He asked questions about the maximum length of suspension or expulsion, whether students received a summary of the evidence against them, whether students could be represented by attorneys, whether the school had its attorney present at hearings, whether the school board held a hearing prior to reaching its final decision, what level of proof the school required prior to excluding a student, and the final outcomes in past hearings. The responses revealed wild variations.[20]

Stone disaggregated the results by districts by geography, distinguishing between urban, suburban, and rural districts. He found that suburban districts were evenly split on whether they provided students a summary of the evidence against them, whereas more than three-quarters of urban districts gave students this information. Likewise, in the written notices of suspension hearings, half the districts advised students of their right to have an attorney present at a hearing. The other half did not. This difference is striking because almost all districts claimed that they would allow students to have an attorney present at the hearing if they brought one.[21]

More troubling variations arose later in the discipline process. For instance, many districts afford students the opportunity to appeal their suspensions or expulsions to the school board, but how this appeal comes about and what it looks like followed no clear pattern. In some districts, the appeal or review before the school board automatically happened. In others, students had to actively seek the appeal. Regardless, the nature of that appeal or review varied tremendously. Sometimes the appeal consisted of an in-person oral hearing with evidence and witnesses. In other instances, there was no hearing at all. Instead, the appeal amounted to a private rubber-stamping of the principal's earlier decision. A rural-urban-suburban divide also surfaced. In rural districts, a student's chance of receiving a hearing amounted to a coin flip. In suburban districts, the general rule appeared to be to provide a hearing. Urban districts swung the other way, offering a hearing only 41 percent of the time.[22]

But even when districts afforded students a hearing, they frequently failed to afford students with basic notice protections or place much of a burden for substantiating the charges on the school. One out of three districts applied a simple preponderance of the evidence standard to determine whether the evidence was sufficient to justify excluding a student. While such a standard makes matters easy for schools, it also means that a student can easily lose his or her education in "he said, she said" situations. All the school needs to do is determine that the accuser is marginally more credible than the student to be excluded.

The absence of deliberative hearings and basic protections like notice and the burden of proof runs counter to the "fair-minded" assessment

Goss expected and is more akin to the charades feared by Wilkinson and Kirp. The outcomes of hearings before school boards, or whoever the final decision maker was, tell this story best. "Upon a school's recommendation to suspend a student, the finding of the disciplinary hearing to suspend the student occurs at a very high rate of 85%."[23] Overall, Stone's study reveals that students frequently do not even receive a hearing before the board or a hearing officer, and when they do, the board or hearing officer sees its job not as adjudicating a deliberate process in which a student can participate but as acting to confirm the recommendation of the principal or previous decision maker.

The sham-like nature of disciplinary processes and school hearings has become so normative that courts do not even recognize it as aberrational. The Sixth Circuit's opinion in *Newsome v. Batavia*[24] offers a prime example. Arthur Newsome was accused of possessing and selling marijuana at school. The only evidence against him was an anonymous accusation by two students. The accusation prompted the principal to question Newsome. Newsome denied the allegations, and yet with no further investigation, the principal suspended him for ten days and referred him to the superintendent for further punishment. Before the superintendent, the same process replayed itself. The principal summarized the anonymous accusations but refused to reveal details or the identity of the accusers.

For some unexplained reason, the superintendent decided to stop the hearing on the first day and continue it at a later date. The intervening time gave Newsome a chance to take and pass a drug test. He presented that test at the follow-up hearing. He also offered testimony from a juvenile court officer who, based on her interactions with Newsome, indicated she saw no need for Newsome to undergo drug counseling. Instead, she said the best thing to do was to return him to school. Rather than reach a conclusion based on that evidence, the superintendent again adjourned the hearing and took another odd step. After the hearing, he contacted Newsome's mother and said he would clear her son's record if he would transfer to a nearby vocational school. She rejected the proposition. The next day, she received notice that her son was expelled for the remainder of the year.

Newsome appealed his expulsion to the school board and was allowed to have an attorney present. The attorney's presence, however, proved practically irrelevant. The principal summarized the anonymous accusations again and added that he did not believe that the accusers were "out to get" Newsome. The superintendent also testified, saying his decision to expel Newsome was based solely on the anonymous accusations. Newsome's attorney asked if he could question the principal and superintendent, but the board refused. The hearing closed with Newsome reiterating that he did not possess or sell marijuana at school and the attorney making a closing argument. Then the school board, with the assistance of the principal and superintendent, reviewed the evidence in private and decided to affirm the principal's decision to expel Newsome.

Newsome then brought suit in federal court, arguing that the district had deprived him of sufficient due process, including the right to cross-examine witnesses, to have his attorney represent him, and to have an impartial decision maker decide his fate.[25] The trial court rejected all his claims and dismissed the case. New information, however, came out during the trial court proceedings. Through court-ordered discovery, Newsome learned that after the school board hearing, the superintendent disclosed additional information to the board that Newsome had never heard. According to the superintendent, a counselor with the county told him that Newsome had confessed to possessing and selling marijuana at school.

The trial court found this closed-door disclosure of new information irrelevant. Fortunately, the appellate court disagreed. The Sixth Circuit wrote, "Such a tactic completely deprived Newsome of any opportunity to rebut the evidence and amounted to a clear deprivation of his right to procedural due process of law."[26] On this basis, the Sixth Circuit reversed the trial court and remanded the case.

This victory, however, was narrow and overlooked the flaw permeating the entire process: a single-minded intent to expel Newsome, regardless of the evidence or process. Had Newsome never sued the school board, he would have never learned that the school board engaged in ex parte conversations with the principal and gathered secret evidence. For that matter, had he not appealed to the Sixth Circuit, the school district still would have gotten away with it.

The appellate court in *Newsome*, of course, corrected the problem by ruling in Newsome's favor on the denial of notice claim. But the denial of notice was emblematic of an inherently flawed and biased process, which the court ignored. Recognizing this, Newsome's claims focused more heavily on the denial of an impartial decision maker and the inability to question those who were feeding information to the decision makers. The absence of these protections infected the entire process. The lack of notice was just one part of the problem.

Newsome emphasized that his principal (and later the superintendent) had conducted the investigation, made the initial recommendation to expel him, and participated in closed-door discussions with the school board. The appellate court reasoned that the multistage involvement of a single administrator does not raise due process concerns. According to the court, Newsome failed to make the crucial showing: "that the principal and/or superintendent possessed either a preexisting animus towards him, or had developed a bias because of their involvement in the incident."[27]

This response belies common sense and the facts of the case. The superintendent gathered information against Newsome, withheld some of that information, and then used it to privately influence the school board. Newsome was deprived of due process not simply because he lacked notice but because the entire school apparatus was arrayed against him. The fact that the superintendent made the conscious decision to go behind Newsome's back may not prove personal animus in the sense that the superintendent specifically disliked Newsome, but it surely showed strong bias toward excluding him through whatever means necessary. Likewise, it would be hard to argue that the superintendent would be entitled to qualified immunity for violating Newsome's due process right to notice. He clearly knew what he was doing and could not be said to be acting in good faith. To the contrary, he was acting in bad faith by hiding information. He hid it, presumably, because he thought it would help ensure a private decision to expel Newsome from school. Yet, on the question of impartiality, both the trial and appellate courts found no problem.

If this level of bias, deceit, secrecy, bad faith, or whatever one wants to label it was driving the process, it is also hard to imagine that notice would have had any effect on the outcome in Newsome's hearing. His hearing never included fair deliberation of his story and interests. That the board was willing to conduct its deliberations and make its real decisions behind a cloak reveals that the open and formal process was a charade. Newsome and his attorney could be present at the hearings, but they were no more than a supporting cast grudgingly allowed to make appearances in a script already written by the school system. Without insisting on procedures that would limit and ferret out ex parte deliberations and bias, notice rights do nothing to protect students in situations analogous to those of Newsome. Even if students sense their process is a charade, they will still have no basis to recognize that their notice rights, or other substantive rights, have been violated.

Newsome is egregious, but it is not anomalous. Other courts would have rejected Newsome's impartiality claim for the same reasons. Courts consistently emphasize that due process hearing officers need not be neutral in all respects and that third parties need not be akin to a judge.[28] Courts accept that the hearing officer may have even prejudged the facts in some respects. Familiarity with the facts of the case before the hearing takes place, including having served as the investigator, does not preclude a person from later serving as a final decision maker.[29] No matter the situation, courts presume that the decision maker hearing the student's case is impartial. The burden rests on the students to demonstrate actual bias if they believe that their hearing officer was prejudiced.[30] As one court in a school discipline case put it, "the Constitution does not guarantee a decision maker free from the appearance of bias[;] it [only] require[s] one who is free of actual bias."[31] As a practical matter, this means the student must show that the final decision maker is *unusually* biased because courts are willing to accept the significant level of bias that is already routinely woven into the process.

Courts also tend to be similarly dismissive of other pleas for procedural protections, even when their absence raises normative questions about whether a disciplinary hearing was meaningful or fair.[32] Take, for instance, the fact that Newsome's attorney was not allowed to question the principal or superintendent. Any number of obvious concerns might support a district's refusal to permit the cross-examination of student or third-party witnesses. Confidentiality, disruption of their education, and basic harassment concerns immediately come to mind. Some of those same concerns might also justify limiting the scope of questions asked of principals and superintendents. But a complete bar on questioning principals and superintendents begs a different justification. After all, these individuals have already made up their minds about what should be done to the accused student and sculpted a rationale and narrative to do it. At a later hearing, they are highly incentivized to leave out details unfavorable to their positions. Only questioning can ferret that out.

Similarly problematic is the fact that principals and superintendents would have been allowed to question the accused student on one or more occasions in and outside hearings, during which time the student may have had absolutely no one on his or her side. When the more formal hearing occurs later, the student would be denied the same basic opportunity to ask questions him- or herself. While this is a typical reality in cases like *Newsome*, stepping back and taking stock of the overall process suggests that such a denial amounts to a deprivation of the "give-and-take" that *Goss* said is essential to the concept and doctrines of due process.[33]

In short, the flexible approach articulated by *Goss*, in which process would vary based on circumstances, has been interpreted by lower courts and implemented by schools in ways that operate in a single direction: one that affords minimal process that is of questionable value. As Stone's data and cases like *Newsome* show, *Goss*'s minimalistic articulation of due process rights is insufficient to ensure meaningful participation or to operate as a serious check on suspension and expulsion decisions. In this respect, these charades not only skirt due process requirements; they make a mockery of the idea of due process itself.

Legitimizing Illegitimate Discipline

Jane Rutherford's work on general due process explores the historical, cultural, and theoretical underpinning of due process.[34] She explains that due process, at its core, is about two things. The first is to ensure that individuals meaningfully participate in the state's decision-making process. The second is to place a substantive limitation on the state's exercise of power against the individual. The simple act of affording some form of process to individuals does not in and of itself accomplish these goals. Rather, in Rutherford's words, "the King at least must consider the [subject's] views," and this requires processes that actually afford the subject meaningful participation.[35] She adds that even when the King affords the subject an opportunity to participate,

> if the governing principle is too vague, the opportunity to participate
> may be meaningless. For example, King John could have adopted a rule
> that all who displeased him would be fined 200 chickens. Such a rule,
> however, would be too vague because those affected might not under-
> stand what displeased him. The mere right to a hearing would not solve
> the problem because the King alone would retain the power to determine
> what displeased him. Hence, part of the purpose of procedural due pro-
> cess is to act as a mechanism to assure that the substantive legal principle
> is adequate.[36]

Rutherford's greatest insight is the notion that the King benefits more from providing some process than he does from providing no process at all. By providing minimal process, the King achieves the appearance of legitimacy and fairness. The very existence of process, regardless of its minimalist nature, can "validate an otherwise inadequate governing principle."[37] In this respect, minimalist process enhances governmental power or, at least, has the effect of marginalizing the position of those who would contest whether the King's exercise of power is legitimate. Without process that both affords meaningful participation and operates as a substantive check on the validity of the principle by which the individual is judged, "those in power are free to be arbitrary."[38] In short, providing minimalistic process allows the King to do whatever he pleases with his subjects.

What does this mean for school discipline? Because neither *Goss* nor any subsequent discipline case articulates a basis on which to evaluate the reasonableness of a school's justification for punishment, *Goss*, as a practical matter, leaves schools free to act arbitrarily. So long as schools follow the minimalistic rules of telling students what they are accused of and offering them a chance to respond, discipline appears fair on the surface and schools are able to punish students however they wish. Even when schools breach the basic rules of process, they stand a good chance of evading judicial sanction because they remain cloaked in legitimacy. The court in *Newsome*, for instance, never questioned the legitimacy of the school's rules or motivations. It simply reasoned that the district should have told Newsome of the evidence it had lodged against him. But as the rest of the opinion makes clear, no process existed by which he really would have been able to question the evidence. Moreover, even had the school afforded Newsome notice of all the evidence against him and the ability to question it, the school could have reached the same result and most likely been affirmed by the courts. In other words, more process would have placed the school in a better position, not Newsome.

Countless decisions like *Newsome* have permitted due process to become no more than the routine through which a school must go to achieve a predetermined result, which is a far cry from the deliberative or collaborative process that due process is designed to further. So long as schools go through the routines, their disciplinary decisions are imbued with validity, and courts find they have complied with the Constitution. And this reality makes it near impossible to challenge not only an individual student's punishment but the substance of the rules and processes by which schools exercise power. In effect, the schools are deemed fair and their discipline policies just for little reason other than that they offer students hearings that give the appearance of opportunities to challenge punishment.

Ignoring the Substance of Rules

At some point, processes become so sufficiently pointless or sham-like that the solution is not more process. As argued earlier, better notice of the evidence against Newsome would have done little to change the quality of the process or the result for him. Rather, the flawed process was emblematic of troubling underlying substantive problems. As Rutherford explains, "the procedural and substantive components of many decisions are inextricably linked."[39] One cannot be fixed without the other.

Picking up on this connection, a few students have sought to raise substantive due process claims in addition to procedural due process claims. Some have even been willing to concede the notion that the district afforded the necessary procedures so as to focus the court on substantive due process. Substantive due process, in theory, is the safety valve for irrational discipline and those instances when schools lack a sufficient justification for punishing or excluding students. This strategy, however, has proven just as ineffective as procedural due process claims.

The problem, like most others in school discipline, stems from the fact that *Goss* did not directly address substantive due process. The only other relevant Supreme Court precedent is *Wood v. Strickland*, which included the problematic warning that federal courts should not insert their wisdom for that of school administrators.[40] While *Goss* explicitly extends procedural due process to school discipline—which inherently requires some level of rationality—and *Wood* imposes liability for those who deprive students of process, lower courts have more often disregarded these basic holdings and interpreted *Wood* as foreclosing substantive due process review. So long as a school followed some sort of process, courts have upheld discipline, no matter how severe or illogical.

The Fourth Circuit's opinion in *Ratner v. Loudoun County Public Schools*[41] offers what may be the worst example. The court refused to scrutinize Ratner's expulsion even when both the court and the school admitted that the student posed no threat to the educational environment. Ratner is the middle school student discussed in the opening pages of this book who took his suicidal friend's book binder because it contained a knife that she was contemplating using on herself. While the school acknowledged his good deed, it expelled him anyway. What was not discussed in the opening pages were the details of the court system's response to Ratner's claims.

Ratner filed a case in the federal court, alleging that his expulsion violated the Due Process and Equal Protection Clauses of the Fourteenth Amendment, as well as the Eighth Amendment's prohibition on cruel and unusual punishment. He got nowhere fast in the district court. The procedural history of the case—something normally apt to put one to sleep—is incredibly telling in and of itself. Ratner filed his claim on June 8, 2000. In less than a month, the school district filed a motion to dismiss. While quick, a motion to dismiss is a common strategy and makes sense assuming the school district's attorney knew how difficult it is for students to win these cases. What is shocking, however, is that, twenty-three days later, Ratner's case was over in the district court.

On the day the school filed its motion to dismiss—July 5, 2000—the court also set a hearing on the motion for three weeks later. Ratner responded to the school district's motion to dismiss on July 18. The school district replied to Ratner on July 25. Just three days later, the trial judge issued a short opinion dismissing Ratner's case. No depositions.

No discovery. No drawn-out oral arguments. Filed on June 8. Dismissed on July 28. Changes in cable service can require more discussion and certainly can take longer to filter through billing cycles. Federal court cases normally move much slower.

Ratner's case moved quickly because the court appeared to give it so little attention. In a short final memorandum opinion, the court curiously focused on Ratner's complaints about inadequate notice as the "crux" of his case. Like Newsome—who had in fact had information hidden from him—notice was the least of Ratner's problems. His biggest problem was the irrationality of the punishment itself.

The only hint that the trial court recognized this substantive problem came in a single sentence. The court wrote, "plaintiffs contend that the suspensions constituted grossly excessive punishment that bore no rational relationship to and without due consideration of the circumstances."[42] The court, however, never even used the phrase *substantive due process* or *rational basis review*, which are the concepts this issue raises. The concept of substantive due process and its distinction from procedural due process appeared all but lost on the court. In dismissing plaintiffs' claim of excessive and irrational punishment, the court's analysis was entirely devoted to whether the district afforded Ratner notice and an opportunity to respond. But those issues, of course, pertain to procedural due process, not substantive due process (or irrationality under equal protection, which Ratner raised as a seemingly interchangeable claim). The court's apparent confusion on this point is further betrayed by the fact that its sole case citation in that part of its opinion was to *Goss v. Lopez*—a procedural due process case. The court's conclusion regarding Ratner's claims was simply that "under these circumstances, plaintiff Ratner had received all the process which was due him."[43] Again, this may answer his procedural due process claims, but it is irrelevant to substantive due process and the question of rationality.

Having lost on all counts, Ratner appealed to the Fourth Circuit. The Fourth Circuit showed little interest in second-guessing the district or digging any further into the relevant law. In an unpublished opinion, the Fourth Circuit wrote,

> The district court also concluded, correctly, that the school officials gave Ratner constitutionally sufficient, even if imperfect, process in the various notices and hearings it accorded him, and we agree.
>
> However harsh the result in this case, the federal courts are not properly called upon to judge the wisdom of a zero tolerance policy of the sort alleged to be in place at Blue Ridge Middle School or of its application to Ratner. Instead, our inquiry here is limited to whether Ratner's complaint alleges sufficient facts which if proved would show that the implementation of the school's policy in this case failed to comport with the United States Constitution. We conclude that the facts alleged in this case do not so demonstrate.[44]

These four sentences are the entirety of the court's evaluation of Ratner's claim. The court jumped to its conclusion without any reasoning on the basis of two simple, but incorrect, premises: (1) the provision of process alone is determinative for purposes of procedural due process, and (2) substantive due process review is beyond the scope of permissible judicial review because it requires courts to assess the rationality of discipline policy. These premises, if correct, would render meaningless the procedural and substantive due process rights that *Goss* and *Wood* held that students have.

As to the first premise, *Goss* explicitly held that the process a student is entitled to varies depending on the circumstances and that expulsions require more formal process. In applying this standard, even the court in *Newsome* felt compelled to go through a relatively lengthy analysis of which particular processes were appropriate under the circumstances. As to the second premise, *Wood* specifically recognized that students are entitled to substantive due process protections but simply warned lower courts not to engage in de novo interpretations of school regulations or facts—neither of which indicates courts should entirely refrain from reviewing discipline. Even if the school did not violate Ratner's rights, that conclusion warrants more explanation than what the Fourth Circuit offered. This point was seemingly lost on all three members of the Fourth Circuit panel, including the concurring judge, who raised concerns about Ratner's suspension.

Troubled by Ratner's suspension, Judge Clyde Hamilton wrote a short concurrence. Oddly though, he was troubled on a personal rather than judicial level. He lamented the fact that a travesty had occurred and that the law could not help. In his opinion, the court was without authority to seriously question Ratner's expulsion. Hamilton wrote,

> The question raised by the facts of Ratner's case is one of degree and the law must be flexible enough so that school officials may intrude upon the right to a free appropriate public education *only* in the most justifiable circumstances. Under a facts/circumstances-sensitive examination of this case, Ratner's nearly four-month suspension from middle school is not justifiable. Indeed, it is a calculated overkill when the punishment is considered in light of Ratner's good-faith intentions and his, at best, if at all, technical violation of the school's policy. Suffice it to say that the degree of Ratner's violation of school policy does not correlate with the degree of his punishment. Certainly, the oft repeated maxim, "there is no justice without mercy" has been defiled by the results obtained here. But alas, as the opinion for the court explains, this is not a federal constitutional problem.[45]

This quote expresses Hamilton's intuitive sense that the school ought to be constrained in expelling harmless and/or innocent students, but he did not take the next step of engaging in the legal analysis that might substantiate his sense or confirm the constitutionality of the school's action. Rather, he, like the majority, assumed the school's action was beyond constitutional reproach.

The basis for Hamilton's and the panel's conclusion regarding substantive due process is highly questionable. Like the trial court, the only case that the judges cite regarding due process is *Goss*. *Goss*'s procedural due process holding and rationale say absolutely nothing to suggest substantive due process claims are foreclosed. To be fair, both the majority and concurring opinion in *Ratner* do echo *Wood v. Strickland*. The majority's statement, for instance, that "federal courts are not properly called upon to judge the wisdom" of school discipline is surely a restated but uncited quote from *Wood*.

No doubt, *Wood*'s admonishment against de novo reviews of school discipline can be interpreted as indirectly discouraging substantive due process review, but *Wood* certainly does not preclude that review (which is the subject of much of chapter 3). Regardless, neither Hamilton nor the full panel offer any other authority for the notion that Ratner has not raised a substantive due process claim or that his problems do not concern the federal Constitution. Judge Hamilton himself wrote that "Ratner's good-faith intentions [were], at best, if at all, [a] technical violation of the school's policy."[46] The notion that a good-faith technical violation of school policy could result in the "calculated overkill" of a semester-long expulsion and warrant no substantive review under the Constitution simply defies logic and any constitutional doctrine that the panel could cite. Yet that is exactly what the court and Hamilton concluded. This refusal to analyze Ratner's punishment, moreover, is not unusual. It is simply the pinnacle of a long line of similar lower-court cases.

Students' Declining Chances of Success

In the decades following the holding in *Goss*, data suggest that lower courts surprisingly grew even less willing to seriously entertain discipline claims. This is true of both procedural and substantive due process claims. Whatever one makes of any particular court's rationale, the overall trend has been to reject more and more student claims. Richard Arum's 2003 study of judicial decisions showed that a student's chance of prevailing in court on a discipline claim in 1990 was at its lowest point since 1960.[47] In 1967, eight years before the Supreme Court decided *Goss*, the probability of student victory was 49 percent. Less than a decade after *Goss*, it had fallen to 39 percent. By 1990, it was 35 percent—lower than in any year in the study prior to *Goss*. In other words, students had a better chance of challenging discipline a decade before the Supreme Court declared they had due process rights than students did decades after they explicitly won those rights.

A 2008 study by Youssef Chouhoud and Perry Zirkel revealed that students' outlooks grew even bleaker in subsequent years. The study also included more nuanced reviews of the cases that suggest that the chances of victory in any given year are probably lower than Arum's study suggested. Chouhoud and Zirkel distinguished between the types of claims students made and whether a court decision was on the merits of a student's claims, whereas Arum's simply evaluated raw results.

Chouhoud and Zirkel found that during the 1990s and first decade of the twenty-first century, students secured conclusive victories in only 10–20 percent of due process cases, while schools secured conclusive victories in about 75 percent of the cases.[48] Even more telling was the finding that among this small percentage of victories for students, very few were on substantive grounds. In other words, students rarely win, and when they do, it is most often on technical grounds.

Notwithstanding the increasingly poor chances of success, the number of due process cases filed made a significant jump in the mid-1990s. The reason is not altogether clear. If lawyers and students knew the chances of success were low, one would expect fewer cases, not more. One explanation is that attorneys were ignorant of the poor prospects of their cases. Chouhoud and Zirkel speculate that attorneys and clients may have been unduly swayed by media and advocacy organizations implying the chances were better than they really were.[49] This, of course, would also assume that attorneys were not doing their research. A quick review of various court of appeals decisions rejecting students' due process challenges would have disabused attorneys of false notions they received from advocates or the media.

The better explanation for the increased litigation is that discipline itself became so draconian that it demanded a response, and litigation was the only means to fight back, regardless of the odds. The widespread advent of zero tolerance during the mid-1990s toward weapons (real or perceived), drugs, and disruptive students did several things to potentially prompt more litigation. As an initial matter, zero tolerance increased the opportunity for litigation by increasing the raw number of suspensions and expulsions. Behavior that was previously handled through informal means now required school exclusion. Zero tolerance also raised the stakes for each excluded student, changing the cost-benefit analysis of litigation. Rather than one-day or one-week suspensions, students were finding themselves excluded for long periods, if not the rest of the school year.

A potential safety valve for the increased stakes and higher numbers in school exclusion would have been some flexibility or discretion in the rules or processes. Flexible responses would have given parents some sense that their concerns were being heard. Instead, zero-tolerance policies eliminated any give-and-take between schools and families. The punishment was nonnegotiable in most instances. These realities created a perfect storm for litigation: more raw school exclusions, exclusions under circumstances that were often ridiculous, and more disaffected and disempowered families. The intersection of these factors screams out for increased litigation.

The important question, however, is not why litigation increased or what the chances of success were. The important question is whether courts were dismissing or failing to take seriously claims that were otherwise valid. None of the data from the studies offers a clear answer to this question, but the declining chances of success after the recognition of student rights in *Goss* is curious. Plaintiffs and lower courts possibly caught school districts off guard in the years leading up to *Goss*. As evidenced by the Ohio statute and the practices of the school in *Goss*, many districts did not afford students any process during the early 1970s. No Supreme Court case explicitly indicated they should do otherwise. The lower-court cases that districts were losing during this period were often cases of first impression. Given the relatively low profile of many of these cases, schools may have been slow to recognize and respond to changes in the law. This would help explain the relatively high rates of success prior to *Goss*.

Following *Goss*, however, districts were clearly on notice and presumably acted accordingly. This could have led to a precipitous drop in the rate of student victories in the immediate years following *Goss*. But this would not explain why the rate of victory continued to fall decades later. Within a few years, the chances of victory should have stabilized, but they did not. Nor would it explain a momentary slight increase in the chances of victory that occurred in the late 1990s. The chances of success were still low in the early 1990s and could not have reasonably gotten much worse, but the chances of success slightly increased thereafter, probably because some courts could not stomach the draconian and irrational nature of discipline at the time. A few courts, like the Sixth Circuit in *Seal v. Morgan*,[50] felt compelled to say enough is enough: schools cannot expel a student who, for instance, happens to be driving a car that contains a knife of which the student is not even aware.

The other possibility for the overall decline in the chances of success could be that plaintiffs began filing more frivolous or poorly conceived cases. This is the most implausible explanation. The number of discipline cases filed in any given year since 1970 has always been relatively small. In the first half of the 1990s, there were forty cases in Chouhoud and Zirkel's study. In the second half of the 1990s, courts reported opinions in sixty-two cases. While this represents a 50 percent increase in filings, it still only amounts to just over one reported due process case in each state every five years.

To further put those numbers in context, over the past decade, schools have suspended about three million students a year and expelled one hundred thousand. Back-of-the-envelope calculations indicate that only about 0.000004 percent of student suspensions led to due process litigation ending in a published court opinion during that time.

If the only cases brought were over expulsions, they would still only amount to about 0.00012 percent of expulsions. This is a far lower rate of case filings than during the 1970s, when there were roughly as many published opinions but only half as many suspensions and expulsions. Thus, in raw numbers and in the percentage of suspended and expelled students, discipline litigation has always been minuscule. This does not rule out the possibility of frivolous litigation as an explanation, but it makes it far less likely.

If attorneys have not gotten more ignorant of the law over time and the claims being raised are not increasingly frivolous, the most likely explanation for the decrease in student victories during a period of draconian school discipline policies is an increase in negative judicial temperament toward discipline cases and the compounding effect of the precedent on later courts. Prior to *Goss*, it was not unusual for courts to expect a school to justify its disciplinary action. Today, courts routinely reject claims with no more than two or three lines of due process analysis. Rather than evaluate and enforce constitutional rights, courts have seemingly adopted the same societal impulses that led to zero tolerance and harsh discipline in the first place—the notion that the general interest in safety and order outweighs the constitutional interest in individual due process, rationality, and fairness. Courts simply defer to schools' suspension and expulsion judgments on the premise that schools pursuing safety and order can do no constitutional wrong.

[3]

THE INSUFFICIENCY OF POLICY REFORM

New Research, New Reforms,
Same Old Problems

The research and data on school discipline have grown increasingly complex and compelling in recent years. No more do they stop with the basic data regarding high rates of discipline, racial disparities, and drop-outs. Newer research shows just how harmful and counterproductive harsh discipline can be for everyone involved: the student who is punished, the school that does the punishing, and the students who are not punished but are part of the community. The harms to the students who are excluded from school have been known for some time, but newer studies show that excluding these students serves almost no purpose at all. It does not improve behavior. It does not improve academic achievement. It does not reduce the likelihood of contact with the juvenile justice system. It does the opposite on all accounts. In short, exclusion is not a wake-up call for misbehaving students, nor does it serve the interests of the overall school community.

To the contrary, newer studies show that harsh discipline practices and high suspension rates can hurt the school and its remaining students. In particular, they undermine the general student population's academic achievement and long-term outcomes. Studies, for some time, have generally shown that overall student achievement is better in schools that take less punitive approaches to student discipline. But the newest studies focus specifically on what we might call "innocent bystanders" and how they are affected by harsh discipline. A 2014 study by Brea Perry and Edward Morris theorized that zero-tolerance policies in schools might produce indirect "collateral consequences" analogous to those that flow from the mass incarceration in certain adult communities. Their suspicions proved right. Relying on long-term data that tracked student suspensions and math achievement across years, they found that higher levels of exclusionary discipline within schools negatively affects the academic achievement of nonsuspended students. This effect is strongest in schools with low levels of violence and high levels of exclusionary discipline.[1]

Another new study looked at specific student behavior that might influence achievement: drug use. The study compared schools with absolute zero tolerance to marijuana use with those schools that took preventative and counseling approaches. Because zero-tolerance drug policies are so prevalent in the United States, the authors were forced to look outside the United States for a context in which schools actually varied their approach to drug use. After applying the data controls necessary to make fair comparisons, the study found that student marijuana use was highest in schools that primarily relied on out-of-school suspension to deal with marijuana use and lower in schools that focused on abstinence and counseling. "Students who attended schools that reported always or almost always using out-of-school suspensions for illicit drug policy violations were 1.6 times as likely to be marijuana users 1 year later."[2] More striking was "that school use of suspensions is associated with increased risk of marijuana use for the entire student body, not just for those who are suspended."[3]

New research has also added nuance to the long-standing finding that minority students are far more likely than whites to be suspended and expelled for misbehavior. Russell Skiba's research has consistently rebutted the notion that minority students simply misbehave more often than whites do.[4] Using highly detailed data sets, he has been able to show that minority students who engage in the same behavior as white students are more likely to be harshly punished. Other researchers have confirmed his finding.[5] Those studies, however, are always subject to some level of dispute, as the data cannot capture the nuance and circumstances under which discipline occurs.

A new blind, controlled study attempts to account for that nuance. It suggests that the individual circumstances surrounding discipline decisions do not explain away the racial bias that Skiba and others have found. In 2015, Jason Okonofua and Jennifer Eberhardt sought to test "the hypothesis that [racial] disparities [in discipline] are, in part, driven by racial stereotypes that can lead teachers to escalate their negative responses to Black students over the course of multiple interpersonal (e.g., teacher-to-student) encounters." Eberhardt explained: "The fact that black children are disproportionately disciplined in school is beyond dispute. What is less clear is why."[6]

To get at this question, Okonofua and Eberhardt conducted experiments in which they presented current teachers with written accounts of student misbehavior. They did not explicitly indicate the students' race in the files but in some records suggested that students were black or white through their names—for instance, DeShawn versus Greg. In the first round of the experiment, after reviewing the files, teachers were questioned about their perception of the misbehavior, how the student should be disciplined, and whether they thought the student was a troublemaker. In the second round of the experiment, teachers were given the files of students who had misbehaved a second time. This time, researchers asked teachers whether they thought the misbehavior was part of a pattern of misbehavior and might warrant suspension.

In the first round of the experiment, the researchers found some racial bias, but it was less than they might have expected. But in the second round, when the student had engaged in misbehavior twice, racial bias became pronounced. Teachers were far more troubled by the second misbehavior when the student had an identifiably black name. Teachers were more likely to stereotype black students as "troublemakers" and want to discipline them more harshly. They also more often inferred that the second misbehavior was part of a pattern that would likely lead to punishment again in the future.[7]

The Office for Civil Rights' new study on preschool discipline offers another troubling wrinkle to Okonofua and Eberhardt's findings. As a general principle, relatively few students are suspended and expelled in the earliest years of school, but the disparities there are just as bad. African Americans are 18 percent of the national preschool enrollment but 42 percent of the preschool students suspended once a year. They are 48 percent of the preschool students suspended two or more times a year.[8] Thus, starting in preschool, African Americans have already triggered a response that Okonofua and Eberhardt's work suggests will just compound racial bias in later years. As they write, race influences how individuals, including school employees, interpret a specific behavior initially, but race also "enhance[s] perceivers' detection of behavioral patterns across time."[9]

Leveraging the Research for Reform

These and other new research developments have not gone unnoticed. More discipline reform has occurred in the past few years than in the prior three decades combined. Advocates have been able to leverage social science research to impressive effect in numerous school districts, a few states, and the U.S. Departments of Education and Justice. In some instances, the shift has even been swift. The UCLA Civil Rights Project, for instance, released a national study of school discipline in 2015 that listed the Oklahoma City Public School Districts as one of the nation's highest suspending school districts. Within days of digesting the report, the school district voluntarily announced it was ordering an audit of its discipline data and practices and would take steps to bring down the exclusion rate. While progress has been painstaking and contested as a general principle, shifts in districts' discipline policies have spread in recent years.

In communities like Toledo, Ohio, schools have recognized that their high rates of suspension and expulsion are inconsistent with their education missions. A few years ago, Toledo took stock of developing research and decided to implement a proactive and preventive approach to discipline. Suspensions dropped immediately in many of its schools.

A school that had suspended 260 students in one year under the old discipline policy suspended only 41 students under the new one.[10] More and more districts are enacting similar policies in hopes of securing better outcomes. President Obama has even played a role in encouraging reform. Through the My Brother's Keeper Initiative, he asked school districts to commit to expanding preschool education, positive behavioral interventions, the number of minority boys in advanced courses, and reducing suspension rates. Sixty of the nation's largest school districts joined the initiative by the summer of 2014.[11]

Los Angeles Unified School District was one of the most prominent members of that group. Prior to the initiative, it had already taken important steps to reform discipline. Under its new policies, the district's school resource officers no longer issue citations for minor offenses such as campus fights, petty thefts, and tobacco possession and instead use alternatives to arrest. The district publicly admitted that its zero-tolerance policies had not made schools safer but had "often push[ed] struggling students to drop out and get in more serious trouble with the law."[12]

Reform has even occurred at the state level in some places. In the summer of 2014, Massachusetts passed legislation that required its public schools to revise their discipline policies to ensure that suspension and expulsion are the last resort.[13] The new state statute specifically provides that "when deciding the consequences for the student, [the principal or relevant decision maker] shall exercise discretion; consider ways to re-engage the student in the learning process; and avoid using expulsion as a consequence until other remedies and consequences have been employed."[14] The statute also limits expulsions to the most serious misbehaviors—students who bring "dangerous weapons" to school, assault school personnel, or are charged with a felony. A few weeks after Massachusetts acted, California also passed legislation to limit the most asinine school exclusions—those aimed at disruptive elementary school students. Under the new statute, school districts cannot suspend students in kindergarten through third grade for disruption or defiance alone.[15]

Connecticut has taken a different, but equally important, route to reform. It does not bar particular suspensions or expulsions but strongly suggests that discipline suspension decisions should be individualized and take relevant circumstances into account. Connecticut's new statute indicates the school administrators should consider multiple factors "in making a determination as to whether conduct is seriously disruptive of the educational process" and warrants suspension.[16] Connecticut's department of education then passed guidelines specifically aimed at lowering the rates of school exclusion.[17] Since then, the state has seen overall suspensions and expulsions decline.[18]

High-profile developments have also occurred at the U.S. Departments of Education and Justice. Both became noticeably aggressive on school discipline in late 2013 and announced new formal policies in January 2014. This shift has, in no small part, led to several of the "voluntary" efforts of districts and states described earlier. The policy changes in Los Angeles, for instance, grew out of long-standing interactions with the Office for Civil Rights (OCR) at the Department of Education. Prior to the changes, OCR had been investigating a number of complaints against the district.

Similarly, the Southern Poverty Law Center (SPLC) filed complaints against five Florida school districts with OCR. The complaints cited serious racial disparities and argued that the districts were abusing their discretion in suspending and expelling African American students for misbehaviors that would otherwise go unpunished. Shortly after filing the complaint, SPLC was able to secure a settlement agreement in Flagler County.[19] The district promised to reduce racial disparities in discipline and minimize exclusions for misbehaviors that could be handled through other means. Flagler also agreed to offer racial-bias training to its staff, which presumably would help reduce the number of minorities referred for disciplinary action. These promises were consistent with the terms of several other settlement agreements that OCR had negotiated over the prior year.

On January 8, 2014, the Departments of Education and Justice went beyond individual enforcement actions and formally announced their policy on school discipline moving forward.[20] The substance of the policy itself was not new, but that the policy was formally articulated clearly signaled that the federal government was taking the policy seriously and would enforce it. The policy guidance distinguished between disparate treatment (treating minority students and whites differently in terms of discipline) and disparate impact (facially neutral policies that result in racially disparate outcomes). It came as no surprise that schools cannot suspend an African American student for fighting and only send his white classmate to study hall. But the guidance on racial disparities was significant.

The guidance indicated that racial disparities may themselves be indicative of implicit racial bias or just poorly conceived policies that require a better justification. The departments announced that they would analyze claims of discriminatory impact in three steps:

(1) Has the discipline policy resulted in an adverse impact on students of a particular race as compared with students of other races? For example, depending on the facts of a particular case, an adverse impact may include . . . instances where students of a particular race, as compared to students of other races, are disproportionately: sanctioned at higher rates; disciplined for specific offenses; subjected to longer sanctions or more severe penalties; removed from the regular school setting to an alternative school setting; or excluded from one or more educational programs or activities. . . . If there were an adverse impact, then:

(2) Is the discipline policy necessary to meet an important educational goal? . . . The Departments will consider both the importance of the goal that the school articulates and the tightness of the fit between the stated goal and the means employed to achieve it. If the policy is not necessary to meet an important educational goal, then the Departments

would find that the school had engaged in discrimination. If the policy is necessary to meet an important educational goal, then the Departments would ask:

(3) Are there comparably effective alternative policies or practices that would meet the school's stated educational goal with less of a burden or adverse impact on the disproportionately affected racial group, or is the school's justification pretext for discrimination? If the answer is yes to either question, then the Departments would find that the school had engaged in discrimination.[21]

The clarity of this framework and the possibility of future enforcement will surely lead more school districts to rethink their discipline policies.

The Limits of Policy Developments

The changes currently occurring at the local, state, and federal levels are all important. They represent the hard work of communities, researchers, policy advocates, and, in some cases, legal advocates. If the past is any indication of the future, these changes will continue to spread. But as important as the progressive changes thus far have been, they only represent small steps toward completing the necessary reforms in discipline. The foregoing policy changes are limited in scope and substance. And even these limited policies have been met with stiff resistance. Thus, while these limited policies may continue to spread, the likelihood that more comprehensive policies would similarly spread is low. Moreover, while suspension rates have fallen in many important places, the crisis in discipline is continuing unabated in most districts. In short, the current regulatory and legal structure is not in place to end harsh discipline and zero tolerance.

The federal policy guidance is the chief case in point. It is the broadest scale attempt to reform discipline to date, but it is still relatively narrow in its focus and application. It speaks only to racial disparities in discipline. No doubt, racial bias exacerbates discipline problems and is the source of racial disparities, but racial disparities are only one facet of the problem. The fundamental problem, whether influenced by race or not, is that schools see fit to exclude students for immature behavior rather than to educate them. In other words, racial bias exacerbates the flaws in the underlying discipline approach. Federal policy, however, does not reach beyond racial bias to address discipline itself. Neither zero tolerance nor overly harsh responses to discipline are subject to direct challenge by the departments. Districts remain free to suspend and expel students for any behavior they wish so long as they do it evenhandedly.

Many of the voluntary efforts of school districts to reform discipline, likewise, reveal only partial responses to much larger problems. A close look at many of the voluntary reforms making news reveals that their focus has often been on constraining law enforcement rather than school officials. The policy changes in places like Los Angeles, Philadelphia, and Broward County, Florida, for instance, limit the circumstances under which a school will refer students to the police department for minor misbehaviors. But policies like these do not limit schools' ability to suspend or expel students for those behaviors. Thus, "disrespectful" students can still be expelled; they just will not be referred to the police for delinquency. To be clear, interrupting the direct pipeline from school to jail and minimizing the role that law enforcement plays in school is vitally important, but school policies that primarily focus on that issue imply that the problem is law enforcement rather than school discipline policy itself. Schools that fail to reform their fundamental approach to discipline will still respond harshly to student misbehavior and will still keep the pipeline to jail running, just less directly.

California's statewide prohibition on suspending students in third grade and below for disruption and defiance similarly misses the point. On the one hand, one might applaud the state for protecting the most vulnerable students from the most senseless punishments. On the other, that such a prohibition was even necessary is telling. Either the state was attempting to grab headlines, or enough elementary schools were suspending disrespectful students that the state had to stop it. Assuming the latter, the legislation reveals the existence of a discipline system so punitive and so unwilling to deal with small children that—save a statutory prohibition—it would send five-, six-, seven-, and eight-year-olds home for multiple days at a time for acting the way most of us know small children act. The statute further demonstrates that California schools will continue to send students who are nine years or older home for acting like nine-year-olds. The statute does nothing to stop that.

These reforms, as limited as they are, have still been criticized and strongly resisted. That resistance will not fade anytime soon. For instance, immediately after the federal government released its school discipline guidance, numerous conservative policy groups and commentators began questioning the guidance. While the government's stated policy on racial disparities purports only to limit discipline policies that lack a legitimate goal or when some other policy is equally effective, critics claimed that government would force schools to keep unruly students in the classroom and undermine positive educational outcomes for everyone else. Andrew Coulson of the Cato Institute's Center for Educational Freedom went so far as to say that "this federal pressure may end up hurting black students far more than it helps them."[22]

The resistance, moreover, runs much deeper than just politics. It comes from teachers themselves. For instance, when Philadelphia's school district directed school police officers to stop responding to calls related to minor student misbehaviors—like failing to follow classroom rules, verbal altercations, and inappropriate public displays of affection—the Philadelphia Federation of Teachers immediately pushed back. Teachers complained that there were not enough resources in their schools to deal with student misbehavior and that much of the misbehavior they experience is not just a classroom management issue to be swept aside.

In teachers' defense, many work in chaotic and inadequate school systems, where behavioral problems stem from student poverty, school funding, teacher quality, and discipline pedagogy. In those situations, simply telling school officials they can no longer suspend students or refer them to law enforcement is not a solution. It leaves other underlying problematic structures in place.

On the other hand, a large percentage of school teachers and administrators are just "winging it" when it comes to discipline.[23] They lack formal training on these issues and are just making decisions based on their gut. When the federal government, the state house, or the district tells them to act counter to their gut, they do not always respond properly because they lack the training to do so. As a result, positive policy change and positive policy implementation can be worlds apart.

The Continuing Crisis

Traditional Public Schools

In states and districts across the nation, the underlying data and reports reveal a discipline system that is still largely punitive. The uplifting stories and initiatives of discipline reform remain exceptions to the rule, not an inevitable new narrative. Students are still being suspended at high rates at all grade levels, in all regions, demographic groups, and types of public schools. In 2006, schools suspended or expelled 3.3 million students.[24] In 2011, that number had crept up to 3.5 million.[25] The bulk of new discipline reforms have occurred since then, and complete data are not yet available to gauge their effect. Regardless, available data and information indicate there is a long way to go in establishing a new national trend.

California reported a 10 percent drop in suspensions in 2014,[26] but impressive drops like this, even at the national level, would not equal success. Suspension rates, even with significant reductions like these, are still roughly twice what they were when the federal government first began tracking the data in the 1970s. The fact remains that schools continue to suspend and expel students at alarmingly high rates and under baffling circumstances. Police and school officials also continue to inflict violence and trauma on students—even the most vulnerable students—that would have been unimaginable two decades ago. And students still have very little recourse. Today's students demand bigger remedies than policies of the current type can deliver.

A recent study of the South by the Center for the Study of Race and Equity in Education at the University of Pennsylvania offers a glimpse of just how strong the commitment to harsh discipline is and how bad the racial disparities that overlay it remain in many communities. Relying on the most recent data, the study found public schools suspended 1.2 million black students nationally. These suspensions were heavily concentrated in thirteen southern states, where 55 percent of all African American suspensions in the nation occurred.[27] Within the South, the study also pinpointed the most problematic school districts. It identified 132 school districts spread across the South that suspended African Americans at rates "five times or higher" than other students.[28] In Mississippi, African Americans made up 50 percent of the student population, but 80 percent of the girls and 70 percent of the boys suspended in the state were African American.

To be clear, these harsh disparities can be found outside the South as well. In fact, our nation's very highest quality school system—Massachusetts—has not necessarily fared much better on discipline than have southern states. Massachusetts students routinely have higher academic achievements than any others in the country. Due to the high-quality education there, the state has also been able to narrow the racial achievement gap more than most states. But when it comes to discipline outcomes, Massachusetts still has serious problems.

In the 2012–13 school year, two-thirds of the state's suspensions were for nonviolent, noncriminal, nondrug misbehavior. Schools reported that these misbehaviors ranged from "dress code violations to acts of disrespect."[29] In other words, Massachusetts regularly excludes students for the same petty reasons as every other state. And as to students of color, Massachusetts was among the worst in the nation. Across the board, the state's racial disparities in discipline were at or below the national average:

> Black students received 43% of all out-of-school suspensions and 39% of all expulsions in the 2012–13 school year, despite making up only 8.7% of students enrolled in Massachusetts. While 1 in 27 White students were disciplined, 1 in 10 Latino students, and 1 in 8 Black students, were disciplined at least once. While Massachusetts' overall out-of-school suspension rate was less than the national average, the same cannot be said for Massachusetts' racial disparities in suspension. Black students in Massachusetts were 3.7 times as likely as their White peers to receive an out-of-school suspension. . . . Latino students were suspended out-of-school at a rate (8.4) higher than the national average (6.8) and were 3.1 times as likely as their White peers to receive an out-of-school suspension— roughly double the national average (1.5).[30]

Equally telling is the fact Massachusetts schools had discretion as to whether to impose in-school or out-of-school suspension for minor misbehavior but were far more likely to impose out-of-school suspension with African American students than whites. White students were given in-school suspensions about half the time and out-of-school suspensions the other half. But "Latino and Black students received out-of-school suspensions almost twice as often as they received in-school suspensions for these more minor incidents."[31]

Charter Schools and No-Nonsense Discipline

Public education is increasingly fragmenting into a system composed of traditional public schools, charter schools, and other choice options, and the fastest growing sector is often taking the harshest disciplinary approach. While still enrolling a relatively small portion of public school students nationally, charter schools are growing exponentially in many locations. In New Orleans, traditional public schools no longer exist. In the wake of Hurricane Katrina, the entire system transitioned to independent charter schools in less than a decade. Many of those schools are premised on a stricter form of discipline, which produces school exclusions far beyond the average in traditional public schools.

Carver Collegiate Charter School in New Orleans, for instance, operates on a demerit system. When students accumulate too many demerits, they are suspended. According to a complaint filed by civil rights advocates, the school's out-of-school suspension rate is 68.85 percent.[32] The behavior leading to demerits and suspensions, however, would go completely unnoticed in almost all traditional public schools, even those employing the harshest zero-tolerance policies.

The civil rights complaint offered this summary of discipline policies at Carver Collegiate and two other charter schools in New Orleans:

> These schools feature a culture of hyper-discipline that is punitive and demeaning to students. The schools demand a uniformity among the students and enforce it with harsh discipline for petty matters such as: (1) requiring all students to firmly shake the hands of their teachers and administrators at the beginning of each day and before each class; (2) walking straight on a line; (3) being required to be silent "at level zero" in the hallways, often at lunchtime or whenever a teacher demands; (4) being required to sit in an upright position all day, hands folded on the desk, feet planted firmly on the floor, and looking straight ahead; (5) being required to raise their hand in lock-elbow position in class or receive demerits if their arm is not straight, (6) being suspended for minor misbehaviors like laughing too much, inappropriate displays of affection such as hugging a friend, and most commonly for being "disrespectful."[33]

The system is so oppressive that some students claim they are depressed, "but they feel they can't speak out because they will get in trouble."[34] The attorneys further allege that the schools do not even bother to offer the basic constitutionally required notice and opportunity to respond prior to suspension.

From the perspective of charter schools, this quick no-excuse, no-nonsense, no-debate approach to discipline is the point. Students must follow the rules, regardless of whether they are arbitrary, and suffer the ultimate consequences when they do not. One wonders, however, whether this harsh discipline is also an indirect method by which to select a "desirable" student body. Most charter school laws require that charters, like any regular public school, serve the students who are eligible to attend. They cannot simply deny a student enrollment because of poor grades, social skills, or behavior. When charters are oversubscribed, they must enroll students based on a lottery. But an overly harsh disciplinary approach could allow a charter to, in effect, deselect certain students after the fact.

The extent to which this occurs is unclear, but some courts have made it relatively easy for charters to do so. For instance, in *Scott B. v. Board of Trustees of Orange County High School of Arts*,[35] a charter school student in California challenged his dismissal. As in charter schools in New Orleans, New York, and elsewhere, the student had accumulated too many demerits under the school code of conduct (although he appeared to have engaged in serious conduct at the end that may have made his removal inevitable). He appealed his dismissal to the school board but was denied a hearing. On that basis, he argued he was denied due process under a state statute. The appellate court rejected his claim, reasoning,

Dismissal from a charter school does not implicate [due process] concerns to the same degree as expulsion. Unlike public schools generally, "OCHSA is a school of choice. No student is required to attend." When a student is dismissed from OCHSA, the student is free to immediately enroll in another school without the loss of classroom time. Thus, dismissal from OCHSA need not and should not delay Scott's education. The May 16, 2011 letter informing Scott's mother of his dismissal instructed her to immediately enroll Scott in another school. Scott's transcripts from OCHSA were attached to the letter. The parties have not cited us to any statute requiring a new school be notified of a dismissal from a charter school.[36]

In other words, charter school students are not entitled to the same due process protections as regular school students. Putting aside for the moment whether the court's holding was correct, the message it sent was clear: charters can punish students however they see fit without even offering students an opportunity to respond.

Statewide data in Massachusetts reveal that the problem there is not just a few rogue charter schools. In 2012–13, while only 3 percent of the state's public school students were enrolled in charter schools, charter schools accounted for 6 percent of the state's suspensions. The statewide suspension rate in public schools was 4 percent. In charter schools, it was more than two and a half times that, at 10.7 percent.[37] A report by the Lawyers' Committee for Civil Rights and Economic Justice also examined the state's highest suspending schools and districts. It found that, notwithstanding the small number of charter schools in the state, charter schools dominated the statewide list of schools and districts with the highest suspension rates. Only one traditional public school district in the state even came close to a suspension rate that matched those of the state's highest suspending charter schools.[38]

Holyoke Public School District's suspension rate was the highest of any traditional public school district in the state, at 21.5 percent, but eight charter schools—which are reported as independent school districts—exceeded that rate. For that matter, Holyoke was the only traditional public school district in the state with a suspension rate above 20 percent, but eleven charter schools exceeded that number. The worst was Roxbury Preparatory Charter School, with a suspension rate of 59.8 percent. Roxbury was followed by City on a Hill Charter, at 40.9 percent.[39] Like Carver Collegiate in New Orleans, very little of the misbehavior that led to suspension in these schools was serious.

Roxbury Preparatory Charter reported that 93.8 percent of its suspensions were for nonviolent, noncriminal, and non-drug-related misbehavior. City on a Hill Charter reported that 93.9 percent of its suspensions were for minor misbehavior. Two of the highest suspending charter schools actually reported that 100 percent of the behavior that led to suspension was nonviolent, noncriminal, and non-drug-related. In contrast, Holyoke—the highest suspending public school in the state—reported far more often that serious misbehavior was the cause for suspension. While Holyoke also suspended students far too often for minor misbehavior, nearly one out of five suspensions was for serious misbehavior.[40]

Law Enforcement Referrals

These minor school misbehaviors continue to lead not only to suspension and expulsion but also to law enforcement involvement and often violence and trauma against students in many schools. While districts like Los Angeles may be seeking to limit the role of officers in schools, countless others clearly still expect officers to harshly police students. In just a two-year period between 2013 and 2015, numerous stories made national and regional news, including stories of school resource officers and officials choking, handcuffing, restraining, and locking up in isolation rooms elementary and middle school students, including those with special needs. This is to say nothing of countless similar routine instances in high schools.

A recent lawsuit in Birmingham, Alabama, revealed that eight area high schools maintained official policies authorizing the use of pepper spray to break up fights, to disperse bystanders, and to respond to verbally disrespectful students. In September 2015, the federal district court ruled against the schools, offering this sad rejoinder and reminder of some schools' hostile approach to students:

> Since the dawn of time, children have engaged in challenging but normal adolescent behavior in school settings. Indeed, this is perhaps the one point on which the parties in this matter agree. For just as long,

presumably wiser, more level-headed adults have responded and have successfully utilized deescalation techniques that are far less violent than those at issue here. As this case has revealed, the adults tasked with ensuring the safety of Birmingham's school children have resorted to using chemical spray to deal with this normal—and, at times, challenging— adolescent behavior. The chemical spray at issue here is . . . described by its manufacturer as "the most intense [] incapacitating agent available today." . . . [Even accepting that there may be circumstances when using the spray is justifiable,] once law enforcement officers have secured the affected individual, they have a legal obligation to decontaminate the individual. Unfortunately, despite established case law requiring effective decontamination and clear instructions from [the] manufacturer, the officers here failed to decontaminate the students, and instead left them to suffer the effects of the chemicals until they dissipated over time.[41]

In the aftermath of the police shooting of Michael Brown and the civil unrest in Ferguson, Missouri, the U.S. Department of Justice studied law enforcement's interaction with youth in local schools, searching for further answers to the lingering question of why the events unfolded there. The department's final study revealed a pattern and practice not entirely different from Birmingham. The department found that Ferguson's middle and high school resource officers too often "treat routine discipline issues as criminal matters and . . . use force when communication and de-escalation techniques would likely resolve the conflict."[42] The Department of Justice detailed one specific, but purportedly typical, example of a middle school student refusing to leave the classroom after getting into a trivial verbal argument. When the student refused to leave, a resource officer Tasered and arrested him, which led to juvenile charges. The school also piled on with a 180-day school suspension.[43]

Nationwide data demonstrate that even if this level of violence against students were isolated, strong ties between school discipline and law enforcement are not. In Virginia, for instance, schools referred nearly 16 percent of all students to law enforcement in 2011–12. Six other states were close on Virginia's heels, referring more than 10 percent of students to law enforcement. More than half of the states referred 5 percent or more of students.

The numbers were far worse for African Americans. Wyoming's schools referred one out of three African American students to law enforcement. Virginia referred one out of four. Six other states referred one out of five. While states varied significantly in their law enforcement referral rates, the national average itself—one in ten African American students referred to law enforcement—reveals that, on the whole, schools continue to refer a large percentage of misbehaving students to law enforcement as a matter of course.[44] To put those numbers in perspective, African American students' risk of being referred to law enforcement is often higher than white students' risk of being suspended. In short, the schoolhouse-to-jailhouse track is as strong as ever in many states.

The Need for Judicial Intervention

New research, policy developments, and data on school discipline form a complicated narrative. Each year, additional studies help advocates and policy makers better understand the scope and source of the problem. These studies offer more compelling reasons for change than ever before. But these studies also reveal how fundamental that change must be. And fundamental change, of course, is the most difficult.

Every year over the past several years, more and more school districts and states take voluntary steps to reform their discipline policies and limit suspensions. These districts and states are a testament to the fact that the overall trend in school discipline can change. On the basis of anecdotal evidence and smaller-scale reports, it is altogether possible that, when the data on current suspensions become available, a national drop will have occurred. But even with a substantial drop, punitive and overly harsh discipline will remain the dominant paradigm. Current policy reforms are simply insufficient to dismantle that paradigm. Most new policy developments operate around the edges of the problem, seeking to limit arrests but not suspensions, expulsions of elementary school students but not high school students, racial disparities in discipline but not harsh discipline itself, suspension rates but not the negative environments that produce them.

Absent clear legal limits on school discipline, policy solutions will be, at best, slow-moving partial solutions. Each year, the number of progressive districts should grow, but it will be years before they are the dominant majority. Even once they are a majority, history strongly suggests that voluntary efforts alone will never eliminate harsh discipline. Punitive responses will persist in several states and districts so long as the law allows. A national consensus began turning against corporal punishment decades ago, but the practice lingers on with alarming frequency in many of the same places where zero tolerance and excessive suspensions are most prevalent. It lingers on because the Supreme Court refused to intervene.

An even bigger tailwind will push the continuation of zero tolerance and harsh discipline. A national consensus has still yet to form against them. A combination of racial bias, overworked school districts and teachers, insensitivity, ignorance, and the inertia of tradition and culture will maintain the harsh practices into the foreseeable future. Charter schools may even make things worse before they get better. A substantial portion of the rapidly growing charter school sector believes that an absolutist approach to student behavior offers disadvantaged students their only chance at academic success.

Unless courts intervene, millions of students will be lost to suspension, dropout, and prison each year while the nation waits on the discipline reform movement to expand. Students are entitled to solutions in their lifetime, not someone else's. Even once policy reform expands, the futures of hundreds of thousands of students will continue to be lost in holdout jurisdictions. And at that point, the stories of these marginalized students will rarely make headlines or reports. The conventional wisdom will be that the nation's discipline problems have been solved. Other issues will demand attention.

When schools deprive these students of their rights, courts have the responsibility to respond, not hope that schools and legislatures will eventually do the right thing. Constitutional rights are the only absolute check on absolutism. This is the very reason we enshrine them in constitutions. They cannot be left to statutes and policies, which will always be prone to expedient thinking. While constitutional rights demand enforcement and compliance regardless of political acquiescence, our courts have failed to carry out the promise of our federal and state constitutions in the context of school discipline. In the 1970s, federal courts meaningfully enforced students' due process rights for a short period, but the doctrines the courts announced were insufficient to stand the test of time and the virulent policies that followed. Rather than revisit and strengthen those doctrines, courts have disengaged from school discipline cases, leaving students with no recourse against the discretion of local school officials or the political whims of the majority.

Chapter 2 detailed this judicial disengagement and the problems it has created. The remainder of the book outlines the theories by which courts can protect students' rights. This is not to suggest, however, that courts can or should resolve our discipline crisis on their own. To the contrary, courts are ill equipped to supervise day-to-day classroom- and office-level decision making. The role of courts is to mark the outer boundaries of permissible school discipline. By doing so, they can take the most problematic discipline policies off the table and prompt policy makers to enact practical and holistic solutions when they otherwise would not. In short, courts must be part of the solution, rather than complicit in the problem.

PART II

COURTS' ROLE IN ENDING THE CRISIS

[4]

MAKING DISCIPLINE RATIONAL

With decades of disengagement by lower courts and little guidance from the Supreme Court, the exact means by which courts should reengage in enforcing checks on school discipline is uncharted. The one thing that is relatively clear, however, is that procedural due process will not lead the way to meaningful reforms. As chapter 2 explained, the primary problem with school discipline is the substance of the rules, not the procedures that schools follow. While more procedures might indirectly force some schools to reconsider the substance of their rules, the rest could just as easily erect more elaborate due process hearing charades. Those charades would continue to obfuscate the underlying irrational decision making and still move students to the preordained punishments set out in school rules and practices.

The remainder of this book maps out the legal theories that could force a substantive evaluation of school discipline policies. Those theories coalesce around two basic constitutional theories. The first is based on the federal Constitution and argues that general substantive due process principles require school discipline policies and practices to be rational. While substantive due process review is deferential, it still requires courts to analyze the rationale behind zero tolerance and harsh discipline. In several respects, those policies are simply too irrational and rigid to survive review. Courts have escaped this conclusion by never starting the analysis. This chapter explores substantive due process's rationality mandate in broad terms and how it applies to school discipline, notwithstanding suggestions to the contrary by some courts. Chapter 5 then identifies the specific inquiries school discipline must address to meet this rationality mandate.

The second theory to force a substantive review of school discipline focuses on state constitutions and argues that precedent in school finance and quality litigation should trigger new analysis regarding suspensions and expulsions. Not all states have favorable precedent, but most do. More than half of the states' highest courts have recognized that students have a constitutional right to education and/or that the state has a constitutional obligation to provide certain educational opportunities. In these states—and arguably more—students facing suspension and expulsion can challenge whether the state has a sufficient interest in depriving them of education and, if so, whether school exclusion is necessary to achieve that interest. Students can also challenge whether dysfunctional school environments that lead to high levels of school exclusion are consistent with the state's obligation to deliver equal and quality educational opportunities. Social science strongly suggests they are not. These state theories are explored in chapters 6 and 7.

Debunking the Barrier to Substantive Due Process Review

As chapter 2 demonstrates, federal courts in recent decades have flatly refused to scrutinize zero tolerance and harsh discipline. For the most part, it is not that their analysis is flawed but that it never occurred. They have operated under the assumption that the Supreme Court's decision in *Wood v. Strickland* prohibited that analysis or scrutiny. The Court in *Wood* wrote, "It is not the role of the federal courts to set aside decisions of school administrators which the court may view as lacking a basis in wisdom or compassion."[1] At best, this language offers an easy excuse for a court wishing to move a discipline case off its docket to summarily deal with the case. At worst, it warns courts against using the Constitution to intrude into school discipline matters. Either way, this language in *Wood* represents an ideological, if not doctrinal, barrier to using the Constitution to substantively reform school discipline. As such, deconstructing *Wood* as a barrier must occur well before any affirmative arguments regarding substantive due process limits on zero tolerance and harsh discipline.

The decision and context in *Wood* are far more complicated than any subsequent court has ever bothered to consider. Rather than sort through the complexities, courts have latched on to that seemingly simple foregoing quote, which, on its face, is not even a statement of constitutional doctrine. Most do not even know what *Wood* was about. Both the facts of the case and the issue before the Court are lost.

The facts of *Wood* are rather remarkable. Peggy Strickland and Virginia Crain were tenth graders at Mena Public High School in Arkansas. Apparently, it had been their responsibility to make sure there was something to drink at a school meeting to discuss extracurricular organizations. The plan was to serve a bowl of punch. Sometime before the meeting, Peggy and Virginia realized the punch had not been made. At that point, the idea of "spiking" the punch came to them. For reasons that most who are familiar with teenagers can appreciate without condoning, they decided this was a good idea. They enlisted the help of a third girl and drove across the state line to Oklahoma to buy alcohol. Their Arkansas county was a "dry" one.

The girls bought two twelve-ounce bottles of malt liquor and a six-pack of soda. They mixed all the soda and alcohol together in a milk jug and went to school. As the meeting approached, a combination probably of excitement, anxiety, and fear caused them to reconsider their prank. But as the Supreme Court wrote, "by then they were caught up in the force of events and the intervention of other girls prevented them from disposing of the illicit punch."[2] So it was served and drunk. There is no mention of whether the girls were pleased or disappointed, but apparently the punch was not very strong. No one noticed or was affected by the alcohol.

As with almost any scandalous behavior, the story eventually got out. Ten days later, a teacher, Mrs. Powell, heard a rumor that Peggy and Virginia had spiked the punch and asked them about it. At first, they denied it, but they eventually confessed when Mrs. Powell said she would deal with their punishment informally. But when the story continued to spread, Mrs. Powell told them that the principal would soon hear about it and that it was best if they went to him first. At least then, they could control the story. They followed her advice and admitted what they had done to Principal Waller. He promptly suspended them for two weeks.

Waller's decision remained subject to school board approval. At an initial hearing, where neither the girls nor their parents were present, the school board voted to expel the girls. The board then held a second hearing to consider the girls' appeal of their expulsions. The girls and their parents attended that second hearing and were represented by counsel. At this hearing, the girls admitted what they had done, expressed their regret, and asked the board to not impose such a substantial punishment. The board contended that its rules mandated the punishment, and it was not going to change its rules. It then affirmed the expulsions.

The girls took their case to federal court. They requested a jury trial and sought a host of remedies. They requested compensatory damages and punitive damages against the district and its employees, as well as an injunction to prevent the district from enforcing the rule against them or noting their punishment in their records. Somehow, they managed to make it all the way to a jury.

The crux of their argument was twofold. First, they argued that the school board lacked the power to expel them because they had not done anything wrong. While the school rule in question authorized or mandated expulsion for bringing intoxicating beverages on campus, they argued they had not done so. They did not deny any of their actions but reasoned, after the fact, that the alcohol content in the punch was too low to be treated as an intoxicating beverage. They pointed to an Arkansas statute that, at the time, defined an intoxicating beverage as one with more than 5 percent alcohol content. But as determined at trial, their mix was only about 0.91 percent alcohol. Thus, they argued they had not violated any school rule. Their second argument was that the district had intentionally violated their rights, as there were some procedural anomalies at the hearing.

After trial, the judge submitted the case to the jury and instructed it that, to enter a decision for the girls, it had to find that the defendants had "acted with malice in expelling them," which the court defined as "ill will against a person—a wrongful act done intentionally without just cause or excuse."[3] The jury, however, was unable to reach a verdict in the case, and the judge entered judgment for the defendants, reasoning there was no evidence on which a reasonable jury could infer that district officials had acted with malice.

The girls' luck was better on appeal to the Eighth Circuit. The Eighth Circuit reasoned that no evidence at either of the school district hearings established the alcohol content of the beverage, and thus, there was no basis on which to legitimately expel them. This, the court found, violated due process. The court also held that the district court's requirement of malice to support damages was too high of a standard. "It need only be established that the defendants did not, in the light of all the circumstances, act in good faith."[4]

This backstory is crucial in understanding what the Supreme Court did and did not intend to do in its holding in *Wood* and why it was seemingly so agitated with the case itself. First, the issues before the Court are not the ones for which lower courts have so often cited *Wood*. There were two issues before the Court in *Wood*, and neither of them was whether courts can entertain substantive due process challenges to school discipline or what the standard might be in such cases. The first issue in *Wood* was whether school officials are entitled to qualified immunity against damage suits, even though they may have violated a student's due process rights. Is "malice" required, a lack of good faith, or something else? The Supreme Court in *Wood* devoted almost the entirety of its opinion to this question and finally offered a simple answer: "A compensatory award will be appropriate only if the school board member has acted with such an impermissible motivation or with such disregard of the student's clearly established constitutional rights that his action cannot reasonably be characterized as being in good faith."[5]

One month earlier in *Goss v. Lopez*, the Court had established, for the first time, that students were entitled to constitutional due process protections in suspensions and expulsions. Thus, the holding in *Wood* simply adds that they are also entitled to damages for deprivations of due process when the school intentionally or in the absence of good faith violates those rights.

The second issue in *Wood* was whether the plaintiffs were entitled to damages under this new precedent. The answer to this question rested on the facts of the case. In particular, this question hinged on whether there was any evidence to support the finding that the students had violated a school rule, not whether the rule made sense or anything else. If there was no evidence of the students violating a school rule, the Court would move to the next step and determine the facts relating to the school officials' intent and whether they had acted in bad faith. But here, the Court emphasized that the evidence was crystal clear that the "girls had brought an 'alcoholic beverage' onto school premises." They admitted to mixing soda with malt liquor, bringing it to campus, and serving it. They also "admitted knowing at the time of the incident that they were doing something wrong which might be punished."[6] In other words, it was obvious that the school had not violated the students' rights in expelling them.

Everything beyond these points in *Wood* is a reflection of the Court's shock that the case had made it this far. Given these undisputed facts, the Court was understandably upset by the fact that the court of appeals had seen fit to set aside the punishment. The court of appeals had only been able to do so by inserting technicality and its own judgment for that of the school district. Rather than accept the school district's own statement or interpretation of its rules, the court of appeals set out to define and interpret the school rules as one would a criminal prohibition.

The court of appeals assumed that, to punish the students, the beverage would have to meet the state's statutory definition of intoxicating beverage. One need not be a lawyer to appreciate how ludicrous this proposition is. Prohibiting students from bringing alcohol of any concentration to school is rational and well within a school's power. No rationale exists to suggest otherwise. Even more ludicrous is the proposition that students might admit to bringing alcohol to campus, serve it to unwitting parents and students—presumably with the hope of getting them tipsy—know they did something wrong, and then escape punishment because it later occurred to them that the drink may not have counted as an intoxicating beverage under an unrelated statute. The students and their lawyers were surely creative in conceiving this argument but also equally juvenile in thinking it appropriate. One would have expected a court to disabuse them of such a notion. The trial court did exactly that, but the court of appeals added to the parade of imponderables by siding with the students.

This context places the *Wood* Court's famous statement that "it is not the role of the federal courts to set aside decisions of school administrators which the court may view as lacking a basis in wisdom or compassion" in an entirely different light. The statement has no doctrinal significance at all. Rather, it is a rebuke of the court of appeals and students' attempt "to relitigate in federal court evidentiary questions arising in school disciplinary proceedings or the proper construction of school regulations."[7] When students clearly violate school rules, which no one questions the validity of, there is no federal question to decide, other than maybe whether the proper process was followed in imposing the punishment.

To read *Wood* as doing more than establishing the rule that plaintiffs can seek monetary damages or that, in the absence of a direct constitutional challenge to the validity of a school rule, courts should enforce school rules as schools write and interpret them is to overinterpret *Wood*. The Court's discussion of substantive due process, or even procedural due process, is almost entirely missing from the opinion in *Wood*. The Court barely even uses the phrase *due process* in the opinion. When it does, it is only in passing or descriptive and never to distinguish substantive from procedural due process. The only definitive statement regarding due process in the opinion was, "Public high school students do have substantive and procedural rights while at school."[8] While the notion that *Wood* forecloses substantive due process review may fit with the tone of the rebuke of the lower court, it is totally inapposite to the issues raised and discussed in the opinion.

In addition, while the lower court had ruled on substantive due process, the Court does not identify any doctrinal error regarding substantive due process. Rather, the lower court's error was in its standard of review and interpretation of the facts. It was only by misconstruing the facts and issues that the court of appeals could create a substantive due process issue. A substantive due process review theoretically may have existed had school rules permitted students to bring low concentrations of alcohol to school and the school had expelled Peggy and Virginia anyway. But, of course, this was not the case.

The Court's reversal of the lower court's substantive due process holding, along with the Court's failure to articulate a standard, may have implied that substantive due process analysis does not apply to school discipline. But that notion is irreconcilable with the Court's explicit statement and citation that students have "substantive and procedural rights." More important, substantive due process is a generally applicable constitutional protection. Courts do not overturn generally applicable constitutional protections indirectly or by fiat. Even if they did, this Court gives no inkling of a rationale by which it would completely exempt school discipline from scrutiny. Substantive due process review might be more deferential in education than, say, in criminal law, but some level of scrutiny still necessarily applies. More to the point, the Court just a month earlier held that students have constitutionally protected due process rights and that, in *Wood*, they could seek damages.

Substantive Due Process Requires Rational Discipline

Debunking *Wood*, however, does not answer the question of what substantive limits the Constitution places on school discipline. Speaking of the general framework for substantive due process analysis, the Court in *Washington v. Glucksberg* explained, "The Due Process Clause guarantees more than fair process, and the 'liberty' it protects includes more than the absence of physical restraint."[9] The Court added that the Due Process Clause "protects individual liberty against 'certain government actions regardless of the fairness of the procedures used to implement them.'"[10] Where the liberty interests are fundamental, the Constitution requires strict scrutiny review. Where the liberty interest is not fundamental, the challenged law or policy need only meet rational basis review, which requires that the government have a legitimate end and that its chosen means of accomplishing that end are rationally related.

In *San Antonio v. Rodriguez*,[11] the Court held that education is not a fundamental right under the federal Constitution—although it reserved the possibility that a minimally adequate education might be protected. Because there is no general fundamental right to education, deprivations of education are subject only to rational basis review under substantive due process. For this reason, scholars have tended to conclude that the efficacy of pursuing substantive due process challenges regarding discipline is low. They, however, may have reached this conclusion too quickly, like lower courts overreacting to *Wood*'s admonishments.

First, rational basis review is not the equivalent of no review at all. Courts and commentators are correct that any legitimate end will suffice under rational basis and that any means that generally achieve those ends are permissible, but they are incorrect in assuming that all school discipline policies and practices would pass rational basis review. Operating on this assumption, they, in effect, forgo thoughtful rational basis review. Such assumptions render the Constitution moot as a practical matter, which is not the intent of Supreme Court precedent, deferential as it may be on substantive due process.

Second, substantive due process includes various background principles that set the outer limits of rationality. In other words, certain things are per se irrational and fail rational basis review without extended analysis of government ends or means. For instance, the Court has emphasized in recent years that a government interest to single out a particular group for unfavorable treatment is impermissible, notwithstanding the state's ability to come up with otherwise-nondiscriminatory reasons for its action. Likewise, even when the government has a legitimate end, when the means it chooses to achieve those ends are arbitrary, they are unconstitutional. Consider, for instance, a school that wanted to stop misbehavior in the classroom and made sitting next to someone who was misbehaving punishable by expulsion. The end is legitimate, and one could argue the means are rational as well. If every student knew that he or she was accountable for stopping misbehavior in the seat next to him or her, misbehavior would probably decrease. In that respect, the policy is rational. Yet the imposition of punishment under these circumstances is entirely arbitrary. Students may lack control over where they sit, and they certainly lack control over their peers' behavior. Thus, the possibility of expulsion is dependent on the luck of the draw: what seats were still available when a student started looking for a place to sit in the cafeteria or where the teacher assigned a particular student to sit in class. Surely, neither scholars nor courts would be so quick to pass on such a policy as imposing legitimate and rational burdens on students.

None of the foregoing is to suggest that substantive due process review of school discipline is easy or straightforward. Substantive due process is unfortunately one of the most controversial and least definitive areas of constitutional law. As such, it has, at times, served as an analytical playground for the Court to impose any rule or policy it liked. During one of the Court's most maligned eras—the *Lochner* era—the Court relied on substantive due process to articulate a "right to contract" that limited state and federal government's ability to intervene in the failing economy. The Court declared everything from minimum-wage and workplace-condition laws to prohibitions on child labor as unconstitutional. It also intervened on an inconsistent basis, reasoning, for instance, that the maximum hour limitations for women were reasonable but regulation of dangerous industries for men was not. In effect, the Court single-handedly prevented government from protecting the poor and stabilizing the economy. Some scholars and jurists claim that the Court repeated this mistake during the 1960s and 1970s with recognition of the fundamental right to privacy, the right through which the Court has protected procreation, abortion, and sexual intimacy.

Whatever the faults and merits of past substantive due process review, zero tolerance and due process do not require courts to wade into the politics or indefiniteness of substantive due process. No new grand theory of substantive due process is necessary for courts to limit egregious disciplinary policies. It is enough to recognize basic existing principles that are either explicit or implicit in substantive due process precedent and to apply them to the disciplinary policies of schools. Schools are subject to the same Due Process Clause and rationality requirements as other state actors are, and certain principles stretch across most all contexts. This chapter identifies these limiting constitutional principles and logical constraints.

At the very least, four distinct substantive due process principles should place limits on zero-tolerance policies and harsh discipline. First, treating dissimilar individuals as though they are the same is irrational. Of course, individuals will always be dissimilar in some respect. Thus, mere dissimilarity is not enough. But when individuals are dissimilar in respects that are of central relevance to their alleged misconduct, it is irrational to ignore these dissimilarities. Second, substantive due process, if it means anything, prohibits the state from disregarding innocence, knowingly punishing the innocent, or otherwise acting in bad faith toward the innocent. Any and all of these innocence risks occur when the state harshly punishes individuals who (1) have not breached the letter of the law or (2) have not engaged in normatively objectionable behavior. Third, distinguishing between dissimilar individuals and avoiding punishing the innocent requires the state to consider, at least, three individualized factors in the context of imposing punishment: the intent of the accused, the culpability of the accused, and the harm caused or posed. Finally, it is not enough for the state to feign attention to intent, culpability, and harm. The state must have evidence of these factors, not simply presuppose they exist (unless there is a strong basis in experience or logic for doing so). In other words, substantive due process prohibits the state from precluding factual deliberation of these issues.

Treating Significantly Dissimilar Individuals the Same

One of the most obvious flaws or irrationalities of zero tolerance and harsh discipline is that they lump so many dissimilar students into the same groups. The first grader whose mother puts a cough drop in his backpack without him knowing is treated the same as the seventh grader who knows that cough drops are prohibited but brings them anyway because his throat hurts and he does not want to miss school. And the seventh-grade cough-drop smuggler is treated the same as the student who brings Advil to school and sells it. And the Advil-distributing student is treated the same as the student who sells steroids or marijuana to his classmates. They are all drug offenders according to their schools and subject to long-term suspension.

Likewise, the kindergartner who brought his favorite pair of scissors to school to create Valentine's Day cards in advance of the holiday would be treated the same as the fourth grader who brought a six-inch letter opener on Valentine's Day to open his cards. And both of them would be treated the same as the sixth grader who brought his new hunting knife to school to show it off to his best friend. And the sixth grader is treated the same as the high school junior who brought a loaded nine-millimeter handgun to school with the intent to harm someone. They are all weapon offenders, threats to the safety of school, and treated as having violent tendencies. Some states and districts would also treat the student who disrupts class three times, disrespects a teacher three times, or wears the wrong shirt to school three times the same as the so-called weapons and drug offenders just described.

Criminal law has traditionally distinguished between all of these students. Under criminal law, some would have done nothing wrong at all. The rest would have done things that carry varying degrees of punishment. Yet, in some states and school districts, all of these students would be subject to the exact same punishment—expulsion or long-term suspension. The difference in the items they carried, their intent, their moral culpability, and their maturity would be irrelevant to the schools, even though the punishment routinely amounts to a de facto educational death penalty.

While substantive due process may be extremely deferential toward schools in the exercise of discretion in setting rules and imposing punishments, schools cannot be free to ignore all fundamental distinctions between students. At some point, individuals are so dissimilarly situated that it is irrational to treat them the same. The Constitution prohibits this irrationality. Both due process and equal protection rest on the fundamental principle that the government must treat similarly situated individuals the same.

This principle rests most obviously in equal protection doctrine, but it is an inherent part of due process as well. In equal protection, equity limits differential treatment based on immutable, illegitimate, or irrational differences between individuals. Because most of the inequities that courts have confronted in the past—racial, gender, disability, poverty, and the like—fall most directly within the framework of equal protection, litigants and courts instinctively move to that analysis. But outside of differential treatment based on immutable characteristics, due process is arguably just as relevant. Insofar as the point of due process is to maintain rules and procedures that lead to rational and fair results in the adjudication of cases and treatment of individuals, equal treatment among these individuals is necessary. In effect, inequity can be irrational and, thus, contrary to due process. The Supreme Court in *Bolling v. Sharpe*[12] made this point explicit. There, the Court held that due process rights include the guarantee of equal treatment and explained, "The concepts of equal protection and due process, both stemming from our American ideal of fairness, are not mutually exclusive. The 'equal protection of the laws' is a more explicit safeguard of prohibited unfairness than 'due process of law,' and, therefore, we do not imply that the two are always interchangeable phrases. But, as this Court has recognized, discrimination may be so unjustifiable as to be violative of due process."[13] Since *Bolling*, the Court has continued to blur the lines between substantive due process and equal protection. As Laurence Tribe explains,

> The conclusions judges have reached . . . [and] the rulings they have actually rendered in the name of substantive due process reveals a . . . narrative in which due process and equal protection, far from having separate missions and entailing different inquiries, are profoundly interlocked in a legal double helix. . . . Certain fundamental facets of freedom have won fierce protection under our Constitution even when they have defied easy labeling and enumeration or one-dimensional characterization in terms of such primary human activities as "speech" or "assembly" or "bearing arms"—indeed, even when they have resisted being named at all.[14]

Kenji Yoshino in "The New Equal Protection" adds,

> Too much emphasis has been placed on the formal distinction between the equality claims made under the equal protection guarantees and the liberty claims made under the due process or other guarantees. In practice, the Court does not abide by this distinction. The Court has long used the Due Process Clauses to further equality concerns, such as those relating to indigent individuals, national origin minorities, racial minorities, religious minorities, sexual minorities, and women. Conversely, the Court has used the equal protection guarantees to protect certain liberties, such as the right to travel, the right to vote, and the right to access the courts. We need to look past doctrinal categories to see that the rights secured within those categories are often hybrid rights.[15]

For the purposes of zero tolerance and harsh discipline, the most important aspect of equity in due process is not ensuring that similarly situated individuals are treated the same but the inverse. If treating similarly situated students differently violates due process, treating dissimilarly situated students as though they are the same also violates due process. As the Court has explicitly recognized, the Constitution requires that "'all persons similarly circumstanced shall be treated alike.' But so too, '[t]he Constitution does not require things which are different in fact or opinion to be treated in law as though they were the same.'"[16] Consider, for instance, a school that sought to adopt discipline policies designed to identify and punish students who engage in violence. Consider further that the school determined that it had too many violent students to punish them all at the same time or, at least, did not want their suspension rate to spike too high too quickly. So instead of punishing all students, it decided it would enforce the policy selectively. On Mondays, Wednesdays, and Fridays, it would punish only violent students who happened to be wearing yellow shirts. On Tuesdays and Thursdays, it would punish only violent students who happened to be wearing blue shirts. Even if this policy somehow allocated scarce resources or kept suspensions down, it is irrational insofar as it makes violence irrelevant on a regular basis. In other words, the dissimilar treatment of similarly situated students is irrational.

The same principle applies to dissimilar students. It would be irrational to treat a nonviolent student and a violent student as though they were the same simply because they both wore blue shirts on the day in question. Consider, for instance, that the school thought the best way to avoid violence was to scare students away from it. Thus, it passed a rule whereby it would harshly punish all acts of student violence plus any other student who happened to wear the same color shirt as a violent student on the day in question. Discouraging and stopping violence is clearly a legitimate goal, and this policy might further it in some small respect; but achieving this goal by treating dissimilarly situated students as though they are the same is sufficiently irrational that it would violate due process.

Fortunately, real-world schools do not adopt policies and procedures that are facially as ridiculous, and thus irrational, as the shirt examples.

The potential irrationality in discipline policies and the imposition of punishment is complicated by the fact that more than just one or two factors are at play. Whereas the shirt example reduces the problem to just a violent act and a shirt color, state actions, including those by schools, may include multiple relevant factors. When multiple factors are relevant, the definition of "similarly situated" varies accordingly. Thus, a more accurate statement of the substantive due process equality principle focuses on whether individuals are similar or dissimilar in relevant respects. This lends itself to prohibitions of two different policies or practices: *treating individuals who are similarly situated in relevant respects differently and treating individuals who are dissimilar in relevant respects the same.*

Zero-tolerance policies vary by state and locality, and many surely include nuances that allow them to be applied rationally. But many, either in form or function, treat dissimilarly situated students as though they were the same. Aggressive zero-tolerance policies lump various categorically different types of behavior together—from trivial to serious misbehavior and from illegal behavior to behavior that is neither illegal nor normatively problematic. For instance, school discipline codes typically lump together alcohol, tobacco, and drugs—including their possession, consumption, intoxication, and sale. All of these items and activities are rightly off-limits for students on school grounds, and schools can punish students who engage in them. But these items and activities are far from similar.

For instance, the student who regularly sells drugs to his classmates in the school parking lot is far different from the student who consumes marijuana, given to him by his wayward uncle, in the basement of his own home. Both students may have engaged in a crime; but in some locations, the latter may have committed no more than a minor misdemeanor that carries a fine,[17] whereas the former may have committed a serious felony.[18] Equally, if not more, important, the latter student would not have involved or endangered anyone but himself, nor would he have entered school property; whereas the former would have transgressed all three concerns. Zero-tolerance policies, however, often disregard distinctions between on-campus and off-campus behavior,[19] as well as distinctions between serious and relatively minor misbehavior.

One might allow that, while distinct, all illegal activities are sufficiently serious that they warrant the same response from schools and, thus, schools need not parse them out. Even if that rationale could be substantiated—which it probably cannot—it does not justify the breadth of zero-tolerance policies. Alcohol and tobacco are legal items, and under certain circumstances, a student might have legal access to them outside school. Minors' access to items such as Ibuprofen, aspirin, cough drops, and other over-the-counter "drugs" is relatively broad. In contrast, items such as cocaine and marijuana are controlled substances that neither adults nor minors can legally obtain (outside of Colorado and Washington and those states that permit medicinal use of marijuana). None of this is to suggest that schools should permit students to bring any of these items to school, but attending school with alcohol or nicotine in one's system or Ibuprofen in one's pocket is far different from having a controlled substance in one's system. The latter student would by necessity have engaged in illegal activity, whereas the former may not have.

Consider the student whose parents allowed him a glass (or two) of wine to celebrate some significant event the night before school or gave him cough drops and Ibuprofen to control a cold at school, versus the student who purchased and smoked marijuana in the school parking lot before entering school. Most zero-tolerance policies by their text would treat the aforementioned wine-drinking or Ibuprofen- and cough-drop-carrying student the same as the pot smoker. Some would treat the wine-drinking student the same, even if he did not enter school with alcohol in his system. Examples such as these, even if rare, reveal the irrationality of zero-tolerance policies that refuse to distinguish between the legal and illegal, the serious and trivial, on- and off-campus behavior, and the innocent and culpable.

The lack of distinction between the legal and illegal, or dangerous and nondangerous activity, is even more problematic in zero-tolerance approaches to weapons. Policies often define a weapon offense in the broadest way possible—"possess[ing] any item capable of inflicting injury or harm . . . to persons or property"[20]—and punish all offenses with long-term suspension or expulsion. The obvious intent of a broad definition of "weapon" (or "drug") is to err on the side of safety and sweep in as much conduct as possible. Legitimate safety motivations, however, do not sanction irrational definitions or practices. Broad definitions treat benign or "innocent" behavior as equivalent to malevolent violence. Some school districts have deemed key chains, staplers, geometry compasses, and fingernail clippers as weapons, expelling students for merely possessing them. No doubt, circumstances could arise in which these items are equivalent to weapons, but those circumstances would involve a student using or intending to use the item as a weapon, not simply possessing the item. Zero-tolerance policies frequently ignore this crucially relevant circumstance and instead focus on the fact that these items share some quality—sharpness or capacity to harm—with actual weapons. But sharing a quality with an actual weapon no more makes a fingernail clipper a weapon than does sharing the characteristic of insanity with the Unabomber make one a terrorist.

It was this exact type of flawed reasoning that led the Court to strike down the detention of an alleged enemy combatant in *Hamdi v. Rumsfeld* in the middle of the Iraq and Afghanistan wars.[21] While Hamdi shared the characteristic of having been seized in Afghanistan—and potentially on the battlefield—with a larger class of individuals who posed a threat to the United States and its soldiers, this fact alone could not render Hamdi an enemy combatant or foreclose the need to inquire further into his situation. To focus solely on that characteristic would fail to account for individuals who are clearly not enemy combatants: "errant tourist[s], embedded journalist[s], or local aid worker[s]."[22] Thus, the Court held that due process prohibited the government from presuming Hamdi to be an enemy combatant and depriving him of the opportunity to prove otherwise.

None of this is to say that a school might not permissibly and explicitly prohibit fingernail clippers in school, but it does not follow that a school can still treat and punish them as though they are weapons. Because fingernail clippers are benign, legal, and particularly useful items, there are any number of reasons why a student may accidentally bring such an item to school. Even though the school might confiscate the clippers or impose some minor punishment for bringing them, no rationale exists by which to punish the accidental possession of a benign, legal, and particularly useful item as one would punish the intentional possession of a hunting knife or firearm, by expulsion. To do so is (1) to irrationally merge nonweapons with weapons and (2) to presume a high level of culpability or intent on the basis of possession where no culpability or intent likely exists.

Finally, putting aside the problems of broadly defining weapons and drugs and conflating possession with use, many states and schools also extend zero tolerance and expulsion to behavior that cannot, under any circumstance, be construed as being as serious or egregious as drugs or weapons. In particular, many disciplinary codes treat tardiness, disrespect, and defiance as a basis for suspension and expulsion. Granted, these policies do not tend to expel students for one instance of tardiness or disrespect, but repeat instances—two or three—can lead to mandatory suspension and expulsion. While these behaviors warrant a response, disrespect, even if repeated, is in no way equivalent to selling drugs at school. Yet some schools effectively treat it as such.

South Carolina's disciplinary statute, while not mandating expulsion for these minor behaviors, captures the irrationality. It provides that a district may expel, suspend, or transfer "any pupil for the commission of any crime, gross immorality, gross misbehavior, persistent disobedience, or for violation of written rules and promulgated regulations established by the district board, county board, or the State Board of Education."[23] On its face, the statute equates a crime with persistent disobedience, authorizing the same maximum penalty for both. But then inexplicably, a subsection of the statute states that a district "shall not authorize or order the expulsion, suspension, or transfer of any pupil for a violation of section 59-150-250(B),"[24] which makes it a misdemeanor for a minor to knowingly purchase a lottery-game ticket.[25] In other words, a district may expel a student for disobeying a teacher's instruction on a regular basis, but it may not even suspend a student who commits the misdemeanor of buying a lottery ticket in the middle of math class. Thus, the statute implicitly recognizes the irrational conflation of substantially dissimilar behavior in one instance—selling cocaine versus buying a lottery ticket—but rejects the more obvious and pertinent distinctions between the classroom clown and the parking-lot criminal. In this respect, the grounds for suspension and expulsion are both over- and underinclusive, a paradigmatic indicator of irrationality.

Making Marginally Relevant Factors Determinative

One might still attempt to defend zero tolerance and harsh discipline on the basis that they still generally achieve some goal of the school, notwithstanding the inequitable treatment they produce. The problem with such a defense is that it glosses over why zero tolerance and harsh discipline wind up treating dissimilar students as though they were the same. They treat students the same because they are based on at least two fundamental logical fallacies, and those fallacies are the direct cause of random and arbitrary punishment, which goes to the very core of what due process was designed to prevent.

The first logical fallacy of treating dissimilar individuals the same is that it is premised on the notion that some characteristic or factor that is entirely irrelevant or only marginally relevant is actually of primary importance. For instance, both shovels and chainsaws have bladed tips and similar curvatures at their ends, but save for some very unique exigencies, choosing to dig a grave with a chainsaw or cut down a mature oak tree with a shovel would be irrational under almost any circumstance one would bother to imagine, even though one could theoretically dig a grave or cut down a tree with either. The items are too dissimilar in other meaningful respects to fashion a logic, under normal circumstances, by which to treat them the same. The logical fallacies were the premise that bladed tips were of importance to either project, when, in fact, some other characteristic was exponentially more important.

The same logic applies to persons. Is there a logic under which a university should interview both the PhD student and a sixth grader to teach a seminar on Mark Twain simply because both attest they are good communicators, have read *Tom Sawyer* and *Adventures of Huckleberry Finn*, and have earned the highest grade in every English course they have taken? Certainly, all those characteristics bear relevance to teaching in an English department, but they have no determinative importance within the pool of persons reasonably qualified for the job. Likewise, is there a logic by which the PhD student should be allowed to compete against the sixth grader in the public library's summer reading-comprehension challenge for students simply because the PhD student attends school and has the summer off?

While these policies and practices may appear to look at relevant factors, those factors are so overinclusive and simplistic that they do not further the government's goal in any meaningfully rational way. When viewed in isolation, the factors become an irrational basis on which to make a decision. Simplistic or overinclusive factors can, at most, serve as triggering or sorting factors that require further inquiry of other determinative factors. But zero-tolerance and harsh-discipline policies elevate simplistic factors to primary or determinative importance: that an item with a sharp edge on it was found on or near a student, that a student possessed an item that contains a pharmacological substance (which may mean nothing more than that it can be purchased over the counter at a drug store), that a student used a word like *gun* or *knife* in a story he wrote or a game he played. These factors are not indicative of much of anything unless they are connected to intent or some other inquiry or examination of the item or activity. Thus, defining disciplinary prohibitions solely in these relatively meaningless respects is irrational. In short, zero-tolerance and harsh-discipline policies regularly treat certain factors as having primary or determinative relevance, when in fact, they do not. Because no argument can be made that they are of primary or determinative relevance, such policies are irrational, both logically and constitutionally.

Ignoring What Matters Most

Relying on these overly inclusive factors intersects with a second logical fallacy that renders zero tolerance irrational: disregarding relevant circumstances. The primary flaw in the foregoing similar and dissimilar treatment examples is not just what they consider but what they do not consider. Those decisions are made in complete or near-complete disregard for the most relevant factors. For instance, assuming that a school does not have a dress code that requires students to wear or not wear a particular color, the color of students' clothing is an irrelevant factor in assessing student behavior. But the earlier example involved the school basing its decision on color while ignoring students' actual misbehavior or good behavior. In other words, the rationality of a school discipline policy is dependent not just on the factors on which it focuses but also on the extent to which it ignores factors that it should consider.

To be clear, a school need not consider every potentially relevant factor, nor is it always prohibited from treating individuals who are dissimilar in some meaningful way as though they are the same. But it is irrational for a government actor to pursue the goal of excluding weapons from school without actually considering what items count as weapons or what characteristics make an item a weapon, rather than just an item with a sharp tip. In other words, governmental goals dictate that certain factors be considered. Ignoring those factors or barring their consideration in administering a rule leads to irrational application of the rule.

This concept of relevant factors and considerations is most clearly borne out in the Court's recent decisions regarding mandatory sentencing guidelines for crimes—the criminal justice system's own version of zero tolerance. The Court's analysis in those cases arises out of the Sixth Amendment right to a jury, but the reasoning is equally applicable to a discussion of what factors substantive due process requires the state to consider prior to imposing punishment.

In *Blakely v. Washington*, the Court explained that fundamental tenets of the common law and our Constitution require that the state prove the facts that justify the imposition of punishment. Quoting Blackstone, the Court wrote, "an accusation which lacks any particular fact which the law makes essential to the punishment is . . . no accusation within the requirements of the common law, and it is no accusation in reason."[26] This basic principle has been so thoroughly accepted by prior courts and all the authorities on which they rely that the Court said it "need not repeat them."[27]

In applying this principle, the Court further reasoned that statutory prohibitions and punishment schemes that prevent juries from considering core facts are unconstitutional. Certain aspects of a crime are inherently relevant to proving that a violation of law has occurred. Thus, juries must have the opportunity to consider them. The statute at issue in *Blakely* had redefined the crime in such a way that juries would not get this opportunity. Rather, juries would make some preliminary determinations of the facts, but other determinations would be held over for the judge. If the role of the jury, however, is to determine whether a defendant is guilty of a crime, such a system is irrational. As the Court explained, one might defend the narrowing of the jury's role by reasoning

that the jury need only find whatever facts the legislature chooses to label elements of the crime, and that those it labels sentencing factors—no matter how much they may increase the punishment—may be found by the judge. This would mean, for example, that a judge could sentence a man for committing murder even if the jury convicted him only of illegally possessing the firearm used to commit it—or of making an illegal lane change while fleeing the death scene. Not even . . . critics [of the Court] would advocate this absurd result. The jury could not function as circuit breaker in the State's machinery of justice if it were relegated to making a determination that the defendant at some point did something wrong, a mere preliminary to a judicial inquisition into the facts of the crime the State *actually* seeks to punish.[28]

The legislative or policy gamesmanship at issue in these mandatory-sentencing cases is eerily similar to that in school discipline. The basis on which a school might exercise its ultimate power to entirely exclude a student from school is that a student has done something gravely wrong. He or she has engaged in violence, directly threatened the safety of the school, or brought an inherently dangerous item, such as drugs, chemicals, or weapons, to school. No one seriously questions schools' authority to severely punish these students. But if those are the bases on which a school exercises the power to exclude, the students whom it excludes must actually fall into those categories. Reaching the conclusion that they fall into those categories necessarily includes the consideration of particular facts. What states and districts have done, however, is attempt to redefine the nature of the infraction in such a way that schools need not consider any detailed facts. The infraction is defined as bringing an item that could be used as a weapon to school, thereby eliminating any inquiry into whether the thing actually was a weapon, was intended to be used as a weapon, or was intentionally brought. But this is the exact sort of activity the court in *Blakely* railed against because it deprives the decision maker of looking at the facts that justify punishment. To permit such action by the state would be to allow it to define anything it wishes as a crime and punish it as severely as it wishes.

The fundamental principle is simple: the government cannot ignore those factors (or proxies) that are most relevant to achieving the goals of its policies without acting irrationally. The rationale and justification for punishing students or adults exists only insofar as the state determines, through the consideration of pertinent factors, that the individual has done something that warrants the punishment at stake. Chapter 5 involves a detailed discussion of exactly which factors are most pertinent. For now it suffices to say that the current discipline policies frequently ignore them all.

Handing Out Arbitrary Punishment

One of the most central concerns of due process, and our Constitution itself, is avoiding the arbitrary exercise of government power against its citizens. Richard Fallon, Jr., one of the nation's foremost constitutional scholars, writes, "In its commonest form, substantive due process doctrine reflects the simple but far-reaching principle—also embodied in the Equal Protection Clause—that government cannot be arbitrary."[29] Without fair rules and reliable process, nothing prohibits executive officers from abusing their power or judicial officers from producing random results. Avoiding arbitrary power and adjudication is why government goes through the administrative hassle of hearings, deliberation, opinion writing, juries, notice, the opportunity to respond, rule writing itself, and all other aspects of procedure. What good would rules be, what good would process be, if the individuals sentenced to jail at the end of the process were just as likely to be innocent as guilty? What good would rules and processes be if top-performing government employees were fired just as often as weak employees were retained? What if the only reliable difference between winning and losing a wrongful-termination case wound up being the number of motions filed in a case? Such a system would be entirely arbitrary and not worth the effort that went into it. The government would be better served to just do away with courts and processes altogether and either bar terminations or bar appeals of terminations. In short, for due process to have any substantive value, it must produce nonarbitrary results and constrain arbitrary power.

In 1884, the Supreme Court in *Hurtado v. People of the State of California* wrote of due process,

> "The provision was designed to protect the citizen against all mere acts of power, whether flowing from the legislative or executive branches of the government." The principle and true meaning of the phrase have never been more tersely or accurately stated than by Mr. Justice Johnson in *Bank of Columbia* v. *Okely*: "As to the words from *Magna Carta*, incorporated into the constitution of Maryland, after volumes spoken and written with a view to their exposition, the good sense of mankind has at last settled down to this: that they were intended to secure the individual from the arbitrary exercise of the powers of government, unrestrained by the established principles of private right and distributive justice."[30]

A century later, the Supreme Court stated it even more simply: "the Due Process Clause contains a substantive component that bars certain arbitrary, wrongful government actions 'regardless of the fairness of the procedures used to implement them.'"[31]

Much of this precedent has focused heavily on what the Court calls abuses of power, which is the arbitrariness against which the Constitution was most directly designed to protect. Traditionally, this meant restricting abuses of executive power. More recently, the Court has increasingly applied the principle in the context of legislative and judicial processes that produce random results. The most poignant examples come from a series of Supreme Court decisions evaluating the constitutionality of punitive damages under the Due Process Clause. In these cases, the Court has consistently held that there are limits to punitive-damage awards, and they must be carefully constrained. While punitive damages in general can further the legitimate government ends of "punishing unlawful conduct and deterring its repetition," the Court explained that when the punitive-damage awards become excessive and arbitrary, they "further no legitimate purpose."[32] As such, they constitute an arbitrary deprivation of property. Christine N. Cimini sums up the Court's thinking in these cases:

> At the root of an analysis of punitive damage awards are concerns about arbitrariness, fairness and predictability. Constitutional limitations promote predictability by requiring notice of the prohibited conduct as well as the severity of the potential punishment. Constitutional limitations also constrain inconsistent sanctions and limit indiscriminate decision-making by juries. Unlike criminal penalties where defendants are afforded a host of protections, civil punitive damage penalties lack significant protections. Without some protections, juries that have wide discretion and are susceptible to bias might indiscriminately award punitive damages.
>
> At the crux of the limitations on punitive damages is the constitutional requisite of avoiding awards that are so grossly excessive as to be either per se arbitrary or amount to an arbitrary deprivation of property. The underlying concern is that without a constitutional floor, individuals will be unable to conform their behavior and jury awards will be irrationally excessive and inconsistent. In order to accomplish this result, courts attempt to monitor the most irrational, arbitrary and inconsistent results and thereby promote the system's fairness and predictability.[33]

In the context of the death penalty, the Court long ago expressed these same concerns under both the Due Process Clause and the Eighth Amendment's prohibition against cruel and unusual punishment. The death-penalty system in Georgia was previously so random that the Court held that it was unconstitutional. The Court did not say that any particular person sentenced to death in Georgia did not warrant the punishment or that the state of Georgia lacked the authority to impose the death penalty. Rather, the Court held that the system overall was too random and irrational to be constitutional. The Court wrote,

> These death sentences are cruel and unusual in the same way that being struck by lightning is cruel and unusual. For, of all the people convicted

of rapes and murders in 1967 and 1968, many just as reprehensible as these, the petitioners are among a capriciously selected random handful upon whom the sentence of death has in fact been imposed. My concurring Brothers have demonstrated that, if any basis can be discerned for the selection of these few to be sentenced to die, it is the constitutionally impermissible basis of race. But racial discrimination has not been proved, and I put it to one side. I simply conclude that the Eighth and Fourteenth Amendments cannot tolerate the infliction of a sentence of death under legal systems that permit this unique penalty to be so wantonly and so freakishly imposed.[34]

Zero-tolerance and harsh-discipline policies raise concerns similar to those voiced by the Court in these punitive-damages and death-penalty cases. The state or school district casts a wide net in terms of things that might be treated as per se weapons, drugs, or misbehavior and punishes them all with the most extreme form of punishment available to the school. To expel a student for bringing scissors to school to work on a creative project is by any measure an extreme punishment. It is just as arbitrary because the student is punished the same as the one who brought a loaded gun to school but different from the student who picked up a stick on the playground and whacked his classmate on the butt. The student with the stick is closer to the one with the gun than the one with scissors, yet the student with the stick might have just been asked to sit on the sidelines of the playground for fifteen minutes while the student with the scissors was expelled. And from the perspective of an elementary school student, the system is entirely unpredictable. An elementary student should readily recognize that hitting someone with a stick would subject him or her to punishment, but unless teachers regularly put students on notice about sharp-edged items, one would not expect a child to think of scissors, nail files, or clippers as weapons. That some students had brought these items to school on numerous occasions with no compunction prior to being punished is particularly telling on this point.

This randomness is the direct result of ignoring relevant factors and making marginally relevant facts determinative. When this happens, punishment can become as random and arbitrary as drawing names out of a hat or being struck by lightning. As one court reflecting on *Wood v. Strickland* hypothesized, what if the school had decided not just to expel Peggy and Virginia for spiking the punch but to expel all of the students who unwittingly drank from the punch bowl because they drank alcohol on campus? Suspending the unwitting students "would not rationally advance the school's legitimate interest in preventing underage students from drinking alcohol on school premises any more than suspending a handful of students chosen at random from the school's directory."[35]

Overly broad and senseless prohibitions can also produce random results when they are not enforced. Consider that many teachers are not prone to blindly follow irrational prohibitions and, thus, surely do not refer all students with scissors and fingernail clippers to the office for punishment. It is, likewise, safe to assume that teachers do not refer all disruptive and misbehaving students to the office and surely do not refer their "best" students to the office a third time, knowing that the third referral can or will result in expulsion in a state like South Carolina or Mississippi. But for the student who is finally sent to the office for scissors or disruption, it may very well be as unexpected as being struck by lightning.

The problem is that zero-tolerance and harsh-discipline policies are never subject to this thoughtful type of scrutiny. The question time and time again, both before schools and courts, is simply whether the student did the thing prohibited by the discipline rules. Or the question might be whether the school has a legitimate purpose in excluding weapons or potential weapons from school. The answers to these questions are obviously yes. But those are the wrong questions. The important questions are whether the policy itself and its application are rational. These questions require a broader analysis than states, districts, and courts have bothered to consider. When these questions are posed, the answers should be relatively clear. The policies are irrational because they treat entirely different students as though they were the same. They completely ignore factors that are relevant to achieving the school's own goals, and as a result, they produce entirely arbitrary and random suspensions and expulsions.

With that said, it is not uncommon for the government to focus on factors that are one or more steps removed from the most relevant factor(s). Governments may need to cast wide nets to achieve broad objectives. Robbing them of wide nets altogether might also rob them of the ability to achieve important goals. The point here is not to suggest that result. Rather, the point is that the rationale of casting a wide net does not support the casting of nets unlimited in their breadth—hence the general principle that government action is random and arbitrary when it is based on factors insufficiently related to its goals, even if those factors correspond in some respect to its goals. The difficult question is determining the point at which a factor is sufficiently irrelevant or relevant that consideration or neglect of the factor renders a governmental decision random or arbitrary. Those questions are taken up further in chapter 5.

Punishing Innocent Individuals Is Irrational

When discipline systems treat dissimilar individuals the same, ignore relevant factors, and randomly hand out punishment, they will inevitably punish innocent individuals. Because no system will ever be perfect, the punishment of innocent individuals cannot be eliminated. But it is a far different thing to say that the state can knowingly and willingly punish innocent individuals or to say that the state can knowingly and willingly punish the innocent because the state believes doing so would be helpful in achieving the state's goals. Processes and rules that by design punish or allow for the punishment of the innocent cannot be reasonably defended under due process.[36] Yet this is exactly what many zero-tolerance and harsh-discipline policies do in the name of safety and order: punish the innocent.

State processes or rules that claim to have reached the correct result for an individual, even though the state knew or should have known an individual was innocent, violate substantive due process. Quite simply, the state lacks a legitimate goal for intentionally punishing the innocent.[37] And while the state might claim that its legitimate goal is punishing the guilty and that the punishment of some innocent individuals is incidental and necessary to that goal, incidentally punishing innocent individuals is justifiable and rational only if it is accidental, not intentional or in reckless disregard for innocence.[38]

To be clear, the meaning of *innocent* is not fixed. Philosophers and scholars have devoted extensive thought to what it means to be innocent. *Innocent* could mean that a person has not done the thing he or she is accused of, but it might also mean that a person has not done anything "wrong." By *innocent*, this book refers to both concepts: individuals who (1) have not breached the letter of the law or (2) have not engaged in normatively (whether morally, socially, or practically) objectionable behavior.

The second concept of innocence generally depends on a whole host of cultural and ethical norms. But for the purposes of due process, fleshing out and evaluating those competing norms is unnecessary. Our Constitution and approach to law carry their own set of norms. As a practical matter, our legal system primarily rests on a normative approach that defines innocence and guilt in terms of mental culpability. A person's actions alone are almost never sufficient to justify punishment, as the person has not necessarily engaged in what society deems repugnant behavior. For instance, it is not a crime to kill someone. It is a crime to kill someone when it is done with certain types of intent.

The only instances in which our laws diverge from this approach are when either the punishment is minimal or the behavior is inherently problematic enough that it speaks for itself. When the punishment is minimal, an assessment of culpability may not be worth the individual's or society's time. In other instances, the behavior is so unique and/or sufficiently problematic that it necessarily carries the requisite mental culpability and, thus, does not warrant special inquiry.[39] Both points are bound up in prohibitions on operating cars in excess of the speed limit. For instance, operating a car in excess of the speed limit poses the same risks and threats to the public, regardless of whether it is accidental or intentional. Thus, low-level regulatory crimes of this sort do not include culpability requirements.

With that said, societal and judicial concern with punishing the normatively innocent never goes away. Regardless of the crime, our laws and courts will tend to construe the prohibitions narrowly so as to avoid punishing the innocent. For instance, a typical speeding prohibition would prohibit "operating a motor vehicle on public roads in excess of the posted speed limit." On its face, the phrase "operating a motor vehicle" eliminates the need for any mental state or culpability. But courts will often still attempt to interpret such a phrase, when necessary, to avoid punishing the normatively innocent. A person driving a runaway speeding Prius might technically be operating the car, but a court could reason that the person was not "operating the car" because the accelerator was out of the person's control. Likewise, numerous criminal statutes make it a crime to "possess" some particular thing, like a weapon or drug. But courts infer that these possession statutes include an intent element because they would otherwise make criminals out of innocent bystanders on certain occasions. In short, even a law that lacks an explicit culpability component tends to be construed as including one. Otherwise, the laws would be reduced to irrational and arbitrary exercises of power.

Yet this is exactly what any number of zero-tolerance and harsh-disciplinary policies purport to do. As described in the introduction to this book, school officials in Knoxville, Tennessee, found a knife in Dustin Seal's car. No one contended that it was his knife or that he knew it was there. He was driving a car that just so happened to have a knife in it. For all intents and purposes, he was innocent of having done anything wrong. The school district, however, insisted that it had to punish him, not because he had done something harmful or wrong but because it had to draw lines in the sand regarding weapons. To further make its point, it initially averred that it would suspend the school valedictorian even if someone slipped, without him knowing, a knife into his backpack as he walked down the hall.

The fact that it was a knife can understandably cloud one's thinking. No question, a dangerous item is on school property and cannot be ignored. But if one moves away from the knife or gun scenario, the problem of innocence becomes quite clear. For instance, the only way by which to characterize the student who accidentally brings fingernail clippers or cough drops to school as other than innocent is to imagine a strict-liability absolutist world in which conduct is permissible or impermissible, not based on policy or reason but based on the fact that the government has "said so." But in our democratic constitutional system, our courts have repeatedly rejected the notion that government or schools can operate as absolutist regimes.[40]

Time and time again, the Court has emphasized that students "do not 'shed their constitutional rights' at the schoolhouse door."[41] And because they do not shed their rights, the Court has emphasized that

state-operated schools may not be enclaves of totalitarianism. School officials do not possess absolute authority over their students. Students in school as well as out of school are "persons" under our Constitution. They are possessed of fundamental rights which the State must respect, just as they themselves must respect their obligations to the State. In our system, students may not be regarded as closed-circuit recipients of only that which the State chooses to communicate. They may not be confined to the expression of those sentiments that are officially approved.[42]

Some schools and their defenders would, nonetheless, insist that policies that punish the innocent are rationally related to the goal of safety. They reason that strict and inflexible rules, even if they punish the innocent, further safety by leaving no potential threat unpunished. This reasoning, however, is seriously flawed because the "innocent" student who unknowingly possesses a nail clipper, or even a pocket knife, is not a "potential threat" any more than a student who does not possess a "weapon." Thus, expelling such a student does not, in any way, serve a school's safety goals. As the Sixth Circuit explained, "Suspending or expelling a student for weapons possession, even if the student did not knowingly possess any weapon, would not be rationally related to any legitimate state interest. No student can use a weapon to injure another person, to disrupt school operations, or, for that matter, any other purpose if the student is totally unaware of its presence."[43] The Supreme Court has further emphasized in other contexts that unchecked and undifferentiated punishment of individuals "carries the potential to become a means for oppression and abuse of others who do not present th[e] sort of threat" the government is seeking to eliminate.[44]

What the school is really asserting when it punishes the "innocent" is an interest not in safety but in convenience or efficiency. It is simply more convenient to punish based on predicate facts that marginally correspond with threats—possessing a sharp object, for instance—than based on actual threats themselves. But efficiency alone is not a legitimate basis to punish the innocent, particularly when the innocent are readily distinguishable. The very purpose of due process is to separate the "guilty" from the "innocent" and to draw reasonable distinctions between those to be regulated. A rule that lumps the guilty and innocent into a single category simply to ease the burden of due process serves no legitimate goal.

Efficiency serves as a legitimate interest in determining how much process a government actor should afford but not in limiting the key inquiries process must pursue. For instance, courts have held that allowing a student to be represented by an attorney and cross-examine witnesses imposes too much of a burden on a school, particularly in regard to a short-term suspension.[45] But even if attorneys and cross-examination are too burdensome, no court has ever suggested that a school, so long as it held some type of informal hearing, could do away with the underlying question of, for instance, which of five students destroyed their teacher's book bag simply because sorting the guilty from the innocent would be burdensome.[46] Zero-tolerance policies that disregard circumstances do exactly that. They disregard innocence and the fundamental question that the Court in *Goss* indicated schools must answer: whether punishment is "unwarranted."[47]

[5]

INDIVIDUALIZING DISCIPLINE

Chapter 4 detailed the irrationalities that substantive due process prohibits and how zero tolerance violates these prohibitions. The question of what due process requires to avoid these irrationalities is a slightly different analysis. In other words, if the key flaw of zero tolerance and harsh discipline is looking at the wrong factors and oversimplifying discipline inquiries, what exactly should our discipline systems look at? What are the precise boundaries of relevance, and what circumstances must decision makers examine?

Numerous factors and circumstances are potentially relevant in determining whether and how to punish a student. Hard lines are difficult to draw because the relevance of factors will vary according to what the student has done and the punishment the school is proposing. A school district might be free to disregard some factors under certain circumstances but not others. For instance, a school might disregard whether a student engaged in disruptive behavior before class or during class and simply punish the behavior the same. On the other hand, a school could reasonably treat in-class disruption as a relevant factor in how serious the misbehavior is. A school might, likewise, be free to disregard whether the student was experiencing trouble in his or her home life at the time of the misbehavior, but it might conversely consider this as a mitigating factor. The point is simply that substantive due process rationality requirements do not dictate every level of school discipline. To the contrary, substantive due process dictates very little.

Zero tolerance, however, narrows the question and increases the stakes by mandating suspension and expulsion. If the punishment for misbehavior is just one hour of after-school detention, the need to carefully consider multiple factors is minimal and a school's discretion more expansive. But when the punishment is suspension or expulsion, due process would require that the school be more careful. When school exclusion is at stake, substantive due process would mandate the consideration of a particular category of circumstances and factors: intent, culpability, capacity, and harm (i.e., danger or disruption to school). Without considering these factors, there is no way to rationally distinguish between the dangerous student who should be excluded from school for a year and the student who accidentally brought something to school that poses no real threat but who warrants some type of reprimand. There would be no way to distinguish between the third-grade student who talks too much in class and the high school student who actively attempts to undermine a teacher's lecture.

The First Pillar of Substantive Due Process: Intent

The most important factor in assessing student behavior and whether a student warrants punishment is intent. In fact, intent is so central that it is the one area where a few courts have been willing to intervene. As a general matter, lower courts have routinely affirmed the suspension or expulsion of students who admit to intentionally breaking a school rule, but students whose violation was unintentional have drawn more interest from courts—enough that a few have reversed the punishment.

The leading case on intent in school discipline is the Sixth Circuit Court of Appeals decision in *Seal v. Morgan*.[1] As detailed in the opening pages of this book, *Seal* involved a student who was expelled for the possession of a knife. While a knife was found in his car, it was undisputed that the student was unaware of the knife because it belonged to someone else who had left it there days earlier.

The Sixth Circuit offered a full rejoinder to the school board's rationale for expelling him. First, the court explained that expelling a student for unknowingly possessing a weapon is "not . . . rationally related to any legitimate state interest" because such a student poses no threat to anyone.[2] Second, the court recognized that laws regularly criminalize or penalize individuals for "possession" of certain items, but those statutes or regulations "ordinarily impl[y] knowing or conscious possession."[3] The court added that courts often infer intent as an element because otherwise the statute or regulation would violate basic due process principles.[4] In other words, it is beyond the authority of legislatures to criminalize certain behavior in the absence of intent. Third, the court responded to the school board's argument that an intent requirement was a criminal "technicality" that did not apply to schools. The court explained that intent is a fundamental precept of substantive due process "so obvious that it would go without saying."[5] Thus, intent applies to punishment and deprivations other than criminal, including expulsion and suspension. On this basis, the court opined that a school could not, consistent with due process, expel a valedictorian who unknowingly had a knife planted in his backpack simply because he was in possession of the knife.[6]

A few courts have followed *Seal's* lead. In *Langley v. Monroe County School District*, a school official found an open can of beer on the floorboard of a student's car. The student later indicated that it was her mother's car and likely her mother's beer can and that she was unaware of its presence. The school, nonetheless, excluded her from school and, in federal district court, argued that her lack of knowledge or intent was irrelevant. The district court disagreed, writing, "In light of the fact that the plaintiffs have presented evidence to indicate that the principal and vice-principal did not believe that Laura knew the beer can was in the vehicle, . . . this court finds that there is a sufficient jury question as to whether Laura's penalty was rationally related to the school board's interests."[7] A Texas appellate court, likewise, held that school officials cannot proceed with the assumption that school removal is mandated for the possession of weapons, when the possession was unintentional (although its reasoning was based on Texas state law).[8]

Other courts, however, have surprisingly been unwilling to endorse *Seal's* approach to intent. This is not to say that they reject *Seal* directly. Rather, they have sought to distinguish the facts in their own cases to avoid the question of whether substantive due process prohibits schools from excluding students without evidence of intent. They have done this by unquestionably deferring to a school's conclusion that intent existed or by stretching the facts to infer that intent existed regardless of what the proceedings in the trial courts suggested. For instance, in *Butler v. Rio Rancho Public School Board of Education*,[9] a school suspended a student for a year under circumstances analogous to *Seal*. A student had borrowed his brother's car for the day and drove it to school. The school found a knife and gun in the car, which the student claimed were his brother's. He also claimed he had no knowledge of their presence until the school found them. The school board expelled him for a year anyway, indicating he should have known that the knife, at least, was there because the butt of the knife was in plain view. On this basis, the Tenth Circuit upheld the punishment and reasoned it did not raise the issue presented in *Seal*. In that respect, one can read *Butler* as consistent with *Seal*, although one could argue that the student in *Seal* "should have known" of the knife as well. If so, the reasoning in *Butler* may be an attempt to minimize the general impact of *Seal*, as a school can almost always make the argument that a student should have known.

Regardless, courts taking an approach more in line with *Butler* than *Seal* often rest their holdings on the notion that *Wood v. Strickland* demands near total deference to schools or that school discipline codes are exempt from the strict constitutional rigor applied to the criminal code. These cases do not purport to offer a substantive due process defense or justification for expelling a student who lacked intent, nor could they. That justification is lacking in zero tolerance and harsh discipline. And this is the important point.

As emphasized in *Seal*, the basic substantive due process doctrine demands intent. While criminal precedent is not directly applicable to education, it does not follow that all constitutional discussions found there are irrelevant. Courts in criminal cases have explored the general contours of intent extensively. Those decisions offer ample evidence that intent is central to substantive due process, whatever the context might be. In those cases, intent is not just a technical requirement of criminal law but a substantive aspect of due process in general.

In the context of criminal cases, courts have recognized only one major exception to the requirement of intent: criminal statutes that seek to regulate behavior related to the general public welfare and dangers to it. For instance, motor-vehicle statutes relating to parking, speeding, and car maintenance may not require intent; likewise, housing codes relating to things such as fire safety may not either. Courts have exempted these "crimes" or prohibitions from intent requirements for two unique reasons.

First, these "crimes" are not traditional crimes like assault, theft, and murder. They are new crimes outside our due process traditions and involve a different set of concerns. As the Supreme Court in *Morissette v. United States* explained, these crimes, in contrast to traditional crimes, involve "neglect where the law requires care, or inaction where it imposes a duty."[10] Thus, unlike traditional crimes, a violation does not turn on the intent to do something. It turns on the failure to do something. The failure to do something or the failure to avoid doing something poses danger to society as a whole. In these respects, these crimes are public-welfare regulations in a class unto themselves.

Second, the "penalties [for public-welfare crimes] commonly are relatively small, and conviction does no grave damage to an offender's reputation."[11] As one court remarked, public-welfare breaches are only crimes in name or form, not function.[12] In other words, the stakes are low enough for the individual and high enough for the public as a whole that dispensing with intent, or at least specific intent, is reasonable. Yet, even with these regulatory crimes, circumstances arise when courts will still require intent if necessary to avoid clearly unjust results.

Beyond these public-welfare and regulation crimes, there are a few other instances when courts have allowed the state to dispense with intent, but those instances are random and limited. In other words, they are truly special instances. For instance, courts have upheld statutory rape laws and prohibitions on automatic-weapon possession, notwithstanding the absence of intent. No clear theory or general rule binds these minor exceptions together. The most that could be said is that they involve or are related to activities that society deems sufficiently repugnant that the law places an affirmative obligation on citizens to avoid that behavior. Yet even this generality does not amount to a reliable rule. With automatic weapons, the rationale would appear to be the serious and intrinsic nature they pose, but the same could be said of any number of other dangerous items for which intent is required. With statutory rape, punishment is premised on the need to protect a particularly vulnerable group from serious risks of exploitation, but again the same might be said of child abuse or sexual crimes. Those other crimes, however, still require intent. Another explanation might be that the crimes are so idiosyncratic that the defendant was, at least, on constructive notice that he or she was engaging in potentially criminal behavior. Thus, he or she could be said to have constructive intent. Yet again, if that were the rationale, one would expect it to extend to a broader set of crimes, which it does not. In short, beyond the public-welfare exceptions to intent, there are no meaningful exceptions that can be extrapolated elsewhere.

Schools Cannot Justify an Exception to Intent

School suspensions and expulsions do not fall within these exceptions. School discipline is distinct from public-welfare regulation in the activity regulated and the punishment to be imposed. Unlike people driving a car, constructing and maintaining buildings, or providing food to the public, students attending school are under no general or affirmative obligation to protect others from harm. They owe no duty to inspect their backpacks throughout the day or to test the chemical content of the liquid in their water bottle before sharing it with a friend or drinking from it themselves. Nor would such an obligation make sense, no matter how much a school official might think this would make his or her life easier.

Affirmative duties do not arise simply because the state desires them. To allow such would give the state the power to seriously erode the liberty that substantive due process intends to protect. The individual must be engaging in an activity to justify a duty. With students, who have not engaged in any intentional misdeed but are simply attempting to receive a state-compelled education, there is no basis to impose an affirmative duty. Their school bags, for instance, do not pose inherent threats of danger or interfere with the operation of school. The only way a book bag presents a danger to anyone or anything is if a student intentionally uses the bag to smuggle some item into the school or swings a heavy bag violently at another student. In other words, an affirmative duty to keep one's bag free of certain items would serve no real end, other than to potentially punish unwitting students for "technical" violations of school rules.

If analogous to anything, the student conduct that schools seek to regulate—fighting, threatening, stealing, and using and transferring drugs—is more similar to traditional crimes: assault, theft, narcotic use and distribution. All of these crimes, then and now, require intent as a matter of due process.

Eliminating intent cannot be justified under the idea that the punishment for students is minor either. Suspension and expulsion are far more serious than a parking fine, housing-code-violation fine, or speeding ticket. First, zero-tolerance and harsh-discipline policies deprive students of more than just the statutory right to attend school (which is important in and of itself). They deprive students of a constitutional right embedded in state constitutions. As chapter 6 details, a few state courts have held that states must have an important or a compelling reason to exclude students from school, regardless of the student's intent.[13] It is not enough that the student has engaged in some form of prohibited misbehavior. The misbehavior must be sufficiently serious and the exclusion necessary to justify cutting the student off from his or her education. To be clear, however, very few state courts, as of yet, have gone this far. Regardless, the point here is that the deprivation of education is the withdrawal of a constitutional right and, hence, a serious punishment.

Second, the withdrawal is not just temporary. Zero-tolerance policies frequently exclude students from school for extended periods of time. That extended loss of education, as a practical matter, can function as the equivalent of an educational death penalty for many students. Students subject to long-term suspensions, for any number of reasons, are increasingly unlikely to get their education back on track. As the Fifth Circuit wrote, expulsion is "the extreme" and "ultimate punishment." It stretches the educational system's "power to act" to its outer boundaries.[14] For these reasons, courts immediately before and after the holding in *Goss* were particularly concerned with schools' substantive justifications for expelling students. The court opinions during this period were entirely inconsistent with any notion that expulsion is a minor punishment or that the nature of student behavior justifies a public-welfare approach. The current failure to treat suspensions and expulsion as gravely serious simply disregards reality.

It would seem, then, that the only way to justify disregard for intent in student suspensions and expulsions would be to argue for an idiosyncratic exception, along the lines of statutory rape or possession of highly and inherently dangerous items. Such an argument has some surface appeal but falls apart upon examination. One might argue, as the school district did in *Seal*, that weapons and drugs pose such a serious threat to schools that rigid lines must be drawn in the sand. Mistakes or oversights cannot be tolerated. As Judge Richard Suhrheinrich wrote in dissent in *Seal*, "Schools act *in loco parentis*. Given this enormous responsibility, and the potentially devastating consequences of weapons on campus, a strict weapons policy is rationally related to a legitimate government interest—protecting our children from the very real threat of violence."[15] The argument clearly draws on both the public-welfare exception and the sui generis exceptions to intent that pertain to extreme dangers or circumstances. The problem is that zero tolerance and harsh discipline do not actually fit the rationale of either exception.

The serious-danger and in loco parentis arguments conflate the school's duty with students' duty. One might marshal a public-welfare or in loco parentis argument for holding a school liable for students' safety, regardless of the school's intent. But as noted earlier, no such argument can be made for holding students accountable, regardless of intent, because students do not owe any affirmative duty to their peers. The fact that a school may have an affirmative duty toward students does not give it the authority to impose affirmative duties on students and subject them to discipline even when they lack intent or would otherwise be protected by due process.

One could argue that weapons and drugs take on a unique and heightened risk in the context of schools and that this risk is equivalent to the risk that automatic weapons pose to society, where intent is sometimes discarded. The comparison, however, rests on sensationalism and emotional appeals, not on the everyday reality of school. In *Seal*, for instance, Judge Suhrheinrich points to the high-profile mass shooting that had occurred a few years earlier at Columbine High School in Colorado to justify the disregard for intent. He wrote that the "massacre and other school shootings have, unfortunately, become part of the national consciousness."[16]

Columbine and other mass shootings, however, do not justify a general disregard for intent. Those shootings, while horrifically tragic, remain isolated events. And while one should always be on guard and protect against them, there is really no basis to assume that such events are likely to occur in any other particular school. To the contrary, schools remain one of the safest places a child can be. Children are more likely to get hurt or killed crossing a street leaving school than they are to be the victim of a shooting at school. Even if the risk of a school shooting were higher, it does not follow that a district should disregard intent. School shootings arise not from accidental or even neglectful actions on the part of a student. They arise from calculated intentional actions.

And even if one disregarded all of these distinctions, the most that could be justified is disregarding intent toward firearms. Mass shootings would not justify the disregard for intent in regard to fingernail clippers, butter knives, and over-the-counter drugs. In other words, even if one could justify an exception to intent in schools, it would only be a narrow exception. In the criminal context, for instance, strict liability applies only to a subclass of distinctively and unusually dangerous weapons, not to weapons in general.

In sum, general deference to schools in administering discipline and ensuring that they operate within the bounds of due process are two distinct issues. Deference is to be afforded when schools operate within the boundaries, not as a basis for changing the boundaries themselves. One of the longest standing boundaries of due process is the requirement of intent. The rationale in *Seal*, legal history, and Supreme Court doctrine all amount to a default rule that substantive due process requires evidence of intent. The exceptions to this rule are few and far between, and the burden should fall on the state to justify any additional exemption it might seek in the context of education.

The Second Pillar of Substantive Due Process: Culpability

The second factor a school should consider prior to punishing a student is the student's culpability. Like intent, the concept of culpability is found throughout our criminal codes, civil liability, and other forms of punishment. Instances in which culpability is irrelevant are exceptions to the general rule. Culpability may not entirely separate the innocent from the guilty in the way that intent might, but culpability plays a huge role in distinguishing among individuals who have done something wrong and determining what the punishment should be. Consider, for instance, the differences between an individual who engaged in an intentional, calculated murder and an individual who started a barroom brawl with his fists but that ended in the death of his victim. Likewise, killing someone in self-defense is fundamentally different from both the premeditated killing and the barroom-brawl killing. All three might involve the intentional act of killing another person, but each has a different level of culpability. Thus, the state-authorized punishment, to the extent there is punishment, is different for each, in both civil and criminal contexts.

The law also recognizes that while individuals might act with the same type of intent, they may have different capacities, which alters an individual's culpability. For instance, the law tends to punish children and adults with diminished mental capacity differently than adults with full capacity, although the exception for adults with diminished capacity is far more limited. An individual may have acted "intentionally" or engaged in some action, but that individual may be in some sense less responsible for his or her actions than other persons are on the basis of capacity. Responsibility tends to be lower when an individual's mental capacity is diminished, the individual lacks realistic options to act differently, or the individual is compelled or persuaded to act for otherwise-legitimate reasons. The law accounts for these factors not because individuals with diminished capacity are innocent in any absolute sense (as is the case when intent is entirely lacking) but because they are the functional equivalent of innocent or, at least, dissimilarly situated from the prototypical offender. Moreover, punishing individuals with diminished mental capacity does little, if anything, to serve the law's objectives, particularly in criminal law. When punishment serves no purpose, punishment is constitutionally irrational and would violate substantive due process.

If there is any group of individuals for whom mental capacity and culpability factor heavily, it is children. Children as a class have diminished mental capacity, and thus, legal rules across the board treat them differently than adults. On the criminal side, the law places juveniles in an entirely different category from adults and assigns them less severe punishments. Their records of punishment are also sealed and/or eventually expunged, depending on the state. In other words, their "crimes" are generally considered youthful indiscretions that should not be punished harshly or haunt them for life (although juveniles are subject to serious punishment).

On the civil side, statutes likewise limit the types of legal obligations that can be placed on a minor and consider age in assessing the liabilities the law might impose. For instance, the contracts that minors enter into are voidable. The law presumes that they lack the wisdom, experience, and intelligence to knowingly enter into contracts to purchase homes, take on loans, or carry out services. And while they can be sued in intentional tort actions for the harms they may accidentally cause, precedent in most states requires that their age, intelligence, and experience be taken into account in assessing their negligence.

The general practice in states' common law and statutory regimes, of course, do not set the baseline for substantive due process approaches to minors, but these practices are persuasive evidence that children's capacity is sufficiently low that substantive due process should prohibit certain harsh punishments for minor misbehaviors. The most explicit indication to this effect was in *Roper v. Simmons*,[17] in which the Court held that sentencing juveniles to death is unconstitutional. There, the Court emphasized three major distinctions between juveniles and adults that placed the death penalty off-limits.

First, "as any parent knows and as the scientific and sociological studies . . . confirm, '[a] lack of maturity and an underdeveloped sense of responsibility are found in youth more often than in adults and are more understandable among the young. These qualities often result in impetuous and ill-considered actions and decisions.'"[18] Second, "juveniles are more vulnerable or susceptible to negative influences and outside pressures, including peer pressure."[19] These influences and pressures make it more difficult for children to avoid those situations that inevitably lead to bad behavior. Third, juveniles are necessarily going through development processes and experiencing enormous changes in their character. Thus, regardless of what they may have done or not done, their character is not fixed as good or bad.

The Court reasoned that, on the basis of these distinctions, society cannot treat juveniles as being among society's "worst offenders" who warrant its ultimate sanctions.[20] The Court further explained,

> The susceptibility of juveniles to immature and irresponsible behavior means "their irresponsible conduct is not as morally reprehensible as that of an adult." Their own vulnerability and comparative lack of control over their immediate surroundings mean juveniles have a greater claim than adults to be forgiven for failing to escape negative influences in their whole environment. The reality that juveniles still struggle to define their identity means it is less supportable to conclude that even a heinous crime committed by a juvenile is evidence of irretrievably depraved character. From a moral standpoint it would be misguided to equate the failings of a minor with those of an adult, for a greater possibility exists that a minor's character deficiencies will be reformed.[21]

In the absence of culpability and capacity, the death penalty does not serve the often-touted ends of deterrence or retribution with minors. Rather, it is vengeance for vengeance's sake or simply irrational.

The Court has returned to these ideas again and again, most recently in *Miller v. Alabama* in 2012.[22] The issue in *Miller* was whether Alabama could automatically impose life without parole on juveniles who had killed someone. The Court did not question whether life without parole could be an appropriate penalty in some instances, but it did question whether the state could presuppose that all juveniles automatically warranted that punishment. The Court held that an individualized hearing to assess the individual facts of the case would be necessary, at least, in the case of minors. As subsequent courts have explained,

> [*Miller* requires that] a "sentencer" ("judge or jury") "follow a certain process" before imposing this harshest possible penalty on a juvenile offender: i.e., consider the offender's youth and the hallmark features of youth (among them, immaturity, impetuosity, and failure to appreciate

risks and consequences); and consider, in an individualized way, the nature of the offender and the offense (for example, as relevant, the offender's background and upbringing, mental and emotional development, and possibility of rehabilitation).[23]

Or more succinctly, "prior to sentencing a juvenile to life without parole, the sentencing court [must] take into consideration all pertinent factors—namely an offender's status as a juvenile and the numerous characteristics that accompany this status."[24]

Josie Brown argues that this Eighth Amendment analysis is equally applicable to harsh forms of school discipline. She writes,

> *Roper*'s reasoning demonstrates adherence to the principles of "dignitary appropriateness" that have repeatedly shaped substantive due process analysis. A governmentally constructed system of consequences can reliably effectuate its legitimate objectives only if it proceeds from an accurate assessment of the person or category of persons on whom such consequences will be imposed. A reviewing court can use relevant professional expertise as a guidepost in its assessment of the "dignitary appropriateness" of exclusion-oriented disciplinary practices that ignore the origins of student behavior and make no effort to fulfill school discipline's central function: teaching students the skills they need to regulate their conduct.
>
> . . . The nature of administrative due process generally and the application of due process norms to schools in particular . . . illuminates that an imperative to acknowledge personal dignity in the conduct of governmental operations is central to due process theory. *Roper*'s animating ethic, recognition that a constitutional duty to respect the dignity of children and youth can be effectuated only through attention to their developmental status, points the way toward a substantive due process attack on school discipline practices that diverge radically from what the best available knowledge about adolescent development would recommend.[25]

The social science community is unequivocal on the relationship between students' developmental status and their decision making. As an American Psychological Association report explained,

> There is no doubt that many incidents that result in disciplinary infractions at the secondary level are due to poor judgment on the part of the adolescent involved. But if that judgment is the result of developmental or neurological immaturity, and if the resulting behavior does not pose a threat to safety, it is reasonable to weigh the importance of a particular consequence against the long-term negative consequences of zero tolerance policies, especially when such lapses in judgment appear to be developmentally normative.[26]

The Court's recent substantive due process precedent regarding civil penalties makes the case for extending the culpability rationale and analysis from *Roper* and *Miller* to school discipline even more compelling. As introduced in chapter 4, the Court's most pertinent recent due process cases have involved punitive damages in civil cases. In these cases, the Court has held that punitive-damage awards that are "grossly excessive" in relation to the state's interest "enter the zone of arbitrariness that violates the Due Process Clause."[27] The Court articulated a three-factor standard in *BMW v. Gore* for assessing whether a damage award is grossly excessive: (1) the reprehensibility of the defendant's conduct, (2) the disparity between the actual harm caused and the punitive damages awarded, and (3) the difference between the punitive damages in the instant case and the criminal or civil penalties imposed in comparable cases.[28] The Court emphasized that "perhaps the most important indicium of the reasonableness of a punitive damages award is the degree of reprehensibility of the defendant's conduct. . . . Exemplary damages . . . should reflect 'the enormity of his offense.'"[29] The Court has since reiterated and reinforced this approach in other cases.[30]

Roper's culpability rationale and evidence fall squarely within *BMW*'s substantive due process limits on punishment, particularly the reprehensibility factor. Together, the cases reflect at least three broad principles. First, culpability cannot be disregarded in assigning criminal or civil penalties. Second, the lack of serious culpability is dispositive when the punishment to be imposed is serious. Third, penalties should be rationally, although not precisely, proportional to culpability, even when the punishment is not extreme or ultimate.

The open question is how exactly this culpability analysis and evidence should apply to school discipline. One might distinguish *Roper* and the *BMW* line of cases from school discipline based on the fact that they involve such extreme forms of state sanction—the death penalty in *Roper* and punitive damages in *BMW* and related cases. To use those cases to further a stringent proportionality principle to all punishments would place the courts in the position of a super legislature, exercising continual and final review of all criminal and civil punishment regimes. The Court has made clear that it will not take up that role.[31] Thus, one could read the principles in the case not as generally applicable standards for all punishment—from the minor to the serious—but rather as limits on extreme outliers within the context of serious punishment.

The fairest reading of those cases, however, suggests that the foregoing culpability and proportionality principles extend beyond the immediate context of those cases, although the principles do not operate as broad limitations on every punishment that the state might impose. The Court's proportionality principle in *BMW* contains its own self-limitation to guard against overreaching later applications. In particular, the Court looked to other punishments that the state imposed for the same or similar behavior under other civil and criminal statutes, finding that BMW's failure to disclose certain information was not punished at all criminally and only minimally by other civil statutes. This would suggest that a $2 million punitive-damages award was excessive. By looking to other state sanctions for comparisons, the Court refrained from exercising its own policy preference as to punishment and instead followed the state's own broader punishment scheme.

With this self-limiting principle, extending the *Roper* and *BMW* analyses poses relatively few concerns. The other two principles relating to culpability—that it cannot be disregarded and that minimal culpability can be dispositive at times—do not provide a basis for judicial review of most punishments. Only when the state ignored culpability altogether or imposed serious punishment for relatively minor breaches of social order would these principles be implicated. As a practical matter, this almost never happens. Because culpability is so rooted in our traditions, the state rarely ignores it. Because extreme punishments are by their nature the exception, the state rarely imposes them.

Zero tolerance and harsh school discipline, however, do present one of the unique contexts in which *Roper's* and *BMW's* principles should be applied. Like *Roper* and the *BMW* line of cases, zero tolerance and expulsion involve extreme punishment. The immediate and long-term effects of school exclusion are extremely serious. In the short term, suspensions and expulsions deny students access to their most important right, place them at risk for academic failure, and potentially set their education back by a year. In the long term, they often amount to educational death penalties and, as the Fifth Circuit termed it, second-class citizenship. As such, zero tolerance and harsh discipline would still fit within even a narrow reading of *Roper* and the *BMW* line of cases that concludes they are premised on exercises of extreme state authority.

The lack of culpability in much of the student behavior that schools punish so harshly, likewise, provides a strong basis for extending the rationale of those cases. Student misbehavior is a result of the same neurological immaturity and social environmental determinism that was involved in *Roper*. In *Roper*, the Court was explicit in reasoning that this immaturity diminished student culpability and, thus, invalidated the basis on which to impose severe criminal punishment. The same should follow for whatever misbehavior a student is alleged to have committed in school. Zero tolerance and expulsion involve serious punishment, but serious culpability is often lacking.

Even worse, zero tolerance actively ignores the issue of culpability altogether. Prior to the Court's opinion in *Roper*, a minor still might have avoided the death penalty by demonstrating diminished culpability or capacity. The Court's opinion was to emphasize that juveniles are per se lacking in culpability and capacity, and thus, the death penalty was inappropriate under all circumstances. Zero-tolerance policies are premised on the exact opposite approach. There is no set of circumstances under which a student could avoid suspension or expulsion because culpability does not matter. In other words, schools are not engaging in any assessment of individual students' culpability (which is necessary in the first instance to warrant judicial deference toward the state's judgment) and are taking a position that cannot be squared with any reasonable articulation of the Court's recent substantive due process principles. In this context, judicial intervention in zero tolerance does not require an expansive interpretation of *BMW*'s holding or *Roper*'s culpability rationale, nor does it require a disregard for schools' judgment.

Applying the other two explicit substantive due process factors articulated in *BMW*—actual harm in relationship to the punishment, and analogous punishments in other contexts—reveals that various applications of zero tolerance and expulsion are not even close to falling within the bounds of permissible punishment. First, schools suspend and expel students even when harm does not exist. Students with fingernail clippers, students with cough drops, and even some students who possess real weapons are harmless. Recall Mr. Ratner, who came to the aid of his suicidal friend. His school even admitted that he posed no danger and that he did the right thing.

When the actual harm these students pose is compared to their punishments—as *BMW* would require—long-term suspension is necessarily grossly disproportionate. As the concurring judge in *Ratner* admitted, school officials "jettison[ed] the common sense idea that a person's punishment should fit his crime in favor of a single harsh punishment, namely, mandatory school suspension. Such a policy has stripped away judgment and discretion on the part of those administering it."[32] The judge then added that expulsion "is a calculated overkill when the punishment is considered in light of Ratner's good-faith intentions and his, at best, if at all, technical violation of the school's policy."[33]

A comparison of potential punishments outside school to those inside school also demonstrates the gross disproportionality of applying zero tolerance to students with minimal culpability. In fact, identifying analogous punishments outside school is difficult because zero-tolerance policies frequently punish behavior for which there would have been no punishment or consequence had the behavior occurred anywhere else. For instance, one would be hard-pressed to identify a place in society where a minor could not take nail clippers other than school. A student could freely take them onto an airplane—one of the most heavily regulated areas in society.

Even where some relatively benign activity or item might be prohibited in society, such as certain liquids or larger sharp items on a plane, the response outside school is to take the item or stop the behavior, not to harshly penalize it. The only context in which relatively benign activities or possessions might lead to punishment is prison. Prisoners, however, are subject to harsher regulation for obvious reasons. They have already committed crimes, demonstrated a propensity toward illicit behavior, and forfeited certain liberty and property rights. Moreover, even if a prisoner him- or herself is not dangerous, he or she is surrounded by other inmates who are and could make use of illicit items taken from others. Schools and students simply cannot be likened to prisons and inmates, and the Supreme Court has directly rejected schools' attempts to draw such comparisons in defending heavy-handed policies. As discussed in chapter 4, the Court has repeatedly emphasized that students do not shed their constitutional rights, schools are not totalitarian enclaves, and schools must justify imposing on students' rights.

In short, it is hard to articulate any basis—much less a compelling one—under the *BMW* three-factor analysis to validate the broad application of zero tolerance and harsh discipline. The debate in regard to applying *BMW*'s holding and *Roper*'s rationale to school discipline should not be whether to apply it but how far. The underlying social science in *Roper*, along with common sense, suggests that substantive due process culpability concerns could and should apply more broadly in school discipline than they do regarding criminal and civil law in general. Aside from older teenagers who intentionally engage in the most serious behaviors, such as bringing a handgun to school, expulsion is a grossly disproportionate and irrational response to student misbehavior, even when the behavior is serious and particularly when it is not. An elementary school student who brings an actual weapon to school, for instance, may have no appreciation of what he has done. His conduct is no doubt serious, but to the extent that his culpability is most likely nonexistent, total deprivation of his education may be disproportionate by *BMW* and *Roper*'s rationale.

If culpability analysis applies to school discipline, the next question is how deep this analysis runs. The answer lies largely within schools' control. If harsh punishments were reserved only for weapon- and drug-related offenses, the analysis might end there. But since zero tolerance and harsh discipline apply to far more misbehaviors in some states and districts, culpability remains relevant. Ignoring culpability is even more problematic as to other misbehaviors because nonweapon and nondrug misbehaviors by students are entirely normal. In other words, they are to be expected.

Adolescents as a class are impulsive, lack self-control, need attention, do not always engage in a conscious decision-making process, and do not fully appreciate the consequences of their actions. As a result, nearly every student—even the valedictorians—will, at some point, engage in disruptive classroom behavior by talking out of turn, whispering in class, passing a note, and even responding to a teacher in a way that could be disrespectful. An informed and objective observer might very well be concerned about a student who was quiet or withdrawn and never got excited enough to breach some minor rule of classroom, playground, or hallway decorum. None of this is to say that classroom disruption should go unaddressed. One of the primary purposes and functions of school is to shape and model good behavior. But extreme and exclusionary disciplinary responses border on sadistic.

A disruptive student has not engaged in aberrational behavior and often may not have acted with any disruptive intent. Nor does such a student generally pose a danger to others or necessarily pose any more risk of future disruption than other students do. Thus, why suspend or expel the student? At best, suspending or expelling the normal disruptive student would frighten his or her peers, but it would not necessarily deter them. If they are like most all other adolescents, they lack sufficient self-control to steer clear of problematic behavior. In other words, the only students that harsh discipline deters are those who probably do not need to be deterred in the first instance.

Recognizing as much, federal special-education laws place specific limits and prohibitions on the suspension of certain students. For students with emotional and behavioral disabilities, some misbehavior is unquestionably expected. If that misbehavior is an outgrowth of the disability itself, the school is more limited in its disciplinary options.[34] Federal statutes would prohibit a school from suspending a special-education student for more than ten days over the course of a single school year without first formally assessing whether the misbehavior was connected to the student's disability. If so, the school would be required to remedy rather than punish the behavior through suspension.

But even at the other end of the behavioral spectrum, a percentage of students with what one might call perfect behavioral control will still predictably misbehave. Some will do it for no reason other than to make a point or protest a school policy or punishment they deem irrational or overkill.[35] In short, expelling or suspending some disruptive students is punishment for the sake of punishment, not for any legitimate educational goal, because these students are not even seriously blameworthy.

Although more controversial, one might also argue that some schools are, at least, partially responsible for or implicated in student misbehavior. Data and social science indicate that some misbehavior is a product of the school environment rather than inherent student characteristics and culpability. Studies show that an individual student will act differently in different classrooms and different schools. These findings reveal a strong correlation between effective classroom management, school environment, and educational outcomes. Thus, as one study found, "when students transferred from a school with a high dropout rate to one with a low dropout rate, their behavior tended to conform to the low rate."[36]

Such findings contradict the notion that good or bad behavior emanates from the "inherent characteristics of students."[37] To the contrary, while some level of misbehavior is behaviorally normal, elevated levels of misbehavior are a function of environment. Schools that offer dysfunctional education settings invite misbehavior. They cannot maintain order by harshly punishing students; they only make matters worse by harshly punishing students. Because suspension and expulsion do not address the underlying environment, some students who remain in the environment soon step up to take the place of the misbehaving student who was recently removed.[38] In other words, harsh discipline in dysfunctional schools begets more misbehavior, not less.

These findings are closely connected to the analysis in chapter 7. The argument there is that, because of the state's role in creating the environment, the state is obligated under state constitutional law to address the environment insofar as the discipline and environment impede students' access to equal and quality education. The argument in the current chapter is not that the state is obligated to rectify the problem. It would be a far stretch to argue as much under federal substantive due process. Rather, the argument here is far simpler: students' culpability for misbehavior is further diminished in dysfunctional schools, as the schools, not just the students, are to blame. As the Supreme Court itself has emphasized in speech cases, one of the primary roles of public education is the "inculcat[ion of the] habits and manners of civility" and the "fundamental values necessary to the maintenance of a democratic political system."[39] Schools that are ineffective in carrying out this role play no small factor in some student misbehavior.

None of this is to suggest that schools should take all the blame and students none or that expulsions are off-limits in these schools. Rather, the point is that when a school is failing to deliver a quality education, it likely bears some culpability for students' misbehavior. Given that students as a class have diminished culpability regardless of environment, only an absolutist or arbitrary state would harshly punish students in the context of a legally and pedagogically deficient environment, without even accounting for culpability.

The Third Pillar of Substantive Due Process: Harm

While intertwined with the concepts of intent and culpability, the harm an individual's behavior poses or causes also has independent importance in assessing the state's justification for punishment. A person might intentionally and maliciously throw a piece of trash onto his neighbor's front lawn, but the harm caused is so minimal that the punishment the state might impose has a relatively low limit. A jail sentence of any length would seem out of the question, but even if not, surely a sentence of one year in prison would violate substantive due process. The most extreme overkills in punishment more directly raise issues of cruel and unusual punishment under the Eight Amendment. The point here is not to suggest that substantive due process supplants the Eighth Amendment on this point. The point here is that, like intent and culpability, harm is a key factor for which the state must account if its punishments are to be rational under substantive due process. For instance, the state can easily articulate a legitimate state end in prohibiting neighbors from throwing trash on their next-door neighbors' lawn, but the state lacks any obvious legitimate reason to imprison individuals for that behavior. In other words, not only should the prohibition itself be rational, but so should the punishment.

The range of reasonable potential punishments is so wide that a principle of proportionality in relation to harm would have little effect on almost all state-imposed punishments. But zero tolerance and harsh school discipline, again, often represent outliers on this measure. The seriousness of a student's behavior and the potential ongoing danger or disruption a student poses too often get lost in districts' disciplinary policies and practices. The basis and justification on which some districts entirely exclude a student from school are often that the student has done something he or she has been instructed to avoid.

Standards and practices as bare as that amount to no less than totalitarianism. Schools must demonstrate some legitimate aim beyond this. Normally, the legitimate basis and justification are that the student has harmed or poses some harm to the educational environment, either in terms of physical danger and disruptive behavior. Either way, the goal should be tethered to real or potential threats. As the Court in *BMW* wrote, a "sanction . . . cannot be justified on the ground that it was necessary to deter future misconduct without considering whether less drastic remedies could be expected to achieve that goal. The fact that a multimillion dollar penalty prompted a change in [the behavior of the defendant or defendant class] sheds no light on the question of whether a lesser deterrent would have adequately protected the interests of [the state]."[40]

Broad zero-tolerance policies do the opposite when they seriously punish students who may pose no threat and require little deterrence. Consider the elementary school student with a pair of fingernail clippers, the middle school student saving his friend from potential suicide, and the Cub Scout who uses his favorite utensil to spread butter on his sandwich. Schools have suspended and expelled all of these students. If the basis for expelling these students is danger, schools are acting irrationally. These students pose no current or future danger. If it is deterrence, schools are still acting irrationally because the punishment sweeps too far afield of intent, culpability, and danger to be related to the deterrence of students who actually pose a danger. And even if intent were present, a far-lesser penalty would be just as effective in deterrence.

When pressed on these points, zero-tolerance advocates have responded with varying simplistic versions of "the rules are the rules" and that the only way to ensure safety and order is to enforce the rules in existence. Districts insist that they must draw hard lines in the sand and have no choice but to expel students when they cross them. This line of argument presupposes a sufficient justification for rules and punishment when none exists. Rules and punishment are not self-validating or self-rationalizing. In other words, line drawing is not a justification in itself. That a rule is written down and demands allegiance addresses only a procedural point of notice. It does not answer the underlying issue of whether the rule itself is valid in substance. For the underlying rule to be valid, it must be based on a proper goal and consider the necessary factors.

When schools defend their discipline policies on no more than the notion that the rules are the rules and they must enforce them unflinchingly, schools are really just arguing that substantive due process protections themselves be dismissed, presumably in the name of deference. The district court in *Colvin v. Lowndes County, Mississippi School District* captured the absurdity of this position and brought together the relevance of intent, culpability, and harm all in one instance:

> [A school district] may not hide behind the notion that the law prohibits leniency for there is no such law. Individualized punishment by reference to all relevant facts and circumstances regarding the offense and the offender is a hallmark of our criminal justice system.
>
> In a system where criminal offenders are afforded individualized punishment upon review of the facts and circumstances regarding the offense, students in our public school systems, who may also face a daunting punishment, should at least be afforded a thorough review of their case, prior to imposition of penalty.[41]

Presupposing Answers to Key Questions

Schools' failure to consider intent, culpability, and harm are the flip side of another fundamental flaw: assuming answers to questions that they do not know. A school might argue that it has, in fact, considered intent, culpability, and harm and that, on the basis of those considerations, it has determined, for instance, that students caught with weapons have necessarily engaged in wrongs sufficiently grievous to warrant expulsion. Thus, they need not inquire any further into the intent, culpability, or harm of any particular student. Surely such an argument might justify some policies, but those policies are rare.

As a general rule, due process prohibits decision makers from deciding students' fates in advance and requires that they listen to what the students say, deliberate the facts, and determine whether further information is necessary before making a decision. This general rule is both substantive and procedural. It is procedural in that it requires the state to afford individuals particular processes prior to imposing punishment. It is substantive in that these processes are aimed at producing a meaningful hearing and fair outcome. The substantive principle is breached when the key inquiries to be determined through individualized due process hearings are decided or significantly prejudiced in advance.

This idea is most clearly teased out in cases where the state has placed the burden on defendants to disprove their guilt or simply prevented an individual from providing counterevidence on some pertinent fact. Take, for instance, the Court's opinion in *Cleveland Board of Education v. LaFleur*.[42] The school board in that case had adopted policies that forced female teachers to take mandatory leave during pregnancy. The rationale was that pregnant teachers would at some point become incapacitated and unable to fulfill their teaching duties. Rather than wait until that point or have it occur abruptly, the school board sought to adopt bright-line rules regarding when teachers must go on mandatory leave. The board required this leave to begin four months in advance of the expected date of delivery.

The Court allowed that the rule might correctly predict the incapacitation of some percentage of teachers, but that was irrelevant. The relevant question was whether "every pregnant teacher who reaches the fifth or sixth month of pregnancy is physically incapable of continuing."[43] This, of course, is not the case. Thus, the central problem with the rule was its presumption. It precluded any "individualized determination by the teacher's doctor—or the school board[]—[regarding] any particular teacher's ability to continue at her job. The rules contain an irrebuttable presumption of physical incompetency, and that presumption applies even when the medical evidence as to an individual woman's physical status might be wholly to the contrary."[44] This, the Court held, the state cannot do under the Due Process Clause.

This holding, moreover, was not groundbreaking. The Court explained that "permanent irrebuttable presumptions have long been disfavored under the Due Process Clause of the Fifth and Fourteenth Amendments."[45] The Court has struck down attempts at irrebuttable presumptions in a number of areas, including, for instance, irrebuttable presumptions regarding a person's residency status, the fault of uninsured motorists involved in accidents, and unmarried fathers' fitness to raise their children.[46]

The Court has even struck down attempts by the state to indirectly presume a fact by shifting the burden of proof to a criminal defendant.[47] While the government may create a "presumption in favor of the Government's evidence," there must be some evidence and experience to justify such a presumption. But even then, the presumption is permissible only when it "remain[s] a rebuttable one and fair opportunity for rebuttal [is] provided."[48]

Zero-tolerance policies breach these substantive principles on any number of levels. Many zero-tolerance policies operate as irrebuttable presumptions that discipline is warranted. When such a presumption is irrebuttable, particularly regarding key aspects of liability, the presumption eliminates the entire substance and purpose of a due process hearing by narrowing the scope of the deliberation too far. Rather than assessing the circumstances surrounding an act, including the intent, culpability, and harm pertaining to it, these inquiries are often merged into a single one: whether an act or event in question occurred.

If, for instance, a weapon was found on a student, many school districts would conduct a hearing in which no issues beyond that fact are considered. As John Garman and Ray Walker write, "the basic concept of the zero-tolerance discipline policy is the near-presumption of guilt founded upon a mere statement of fact."[49] From this presumption or finding flows the second and more explicit irrebuttable presumption: that the ultimate sanction of exclusion is per se the appropriate response to a student's behavior. In effect, the school is just going through the motions of process, with no intent to actually deliberate on the facts and issues at hand because it has already decided the outcome. This prejudgment, or sham-like process, violates due process.

The only plausible justification schools can offer for these irrebuttable presumptions is that "efficiency calls for swift, decisive discipline that will fix the immediate problem."[50] Efficiency and speed, however, cannot be justifications for thoughtless disregard for the facts of a case or for making presumptions not grounded in reality. Efficiency and speed are justifications for limiting the exact type of process a school will provide, as more formalized processes can be burdensome. They are not legitimate justifications for presuming answers to substantive questions and making the presumptions irrebuttable. As one court reasoned, the aim of due process is

> to require school boards to fully consider the circumstances surrounding the misdeed as well as the penalty to be prescribed. . . . Employing a blanket policy of expulsion, clearly a serious penalty, precludes the use of independent consideration of relevant facts and circumstances. Certainly, an offense may warrant expulsion, but such punishment should only be handed down upon the Board's independent determination that the facts and circumstances meet the requirements for instituting such judgment.[51]

Likewise, the Supreme Court stated in *LaFleur*, "The Constitution recognizes higher values than speed and efficiency. Indeed, one might fairly say of the Bill of Rights in general, and the Due Process Clause in particular, that they were designed to protect the fragile values of a vulnerable citizenry from the overbearing concern for efficiency and efficacy that may characterize praiseworthy government officials no less, and perhaps more, than mediocre ones."[52]

While it might be easier for the school boards to conclusively presume that all pregnant women are unfit to teach past the fourth or fifth month or even the first month of pregnancy, administrative convenience alone is insufficient to make valid what otherwise is a violation of due process of law. The Fourteenth Amendment requires school boards to employ alternative administrative means, which do not so broadly infringe on basic constitutional liberty, in support of their legitimate goals.[53]

In short, while schools' judgments are accorded deference, due process requires that those judgments be based on an individualized consideration of inherently relevant facts. No predetermined set of rules or decisions can validly eliminate this adjudicative function. Moreover, without a consideration of, for instance, the harm posed by a student, the basis on which a student is to be legitimately punished falls apart.

Once one recognizes that these central pillars of due process have been stripped from much of school discipline, then one realizes that the discipline policies are but empty shells. The policies are not based on substance, do not have real justifications, have not been formed on real exigencies or real experiences, and make almost no attempt to afford processes to determine whether individual students actually warrant punishment. Instead, they are processes with heavily tilted scales masquerading as adjudications. The only possible way they can survive substantive due process scrutiny is for courts, under the guise of deference, not to scrutinize them at all.

[6]

THE CONSTITUTIONAL RIGHT TO EDUCATION

Can the State Justify Taking It Away?

When the Supreme Court decided *Goss v. Lopez* in 1975, the right to education had yet to fully develop. Two years earlier, in *San Antonio v. Rodriguez*, the Court held that education is not a fundamental right under the federal Constitution. And while today more than half of the state supreme courts have recognized education as a fundamental or constitutional right, only one state supreme court had clearly recognized such a right in 1975. Thus, the Court in *Goss* analyzed education only as a statutory right. To withdraw a statutory right, a school need only pass rational basis review. Under rational basis review, a school need not articulate any significant governmental interest or follow procedures beyond basic notice and an opportunity to respond in order to exclude a student from school.

The development of the right to education in state courts since *Goss* potentially changes everything. In those states where courts have held that education is a fundamental right or that students have a constitutional right to some qualitative level of education, students should be able to challenge their suspensions and expulsions on new, more persuasive grounds. Students whose disciplinary hearings before administrators and school board members resembled the shams described in chapter 2 should now be entitled to more formal and protective hearing processes prior to exclusion. In *Goss*, the Court balanced students' rights against those of the schools and reasoned that the schools' interest in avoiding administrative burdens outweighed students' interest in more protective processes. A constitutional or fundamental right, however, weighs far heavier than a statutory right to education and, presumably, would require schools to provide more formal discipline hearings than they currently offer. Yet school discipline is unlikely to be reformed simply by creating more procedural hoops for schools to jump through. Rather, real reform requires that the environments in which students misbehave and the reasons why schools exclude students for misbehavior be substantively examined. Those substantive concerns fall squarely under new potential state claims.

Under state law, deprivations of the fundamental or constitutional right to education are theoretically subject to strict or heightened review. Heightened review would require the state to offer an important, if not compelling, justification for excluding students from school. Realizing this possibility, plaintiffs have already begun to make these claims in a few state courts. Thus far, the few courts to hear these claims have not been entirely receptive, but plaintiffs' theory remains solid and straightforward.

In other nondiscipline cases, a majority of courts have already declared that education is a fundamental or constitutional right under state law. If deprivations of that right due to funding inadequacies or inequities have triggered heightened scrutiny, deprivations of education through school discipline should trigger the same review. Serious educational harm exists in both contexts. While the cause of that harm differs between school funding and discipline, state policy is a substantial cause in both. Those similarities alone justify heightened scrutiny for discipline. That the state may have a good reason for excluding students—whereas it lacks a good reason for underfunding schools—speaks to whether the state can survive heightened review, not whether heightened review applies in the first instance.

A less straightforward but far more interesting and powerful theory involves using school finance precedent (in those states where it has been successful) to reconceptualize school discipline and student misbehavior as functions of the environment and educational quality available in a school, rather than merely functions of individual students' decision making. This theory draws heavily on the notion that state constitutions require the state to deliver a certain level of education to all students and that state policies that fail to ensure that students receive this education are unconstitutional.

In successful school finance cases, students' academic outputs—achievement scores, graduation, and college enrollment—are typical measures of whether students are receiving a quality or equal education. These academic outcomes depend on two factors: students' individual capacities and challenges, and schools' responses to students' needs. The state may not be able to control the former, but it is entirely responsible for the latter. Thus, when students systemically fail to succeed in school, courts have rejected states' attempts to blame students—or even local school personnel. Courts reason that students' academic failure is also the state's fault when it has failed to provide the supports reasonably necessary for students to succeed academically.

The same reasoning could apply to school discipline as well. Numerous studies show that a school's discipline rate is closely connected to its achievement. Not only do suspensions set the excluded student back academically, but suspensions set the entire school back when they become endemic. The environment becomes caustic, undermining achievement and incentivizing more misbehavior. In other words, in addition to quality teachers, safe facilities, a strong curriculum, and academic support services, positive educational outcomes depend on effective discipline. Thus, the state should have a duty to create discipline policies and foster environments that support academic achievement. Only then can a state ensure that students receive the educational opportunities its constitution mandates. When the state fails to carry out this duty, it becomes a contributing cause of student misbehavior and exclusion.

This chapter describes the first theory—that suspensions and expulsions require important governmental goals and carefully chosen means to achieve them. Chapter 7 details the theory that high discipline rates interfere with the delivery of the educational opportunities required by state constitutions and warrant a response by the state. But first, a caveat is in order.

While school finance cases have been tremendously successful in expanding the constitutional rights and duties in education, implementing those rights and duties have been far more difficult. Courts cannot, for instance, force legislatures to pass legislation to increase school funding. The most they can do is declare current practices unconstitutional and potentially penalize legislatures that refuse to act. Knowing this, some courts have been less than forceful in their opinions, and legislatures less than receptive. As a result, the fact that plaintiffs have succeeded in school finance litigation in more than half of the states has not been enough to eliminate inadequate and unequal educational opportunities. Nonetheless, the constitutional right to education and courts' enforcement of it have created a framework through which to hold states publicly accountable and to press for reform—and reform has, in fact, occurred. As the following sections and chapters detail, school discipline presents a more compelling basis for judicial intervention and potentially more manageable remedies than those raised by school funding litigation.

Evolution of the Constitutional Right to Education

In 1954 in *Brown v. Board of Education*, the U.S. Supreme Court declared racial segregation in schools "inherently unequal" and struck it down as a violation of the federal Constitution's guarantee of equal protection of the law. In reaching that conclusion, the Court wrote,

> Today, education is perhaps the most important function of state and local governments. Compulsory school attendance laws and the great expenditures for education both demonstrate our recognition of the importance of education to our democratic society. It is required in the performance of our most basic public responsibilities, even service in the

armed forces. It is the very foundation of good citizenship. Today it is a principal instrument in awakening the child to cultural values, in preparing him for later professional training, and in helping him to adjust normally to his environment. In these days, it is doubtful that any child may reasonably be expected to succeed in life if he is denied the opportunity of an education. Such an opportunity, where the state has undertaken to provide it, is a right which must be made available to all on equal terms.[1]

While some jurists and scholars read this quote as signaling a potential willingness to recognize education as a fundamental right, the Court's strict holding was only that racial discrimination in education violates equal protection. As the final sentence in this quotation indicates, the provision of education was understood as a voluntary act by the state.

After two decades of school desegregation, some education advocates returned to the idea of an affirmative right to education or a general prohibition on education inequality that extends beyond just race. Advocates had begun to make significant strides in desegregating schools but were concerned with the continuing vast funding inequalities that persisted within and across states. They believed these funding inequalities were potentially as important as racial segregation itself. If these funding inequalities remained, they might lock in unequal educational opportunities long after the end of de jure segregation.

The first attempt to address these inequalities was to argue what *Brown* had implied: that education was a fundamental right under the federal Constitution. If so, strict scrutiny should apply to funding disparities. This theory had a lot going for it. The Court, for two decades following *Brown*, had proven particularly receptive to increasingly aggressive challenges to racial inequality in education. In addition, *Brown*'s statement that education was "the most important function of state and local government" had been repeated by the Court in *Wisconsin v. Yoder*—another school case—and was soon repeated again in several other Supreme Court cases. In fact, when the Court was internally debating its rationale for striking down segregation in *Bolling v.*

Sharpe—the companion case to *Brown* that struck down segregation in the District of Columbia—a majority of the Court may have been poised to recognize education as a fundamental right or something akin to it.

Chief Justice Warren's initial draft opinion in *Bolling* argued that education was a fundamental liberty under due process. That draft cited several First Amendment and liberty cases that struck down state attempts to interfere with or restrict parents' control over their children's education. Warren wrote, "We have no hesitation in concluding that segregation of children in the public schools is a far greater restriction on their liberty than were the restrictions in [other] school cases [in which we have intervened]. . . . [In addition,] we have declared that the Constitution prohibits the States from maintaining racially segregated public schools. It would be unthinkable that the Federal Government should have a lesser duty to protect what, in our present circumstances, is a fundamental liberty."[2]

However, the second and final draft omitted references to education as a fundamental liberty, apparently due to pressure from just two justices who would have compromised a unanimous decision.[3] This excise was accomplished by simply deleting the words "fundamental liberty" and rephrasing the final sentence in the preceding quote to read, "In view of our decision that the Constitution prohibits the states from maintaining racially segregated public schools, it would be unthinkable that the same Constitution would impose a lesser duty on the Federal Government."[4] As Dennis Hutchinson explains in his thorough review of the Court's internal memoranda, "With a flick of the wrist [Justice Warren] changed *Bolling v. Sharpe* from an education case into a race case."[5]

In 1973, in *San Antonio v. Rodriguez*,[6] the issue *Brown* had avoided returned. This time it was squarely before the Court. Plaintiffs made two claims: (1) education is a fundamental right under the federal Constitution, and (2) poor students are a suspect class, against whom unequal funding practices discriminate. The Supreme Court rejected both claims, holding that education is not a fundamental right and poverty is not a suspect class. With this resounding and somewhat surprising defeat, advocates abandoned school funding litigation in the federal courts and focused exclusively on state courts.

In a few places, the state litigation was already under way. Advocates had been prescient enough not to rest all of their hopes on the federal Constitution and had filed state claims while *Rodriguez* was proceeding through the federal courts. The state claims were theoretically and factually the same as those in *Rodriguez* in all respects but one. The state claims were based on education clauses in state constitutions. While the federal Constitution does not mention education at all and operates primarily as a restriction on government power, state constitutions affirmatively obligate states to do certain things, the most important of which is to deliver education. In fact, all state constitutions include specific provisions mandating that the state establish and maintain public schools.

Each state education clause has a unique history and articulation, but scholars have identified four potential categories into which most roughly fall. The first group includes state constitutions with very basic clauses, requiring only that the state "establish and maintain a system of free public schools wherein all the children of the State may be educated."[7] A second group of state constitutions add some qualitative component that the education system must reach. Some constitutions define this as "a thorough and efficient system of public education to serve the needs" of the citizens and state.[8] Others characterize it as an adequate, sufficient, or high-quality education. A third group of state constitutions are "stronger and more specific [in their] education mandate."[9] They include a statement of purpose for the educational mandate.[10] For instance, the California Constitution emphasizes that "a general diffusion of knowledge and intelligence being essential to the preservation of the rights and liberties of the people, the Legislature shall encourage by all suitable means the promotion of intellectual, scientific, moral, and agricultural improvement."[11] In other words, the qualitative mandate might be measured by the education system's ability to promote particular student outcomes. The final category of state constitutions specifically declares education to be a fundamental right or the state's foremost obligation to its citizens.[12]

Litigation based on these education clauses was immediately successful. In 1973, just weeks after the U.S. Supreme Court decided *Rodriguez*, the New Jersey Supreme Court held that funding inequities violated students' state constitutional right to a "thorough and efficient" education.[13] The California Supreme Court had suggested the same before *Rodriguez* was even decided but made the point explicit in 1976, holding that education was a fundamental right under the California Constitution and that funding inequalities violated that right.[14] With California and New Jersey leading the analytical way, courts in Arkansas, Connecticut, Washington, and Wyoming followed, recognizing a fundamental right to education under their own state constitutions.[15]

In the 1980s, school funding litigation entered a third phase that focused more heavily on quality and less on formal equity. Some advocates began to question the potential limits of equity theory and noted that many state constitutions contained rich language that spoke to the quality of education. Those two factors combined with the "standards-based reform" movement occurring in education policy at the time. Beginning in the 1980s, a series of reports, national summits, and popular media began charging that students in the United States were not mastering basic core educational concepts and were falling behind their international counterparts. The most notable was the National Commission on Excellence in Education's 1983 report, self-explanatorily titled *A Nation at Risk*. Six years later, President George H. W. Bush called for and hosted the first national education summit of state governors since the Great Depression. The purpose of the summit was to set national educational goals that would reverse the nation's declining educational standards and outputs. States responded to these and other developments by creating core academic standards that all students would be required to meet.

Those academic standards and students' scores on tests of those standards soon found their way into plaintiffs' legal claims. Plaintiffs argued that state constitutional phrases such as "efficient," "thorough," and "sound basic" education obligated states to provide children with a qualitative level of education that could be measured through the academic standards and tests that states had developed. While a few courts had already begun moving in this direction prior to 1989, that year, in *Rose v. Council for Better Education*,[16] the Kentucky Supreme Court became the first to fully articulate a qualitative right to education. The court held that a constitutionally adequate or "efficient" education included several specific skills and outcomes in each of the major subjects of school curriculum. The court reasoned that an efficient education requires

(i) sufficient oral and written communication skills to enable students to function in . . . civilization; (ii) sufficient knowledge of economic, social, and political systems to enable the student to make informed choices; (iii) sufficient understanding of governmental processes to enable the student to understand the issues that affect his or her . . . nation; (iv) sufficient self-knowledge of . . . mental and physical wellness; (v) sufficient . . . arts [education] to enable each student to appreciate [his or her] cultural and historic heritage; (vi) sufficient preparation for advanced training in either academic or vocational fields . . . ; and (vii) sufficient levels of academic or vocational skills to enable . . . students to compete . . . in the job market.[17]

Following *Rose*, numerous other state courts, including Alabama, Arkansas, Idaho, Massachusetts, New Hampshire, North Carolina, South Carolina, and Texas, borrowed from *Rose*'s standards or followed *Rose*'s approach in defining their own.[18] With these litigation successes and the continued emphasis on standards-based learning, quality-based litigation quickly became, and has since remained, the primary form of constitutional education litigation.

Equity litigation, however, did not abruptly end. Over time, the lines between "equity" and "adequacy" litigation have increasingly blurred, and litigants now often include both theories in their claims. The point here is simply that a new form of litigation took hold and was successful. *Rose* marked the beginning of twenty-seven school finance cases—most of them premised on adequacy—that were filed between 1989 and 2006. Plaintiffs prevailed in nearly 75 percent of those cases, as compared to the success rate of less than 50 percent prior to *Rose*.[19]

Several important ideas and principles developed in school finance litigation that have direct bearing on school discipline. Some of those principles—particularly the notion that the state is ultimately accountable for the quality of education that students receive and obligated to help students overcome disadvantages that might prevent them from succeeding in school—are explored in chapter 7. The most important point for this chapter is also the simplest: courts have held that education clauses in state constitutions create educational rights and/or duties. The implications for discipline should be obvious. When a student is removed from school, the student is not simply losing access to some statutory benefit that the state is free to condition or limit; the student is also losing access to an opportunity that the state is constitutionally obligated to deliver.

In the context of school funding, courts in a majority of states have enforced this right or duty. Those courts that have refused to enforce this right or duty have done so primarily out of deference to the legislature. They have not suggested that the state is free to disregard its constitutional obligation to deliver an equal or quality education or that the state can carry out that duty with anything less than full good faith and effort. Those courts that refuse to intervene most often do so because they reason that they lack the authority and competency to question or evaluate the state's actions in carrying out its education duty.

Were there any doubt that this right—where enforced—could extend to school discipline, school finance precedent is clear that principles developed there are not limited to money. To the contrary, while money is important, money is only a means to an end. The precise right at stake in school finance cases is the right to equal educational opportunities or adequate educational opportunities, depending on the particular state. Money has taken center stage only because it substantially affects educational opportunity in general and those critical inputs that make educational opportunity meaningful: quality teachers, small class sizes, modern technology, safe facilities, and support services, to name a few. The cases spend just as much, if not more, time addressing substantive issues relating to these key inputs as they do money. In short, although money is frequently implicated in education litigation, the precise legal challenge in many cases is based on inadequate educational inputs and opportunity, not money. Those inputs and opportunities matter because students have a constitutional right to education and the state has a duty to deliver it to them.

With discipline, however, the issues are far simpler. Suspended and expelled students are necessarily being deprived of educational opportunity. Plaintiffs need not demonstrate that the state has failed to deliver a quality education, that certain inputs affect educational outcomes, or that the education available in some other district is better. To trigger serious judicial review, plaintiffs in discipline cases need only point to the uncontested fact that the state has taken their education away. The difficult question ought not be whether students have a constitutional right that triggers scrutiny but whether suspensions and expulsions under questionable circumstances can survive that scrutiny. In other words, school finance precedent should apply; the only question is how. Do disciplined students somehow forfeit the right to education by misbehaving? What state interests might justify the deprivation of the right to education? Are there ways to achieve the state's interests other than by excluding students from school? Does the provision of alternative education moot a student's claim against the state?

Following a decade of favorable precedent in school funding cases, litigants in the late 1990s began to seize on the idea that they could use the principles from those cases to challenge harsh school discipline. Yet, like school funding litigation, discipline litigation was idiosyncratic and not strategically coordinated across states. Thus, relatively few cases were filed and even fewer high-court decisions reached. Those few states that have decided discipline cases have afforded the key issues varying degrees of attention and reached conflicting results. This has left the intersection of discipline with the constitutional right to education grossly underdeveloped. A few courts have treated the development of the constitutional right to education as irrelevant to discipline, finding that the existence of a constitutional right to equitable or adequate educational opportunities does nothing to increase the protections afforded to suspended and expelled students in those states. In other words, school finance precedent applies to school finance cases, and the general rules of school discipline continue to apply to school discipline cases. Other courts have simply reasoned that whatever the constitutional right to education might mean in school finance, misbehaving students forfeit their rights. The few remaining courts simply assume, without any serious explanation, that school finance precedent does establish an individual constitutional right to education. Yet these final courts also disagree among themselves regarding whether heightened scrutiny should apply to suspensions and expulsions.[20]

Asking the Right Questions

Part of the explanation for muddled, if not negative, precedent lies in the fact that these courts have been distracted by the fact that the plaintiffs in these cases have sought access to alternative schools. Rather than directly challenge schools' authority to exclude students from regular public school itself, plaintiffs have merely asked that the state assign them to alternative school. But when courts or legislatures order districts to provide alternative education, the state can argue that neither procedural due process nor the constitutional right to education is implicated. Some schools and districts argue, for instance, that they have only transferred a misbehaving student from one school to another. Thus, they have not actually expelled a student from school or deprived a student of the statutory or constitutional right to attend school. While this reasoning suffers from a number of flaws, it has been enough to undermine a clear framing of the constitutional interests at stake.[21] The second, more practical explanation for the negative outcomes in prior cases is the particular facts of the cases themselves. All of them involved students who admittedly engaged in serious misbehavior that potentially posed a danger to others or themselves. Their offenses included firearm possession, alcohol consumption, selling marijuana, a multiperson brawl, and a switchblade knife. Cases involving serious misbehaviors make the cases easier to litigate and get before a high court quickly, but the facts operate to the disadvantage of expanding discipline rights. With serious misbehavior, the deck is heavily stacked against the students before the briefs are even filed. Students are hard-pressed to argue that the school cannot remove them for their behavior.[22] The schools clearly have a substantial or compelling interest in safety that demands a response to dangerous behavior.

If school discipline is to be reformed and the constitutional right to education meaningful, advocates must challenge suspensions and expulsions for minor misbehavior. Exclusion for minor misbehavior presents a far more compelling case for courts to closely examine discipline policy. Moreover, data show that drugs and weapons offenses account for only about 5 percent of all suspensions and expulsions.[23] Thus, the real problem with school discipline lies in the other 95 percent of suspensions and expulsions, where the misbehavior is minor.

If subjected to heightened scrutiny, minor misbehavior would present a far more favorable analysis for students than would a weapon or drug case. The students who, for instance, have disrupted class several times, disrespected a teacher, or defied authority do not pose an obvious danger. A school that sought to exclude these students could face two substantial hurdles. First, the school does not have an obvious substantial or compelling interest in exclusion. While real weapons or drugs might easily cross that threshold, a school's interest in maintaining an orderly environment is far more contextual. Do suspensions and expulsions actually improve school order? Are students more respectful when that respect is compelled by threat? Does a single act of disrespect actually undermine order in school? At least on these questions, the literature indicates the answer is no, which suggests that the school's goal may actually be something other than order or safety.

Even giving a school the benefit of the doubt on its interest in excluding a student—a deference that generally would not exist under heightened scrutiny—the school's second problem would be the difficulty in demonstrating that exclusion is a narrowly tailored way to achieve the school's interest. Any number of moderate responses and punishments short of long-term suspension and expulsion are just as—or more— effective. A short in-school suspension, after-school detention, lost privileges, extra school work, or simply a private conversation with a thoughtful teacher, counselor, or principal all come to mind as moderate punishments that could improve behavior just as well as more serious punishment. And those are just the low-cost ways of dealing with misbehavior. As a large body of research shows, schools could also institute various positive behavioral support or restorative justice programs that are far more effective. To the extent schools do not have the resources or people in place to carry out the programs, a court might order them as a less intrusive way for schools to achieve their goals. In short, the leeway and defenses afforded to schools regarding students who bring weapons or drugs to school do not exist with the run-of-the-mill misbehaviors that lead to most school exclusions.

Given these fundamental distinctions between serious and minor misbehavior, prior discipline cases' analyses of the constitutional right to education is easily distinguishable. Those cases answer entirely different questions than those raised by minor misbehaviors. And while those prior answers are relevant to the questions of whether education is a fundamental right in the context of discipline and what scrutiny applies, other questions remain open. Do schools have important and compelling interests to remove students who engage in minor misbehavior?

Are suspension and expulsion narrowly tailored responses to minor misbehavior? Is assignment to alternative school a narrowly tailored response to minor misbehavior? These are the important questions, not whether students with firearms have a right to alternative school.

Yet even this framing of the issues is slanted in the state's favor. If school finance has taught anything, it is that a duty lies with the state to deliver equal and adequate educational opportunities to students. This duty is not conditioned on those students being well behaved and ready to learn when they arrive at school or the state's interest in delivering education in the way it finds most convenient for its own bureaucratic interests. Rather, the duty obligates the state to meet students where they are and exert the effort necessary to get them to the positive educational outcomes. In short, the development of a constitutional right and duty in education means that courts should ask not simply whether the state can take education away from a student but whether the state has done enough to provide students with a quality education. Until the state can answer the second question affirmatively, courts should not seriously entertain the first. The question of the state's duties in regard to discipline is the subject of chapter 7.

[7]

ENSURING QUALITY EDUCATION
THROUGH DISCIPLINE

Fixing Dysfunctional School Environments

Focusing on discipline from the perspective of individual students and the idea that suspensions and expulsions take something away from students only captures half the story of school discipline and only part of the students' interests at stake. Student misbehavior is a function of individual choices that students make, but individual student misbehavior is also a function of the structure and environment of schooling in which those students act. Quality schools and orderly environments consistently produce higher student achievement and less misbehavior. Low-quality schools with disorderly, hostile, and punitive environments produce lower student achievement and higher rates of suspension and expulsion.

On one level, the connection between discipline and student achievement should be obvious. The amount of time a student spends in school, along with the quality of that time, necessarily affects achievement. If students are in environments that interfere with their ability to focus on school work, they score lower. If they are not in school at all because they have been suspended or expelled, they score lower. If their teachers are regularly pulled away from instruction to deal with discipline, they score lower.

At the most general level of analysis, a 2003 study revealed that statewide test scores in math, writing, and reading on the National Assessment of Educational Progress closely tracked states' suspension rates.[1] A more nuanced study in 2005 reached the same finding.[2] Even after race, poverty, and other demographic factors were accounted for, the fact remained that schools that exclude the most students score the lowest. This correlation makes perfect sense. Suspended and expelled student are necessarily exposed to less instruction and experience a disjointed learning experience. If we follow the basic maxim—which social science strongly supports—that the more a student puts into education, the more the student will get out, school exclusion directly lowers achievement. Excluded students are simply prevented from putting in as much as others, and they also receive less from their schools.

The research, however, is more powerful than the simplistic notion that if students are not in school or the environment is not orderly, students learn less. If that were all the studies revealed, schools might reasonably justify excluding the misbehaving student because doing so preserves the educational environment for others. But studies indicate that a school's approach to discipline and decisions to suspend or not suspend students predict a substantial portion of overall student achievement. In other words, schools—not just misbehaving students—set the environment. Consistent with this notion, Karega Rausch and Russell Skiba found that "a school's out-of-school suspension rate predicted a unique amount of the variance in achievement scores even after accounting for the influences of poverty, minority composition, and school type."[3] More specifically, school suspension rates explained 36 percent of the total variation in student achievement scores across schools. With all other things being equal, those schools with higher suspension rates had lower achievement. Interestingly, while individual poverty, as well as the poverty level among the school's overall student body, heavily predicts student achievement in a school, researchers found that, after poverty, "out-of-school suspension is the next strongest predictor of achievement, even stronger than a school's percent minority enrollment and level (elementary vs. secondary)."[4]

Linda Raffaele Mendez and her colleagues conducted a smaller-scale study of students in a single school district. The narrower scope of the study allowed the research team to dig into individual students' disciplinary and achievement records. They found a similarly strong correlation between a school's suspension rate and its students' achievement in reading, math, and writing.[5] They explained that "serving a high percentage of poor minority children does not mean that a school will *necessarily* have a high suspension rate,"[6] but having a high suspension rate does seem to mean that achievement will go down. Looking at individual students, they found that the very act of suspending a student, even for a short period of time, had long-term effects on the student's behavior and achievement, both of which were negative. They tracked this trend across multiple years of students' academic careers.

This macro-level connection between suspension and achievement raises important questions. How would excluding a misbehaving student negatively affect others? What exactly is going on inside schools with high suspension and expulsion rates to produce these counterintuitive results? The answers to these questions relate to the overall school climate associated with high suspension rates. The evidence is pretty clear that high suspension rates negatively affect the general student body's perception of school authority and the school's climate. Rather than improving the environment in which students learn, aggressive suspension practices can degrade it and make school less inviting for everyone. The National School Boards Association recognized three decades ago that "traditional approaches—such as punishment, removing troublemakers, and similar measures— . . . often harden delinquent behavior patterns, alienate troubled youths from the schools, and foster distrust."[7]

Newer research shows that those negative reactions are not confined to the students on whom discipline is meted out. On the basis of extensive analysis of student and school responses to surveys about discipline and school climate, Richard Arum found that as discipline becomes overly strict or harsh, the general student body, including students who are not misbehaving, begin to perceive it as arbitrary and unfair.[8] At that point, students may have any number of negative reactions, including resentment, opposition, fear, and disillusionment.

As these student reactions to harsh discipline occur, the school environment becomes more, rather than less, disorderly. Arum found that students who perceived school discipline as unfair "had a 35 percent likelihood of expressing a willingness to disobey rules," whereas the willingness to disobey rules was 5 percent or less when discipline was perceived as fair.[9] In other words, schools cannot simply suspend their way out of discipline problems. As they rid themselves of one purportedly problematic student, another takes his or her place. Those schools that persist in the idea that the problem is solely misbehaving students, rather than the climate the school fosters, can spiral into complete dysfunctionality. This out-of-control dysfunctionality helps explain why some schools in Washington, DC, and New Orleans can have 50 and 75 percent suspension rates. These schools do not have the worst students in the nation. They have the worst school climates.

The effects of disorder and negative climate are visited on teachers as well. Negative environments make teachers more likely to be absent from school, transfer schools, or quit teaching altogether. These teacher effects bring the problem full circle. Negative educational climates, higher teacher absenteeism, higher teacher turnover, lower teacher quality, and negative school environments all have negative reciprocal effects on one another, with each individually and collectively also negatively affecting student achievement.[10]

A 1994 study, on the cutting-edge of these issues at the time, found that among all the variables examined, teacher absences had the strongest connection to African American males' academic achievement: the higher the teacher absences, the lower the student achievement.[11] Even reflecting back from afar, this finding appears curious at first glance, but what this early study stumbled on was the environmental interaction between climate, student discipline, student achievement, and teacher engagement. Later research in each of these discrete topics has helped close this gap and suggests that once these factors begin to negatively interact, a vicious cycle can form, from which it is hard to escape.

How Schools Approach Discipline Matters

The key takeaway from past research is that states, districts, and schools have a choice in how they approach discipline—and that choice matters. While some level of student misbehavior is a given, how educators respond is not. One might assume that schools are passive participants in suspensions and expulsions, simply reacting to the unfortunate environment and circumstances they face. From this perspective, low academic achievement is a natural consequence of misbehaving students who are distracting themselves and others from learning. If so, it would be no surprise that schools with the most misbehavior have the lowest achievement. Per this line of reasoning, misbehaving students must be removed.

The data and research indicate that this perspective is wrong and part of the problem. Karega Rausch and Russell Skiba offer this overview of the findings of several different studies:

A school's use of suspension and expulsion is not simply a direct administrative response to student externalizing behavior problems. To be sure, some portion of a school's suspensions and expulsions are due to student misbehavior and anti-social attitudes. Yet administrative responses to student behavior represent a complex and multi-determined process. Thus, studies have also found rates of disciplinary removal at the school level to be (1) extremely inconsistent from school to school even given a similar student population, (2) strongly related to school factors independent of individual student factors such as teacher attitudes, administrative centralization, and school governance, and (3) attributable to variability in principal attitudes toward discipline.[12]

The first trend in the research noted by Rausch and Skiba is the most persuasive and one from which those who would entirely blame students for misbehavior cannot run: data and student records indicate that students are treated differently in different classes and in different schools.

For instance, one study demonstrated that students who get sent to the office for misbehavior are not necessarily the inherent troublemakers one might otherwise assume. The study found that many students get in trouble only in particular teachers' classes. In one school, two-thirds of the office referrals for the entire school came from a relatively small group of teachers.[13] Either most teachers tolerate misbehavior that a small group of teachers will not, or students respond differently to different classrooms. The former is possible and would be indicative of a dysfunctional school, whose disciplinary responsibility is left to a few. The latter possibility, which the authors of the study indicate is more likely, is that teachers who do not refer students to the office on a regular basis tend to deal with student misbehavior in constructive ways, which includes fostering learning environments in which misbehavior is less likely to occur.[14]

The data on students who transfer schools are smaller and harder to track, but they again reveal that students' behavior and chances of suspension are significantly influenced by the school they attend. If certain students are inherently predisposed to misbehave or if the only way to deal with that behavior is suspension, one would expect the discipline rates of students who transfer schools to remain relatively steady. In other words, misbehavior would follow the student, not the school. But it does not. Transfer students' behavior and/or chances of suspension tend to track the school in which they are enrolled.[15]

Likewise, study after study reveals that there are schools that appear the same in all important respects but have very different discipline rates. Randomly pick any state and any demographically similar group of schools and the trend repeats itself. In South Carolina, for instance, C. A. Johnson, Calhoun County, Kingstree, Fairfield Central, and Military Magnet Academy high schools are roughly the same in terms of race, poverty, and size. All are medium-sized high schools. All have poverty levels between 85 and 88 percent. All are predominantly African American schools. Calhoun is 80 percent African American, with the rest of the schools falling between 87 and 94 percent African American.

In 2011, however, the suspension rates at these schools were all over the place, varying from 14 percent at Fairfield to 50 percent at Kingstree.[16]

At the other end of South Carolina's demographic spectrum were Nation Ford, Riverside, Fox Creek, Hilton Head, Indian Land, and Eastside high schools. These schools are all predominantly middle-income schools, at 71 to 80 percent middle income. They are all predominantly white. They all have relatively small African American student population, ranging from just 11 to 16 percent. But in 2009–10, their discipline rates varied wildly.[17] Three of those high schools had suspension rates well below the state average. Riverside's suspension rate was only 5 percent, followed by Nation Ford and Fox Creek at 7 and 8 percent, respectively. The other two high schools—Hilton Head and Indian Land—had suspension rates that were three to four times as high as those at Riverside, at 18 and 21 percent. At that level, moreover, Hilton Head and Indian Land had suspension rates that mirrored or exceeded the suspension rates at Fairfield and Military Magnet—the predominantly poor, predominantly African American schools noted earlier. In other words, these predominantly white, middle-income schools had the same suspension rates as two of South Carolina's poorest and almost entirely African American schools.[18]

How else can one explain the discipline variations between demographically similar schools than by differences in school leaders' responses to student behavior in those schools? How else can one explain the similar discipline rates of schools so demographically different other than the approach to discipline in those schools? As Shi-Chang Wu and his coauthors remarked in their 1996 empirical study, "Suspension rates cannot be regarded as a simple reflection of student misbehavior in school, but rather as the result of a complex of factors grounded in the ways schools operate. Suspension rates are best predicted by (1) knowing the kind of school a student went to, and (2) knowing how that school was run."[19] After reviewing national-level data and the literature on the topic, they concluded that if students were "interested in reducing their chances of being suspended, . . . [they would] be better off by transferring to a school with a lower suspension rate than by improving their attitudes or reducing their misbehavior."[20]

When schools understand that suspension rates and the academic achievement that follows them are a function of not just the students but also the school climate and disciplinary approach, the need for change becomes imperative. Mendez and her colleagues found that the difference between schools with high and low suspension rates were "(a) use of primary and secondary prevention strategies to curtail inappropriate behavior (e.g., social skills training for students, behavior management training for teachers), (b) opportunities for parent involvement, including involvement in the development of the school-wide discipline plan, and (c) a belief that responding to students' needs and treating them with respect is effective in reducing problematic behavior."[21] That last point, in particular, has been consistently reaffirmed in recent years. Whether it is "positive behavioral support," "restorative justice," or some other progressive strategy, studies have shown that schools reduce misbehavior and improve achievement not through punitive responses to misbehavior but by taking steps to prevent misbehavior in the first place.[22] Research also confirms that misbehavior is often a sign that a student is experiencing academic challenges.[23] The way to address academic challenges is certainly not by excluding a student from school. It is to provide academic support. Moreover, progressive disciplinary approaches, unlike punitive approaches, are better suited to ferret out the causes of misbehavior, whether they be academic, social, or both.

Disparate Discipline's Role in the Racial Achievement Gap

While the connections between school climate, school exclusions, and academic achievement are important for all students, they are particularly important for African American students. As detailed throughout this book, African Americans are suspended at much higher rates than other students are. In addition, as a group, their academic achievement lags behind others. Too often, however, racial disparities in discipline and the racial achievement gap are framed as distinct problems. For nearly half a century, significant amounts of research have been devoted to the racial achievement gap. For going on three decades, significant amounts of research have been devoted to racial disparities in discipline. And as the previous section shows, a growing body of literature has been devoted to the connection between discipline and achievement in general. But very little research has explored the extent to which the racial disparities in discipline explain the racial achievement gap. Recently, a few studies have suggested that the two may be intricately intertwined and that the solution to high African American suspension rates may also be a solution, in part, to the racial achievement gap.

One of the earlier studies to consider this connection was a 1989 study by Valerie Lee and Anthony Bryk. They sought to identify those school contexts in which students achieve best but also those contexts in which achievement gaps between advantaged and disadvantaged students were the smallest. As to the first point, they predictably found that "high average achievement is related to school social composition and to the school's academic emphasis."[24] As to the second point, they found that, when controlling for other relevant factors, the achievement gap for African American students was lower in Catholic schools. The reason why revealed something far more important.

The disciplinary climate in Catholic schools, on average, was better than that in other schools. This fact, more than anything else, explained African American's higher achievement there. The authors explained that the average achievement gap was smaller in Catholic schools than in public schools, but the difference between the schools disappeared once they "took into account the disciplinary climate of schools. The minority gap is largest in schools in which there is a high incidence of disciplinary problems. This finding suggests that the minority gap is smaller in the Catholic sector because the environments are more orderly and less disruptive."[25] To state it another way, public schools exacerbate the achievement gap by more often exposing African Americans to problematic environments.

In 2004, Xin Ma and Douglas Willms investigated the connection between the racial achievement gap, discipline, and environment more closely. They found that the percentage of low-income or middle-income students in a school strongly correlated with the disciplinary climate and academic achievement in that school. From that finding, they concluded that "if the extent of segregation in school districts or communities increases, . . . there will be an increase in the variation of both disciplinary climate and academic achievement at the school level. In schools where advantaged students are concentrated, there will be fewer discipline problems and higher achievement levels, whereas schools serving disadvantaged students will have even worse discipline problems and lower levels of academic achievement."[26]

Richard Arum and Melissa Velez reached the same conclusion. "Schools with more than 50 percent of students from economically disadvantaged homes have significantly higher levels of principal reports of disciplinary disengagement."[27] By "disciplinary disengagement," they mean a school where principals, or the teachers they supervise, are not committed to maintaining an orderly environment. Arum and Velez, however, pushed the analysis even further. They sought to quantify how much of the racial achievement gap is attributable to socioeconomic segregation and how much might be attributable disciplinary environments. The precise answer to that question is hard to reach because so many factors are at play in the achievement gap, but Arum and Velez managed to tease out several important subsidiary findings that suggest segregation and counterproductive discipline are linked.

First, "a large and significant component of the negative effects of attending economically disadvantaged schools on test score performance is associated with the dysfunctional disciplinary climates that exist there."[28] Second, because African Americans are disproportionately consigned to high-poverty schools, they are also disproportionately consigned to dysfunctional disciplinary climates. As the Civil Rights Project's studies consistently emphasize, the typical African American student attends a school in which 59 percent of his or her peers are low income.[29] Third, while attending a predominantly poor school strongly correlates with lower African American test scores, Arum and Velez found that nearly half of that correlation was canceled out when disciplinary measures were included in the statistical analysis. In other words, decades of social science documenting the negative interaction between segregation and African Americans' academic achievement might be explained by the fact that African Americans experience very different disciplinary and school climates than whites do. These differences in climate depress African Americans' achievement.

Past research has attributed the racial achievement gap to poverty segregation in general. That research posits several explanations for why students benefit from attending a middle-income versus a high-poverty school: peer-to-peer learning, the ease of recruiting higher-quality teaching staffs, the availability of more resources, higher academic expectations, and parents who can hold school leaders accountable, all of which set a positive school climate. Arum and Velez do not question these explanations, as they all surely remain relevant, but their findings suggest a reordering of these explanations.

Arum and Velez evaluated two different sets of data—one based on information submitted for domestic comparisons and a second based on information that was internationally benchmarked. As to the first data set, they found that 45 percent of the variance in the achievement between African Americans attending high- and low-poverty schools is attributable to the differences in the disciplinary environment in those schools.[30] Moreover, when data on the disciplinary environment are included, the effect of attending a high- or low-poverty school on African American achievement becomes statistically insignificant.[31] As to the second data set, they found that, as the disciplinary climate improves, "the gap between African American and white test scores decreases. Notably, the gap is diminished to nearly zero" in the more orderly environments (after controlling for other relevant factors).[32]

From Arum and Velez to the studies discussed at the beginning of this chapter, increasingly sophisticated analysis of school discipline and student achievement is reframing the nature of the problem. Student misbehavior is not just about students making bad choices or schools overreacting to those choices. Student misbehavior is contextual and depends on the quality of the social and academic environment. Likewise, students' academic achievement is not just about how hard students study or how qualified their teachers are. Academic achievement is a function of the social and disciplinary environment in the school. Understood this way, states and schools have far more leverage to improve discipline and academic outcomes than one might otherwise assume. In fact, schools are and have been leveraging their power for some time. The problem is that they have too often used that leverage to suspend and expel students, which has undermined both the discipline climate and academic achievement.

The Intersection of School Discipline and the
Constitutional Duty to Deliver Quality Education

Several important ideas and principles developed in school finance litigation have direct bearing on school discipline. The most obvious—the recognition of a constitutional or fundamental right to education—was detailed in chapter 6. Whatever the potential successes or failures of using that right to limit school exclusion for individual students, school finance litigation's concern with school quality and academic outcomes fundamentally intersects with other attempts to reform school discipline. As the foregoing social science demonstrates, positive academic outcomes and positive discipline environments are directly linked. The still-unexplored question is how school finance movements and discipline reform might be aligned not just in theory or research but in practice.

A close look at the framework through which school finance litigation is conceptualized and litigated indicates that this integration is possible. First, as discussed in chapter 6, the inquiries and remedies secured in school finance litigation are not limited to money. The cases are about the right to equal educational opportunities or adequate educational opportunities. Money is highly relevant in accessing those educational opportunities but not singularly determinative.

Second, because the right at stake in these cases is an adequate or equal education, not adequate or equal money, the right is broad enough to include almost any educational policy that significantly affects educational opportunity. Past litigation has involved remedies for those obvious things that money can buy, such as teachers, technology, and buildings, but it has also included remedies that money cannot buy. Most notably, plaintiffs in *Sheff v. O'Neill* successfully demonstrated that racial segregation between school districts was the cause of educational inequality in Hartford.[33] Thus, the court struck down the rigid segregation as a violation of students' state constitutional right to an equal education. The final remedy was to offer students the opportunity to escape segregation and cross district lines.

Litigants in other states have also recently attempted to use school finance precedent to reform policies that go well beyond the bounds of improving schools' resources. They have sought to change the substance of state education policy. In California and New York, plaintiffs have challenged teacher tenure and seniority policies. They argue that tenure and seniority deprive students of equal and adequate educational opportunities because they keep grossly ineffective teachers in the classroom. Those teachers fail to provide students with the necessary learning opportunities. A trial court in California ruled in the plaintiffs' favor on this theory in 2014.[34] The New York plaintiffs have yet to go to trial but have survived a motion to dismiss. Litigants in Massachusetts have employed a similar strategy in challenging the state's cap on the number of charters. They argue that the cap deprives students of a constitutionally sufficient education because it prevents them from exiting their constitutionally deficient traditional public schools for better charter schools.

These court decisions and plaintiff theories demonstrate how flexible the right to education can be in challenging state educational policies.

Whatever the merits of these newest claims—some of which scholars have called into question on evidentiary grounds[35]—the case for extending school finance precedent to discipline is compelling. The foregoing studies solidly establish a close connection between discipline, the environmental climate, and academic outcomes. Once plaintiffs pinpoint specific state discipline practices and policies that impair their access to a quality or an equal education, the structure and substance of their claim would be no different than the various other successful school finance cases filed over the past several decades regarding teachers, facilities, technology, and the like. They would simply be asking for an environment that affords them the opportunity to receive the education that the state's constitution obligates it to deliver.

Third, school finance precedent solidly affirms the principle that the state has the final responsibility for the educational opportunities that students do or do not receive. Thus, while variations in educational opportunity and students' academic achievement may be random in some respects, the state has the responsibility to monitor educational opportunity and intervene to address policies and practices that interfere with students' ability to receive an equal or quality education.

For decades, states abandoned local districts in many respects, leaving them to fund education largely on their own and deliver whatever level of academic rigor those funds allowed. When things were bad, the state blamed school districts and/or the students. According to the state, school districts squandered their resources, hired poor leaders and teachers, or had students who were simply too disadvantaged to achieve at high levels. Whether the fault rested with the districts or the students, academic failure was not the state's fault.

School finance decisions, however, rejected states' attempts to shift blame in these ways. Courts have held that the responsibility for academic success and the school funding necessary to deliver it falls primarily on the state. If districts lack the funding to deliver a quality education, the state has the duty to directly supplement struggling districts. When the problem is widespread in a state, courts have ordered states to develop entirely new statewide funding schemes that meet the needs of all districts. In other words, if local districts cannot secure sufficiently qualified teachers, the state has the responsibility to raise the funds or develop the recruitment tools so that districts can hire those teachers. If local districts waste the resources they have, the state has the responsibility to stop them.

The Supreme Court in *Rose* makes this point clearly:

> The sole responsibility for providing the system of common schools is that of our General Assembly. It is a duty—it is a constitutional mandate placed by the people on the 138 members of that body who represent those selfsame people. The General Assembly must not only establish the system, but it must monitor it on a continuing basis so that it will always be maintained in a constitutional manner. The General Assembly must carefully supervise it, so that there is no waste, no duplication, no mismanagement, at any level.[36]

Fourth, states' ultimate responsibility to monitor and help districts in need arises from their more important obligation to help students in need. If a particular demographic group faces unique challenges to academic achievement, the state has a duty to implement policies to address those challenges. As the Court in *Abbott by Abbott v. Burke* wrote, "If the claim is that these students simply cannot make it, the constitutional answer is, give them a chance."[37] Even if the state cannot eliminate students' challenges, "students are constitutionally entitled to . . . help,"[38] and "in some cases for disadvantaged students to receive a thorough and efficient education, the students will require above-average access to education resources."[39]

The state's ultimate obligation to ensure that schools are delivering adequate and equal educational opportunities, particularly for disadvantaged students, could easily entail an obligation to better manage school discipline and related policies. The existence or nonexistence of behavioral supports will for a substantial portion of students determine whether they achieve at grade level and graduate or, conversely, are suspended and eventually drop out of school. Moreover, schools' responses to these students who are most at risk will also have spillover effects on the rest of the student population. To the extent these other students are not consistently reaching adequate educational outcomes, the state may owe them a better discipline system as well.

As noted earlier, studies also show that students who are academically struggling tend to be the ones most likely to be suspended and expelled. For these students, misbehavior is a response to the academic challenges they are facing. These students either want to avoid the stress of the challenge or believe they cannot meet the challenge. Either way, their misbehavior is a signal that the state has failed to intervene with the academic supports that school finance precedent would have otherwise indicated should have been in place.

Finally, student achievement data, including substantial achievement gaps between student groups, has served as significant evidence of states' failure to provide students with an adequate or equal education. Generally poor achievement or large achievement gaps are, in effect, the result of the state's failure to ensure sufficient access to the various educational inputs that matter, such as access to quality teachers, quality curriculum, and support services for at-risk students.

The same reasoning follows from discipline data. Data show that the overall academic achievement of a school is closely correlated to the discipline climate and suspension rate in the school. In both cases, discipline reform—not just academic reform—is a necessary policy intervention for ensuring adequate education opportunities and outcomes in some schools. Schools' harsh response to misbehavior and their failure to foster a positive climate actively undermine achievement. Students in these schools have some of the largest achievement gaps to be found. As Arum and Velez emphasize, the achievement gap between students attending predominantly poor and predominantly middle-income schools is largely explained by disciplinary environments they encounter in those schools. Thus, the achievement gaps that frequently prompt school finance courts to demand reforms in funding, staffing, and academic programing should also prompt a close examination of school discipline. Where high suspension rates prevail, data indicates low achievement is likely to follow.

Overall, school finance and quality frameworks align so closely with social science research on discipline that raising discipline concerns in the context of this litigation would not necessarily require any doctrinal development. Unlike the theory to force the state to justify suspension that was explored in chapter 6, connecting discipline to school quality and achievement would not require discipline advocates to extract the constitutional right established in school finance and resituate it in the context of discipline. Rather, plaintiffs would theoretically only need to present discipline data and studies as additional evidence of the causes of unequal and inadequate education. Under the current basic principles of school finance litigation, that evidence could become a central inquiry of courts and a source of the basic reforms that they might order.

Mapping a Discipline Claim in the Context of School Finance Precedent

Once a court accepts the notion that discipline studies and the concerns they raise are aligned with the fundamental tenets and frameworks of past litigation, the basic discipline claim could follow the pattern established in numerous school quality or finance cases. Those cases require plaintiffs to establish four different elements of a constitutional violation. First, plaintiffs must identify a constitutional duty by the state to deliver education. All state constitutions include that duty. The only variance is between those state supreme courts that hold they have the authority to enforce some equality or adequacy component of that duty and those that do not. The judiciary in more than half of the states has held that courts have that authority. Thus, so long as plaintiffs bring a claim in one of those states, establishing an educational duty that the courts will enforce is not a barrier.

Second, plaintiffs must establish that they have suffered harm. The requirement here is that harm suffered is not de minimis but rises to the level of consistently interfering with students' ability to learn and achieve. The social science demonstrating the connection between achievement, discipline, and climate would be central on this point. The studies detailed earlier reveal consistently lower academic achievement and larger achievement gaps in schools with high suspension rates and problematic school climates.

Those studies do not assess the extent to which students in particular school districts with problematic discipline are achieving below grade level or failing to graduate, but the findings in those studies strongly suggest that plaintiffs could establish the requisite harm in particular schools and districts. For instance, data already show a significant achievement gap between predominantly poor and predominantly middle-income schools. Arum and Velez's work further indicates that, for African Americans, about half of that achievement gap is attributable to discipline. At that level, it is hard to imagine that the harm suffered is minimal or random. Plaintiffs' task would be to identify these types of trends in specific schools and districts, which presumably would reveal academic outcomes that fall below constitutional expectations.

Third, plaintiffs must establish that state action or policy is the cause of these harms. In the context of school quality and finance litigation, this has typically involved two distinct causal showings: (a) that a state policy or practice has a causal effect on local conditions, such as insufficient resources, teachers, or facilities; and (b) that those local conditions have a causal effect on educational outcomes. In more practical terms, plaintiffs have, for instance, been required to show that state funding policy was a significant cause of low-quality teachers in particular school districts and that those low-quality teachers were a significant cause of poor academic outcomes for students.

While this causal inquiry sounds straightforward, it has been a source of serious contention and finger-pointing for decades. In almost every case, the state has disputed the causal connection between the policies plaintiffs are challenging and educational outcomes. Most notably, states have argued that money is not causally connected to educational quality or outcomes. Rather, they argue that educational outcomes are more directly a product of student demographic variables and student effort. States have also argued that, to the extent money matters, the state has provided districts with sufficient funds. The problem, states argue, is local mismanagement. For the most part, courts that have adjudicated the merits of these cases have rejected states' arguments, but the issues never entirely go away because causation is sufficiently complex and contested.

With discipline, the debate would be no less intense, but the causal analysis would be much cleaner. The state would be hard-pressed to disprove the evidence that suspension rates and school disciplinary climate have a significant effect on educational outcomes—which speaks to the second step in the causal analysis. States' primary defense would be on the first causal step. They would argue that state action does not cause student misbehavior and negative climates. Rather, students and/ or misguided teachers, administrators, and school boards are the cause.

Shifting blame to students has obvious appeal. As noted in chapter 6, some courts have reasoned that individual suspensions and expulsions do not warrant scrutiny under the traditional fundamental rights analysis because misbehaving students forfeit their education rights.[40] In the context of a school quality or equality claim, however, shifting blame to misbehaving students is more difficult. The claim could be brought on behalf all students, not just misbehaving students. Or it could be brought on behalf of innocent bystanders alone. In the context of these potential claims, both the logic and rhetorical value of shifting blame onto students would disappear. Equally important, studies indicate the facts simply would not support a state claim that students are to blame. While student misbehavior is a product of individual choice, it is heavily influenced by context. Schools that maintain negative climates and punitive discipline policies are, in effect, the cause of additional misbehavior and lower student achievement. If plaintiffs establish that school climate and discipline policies influence student behavior and academic achievement, plaintiffs will have established the necessary causal connection between state policy, school discipline, and educational outcomes.

The state's claim that local school actors are to blame should be even easier to overcome. Prior courts have emphasized that states have a duty to ensure an adequate or equal education. That duty cannot be shirked by delegating authority or responsibility to others. If problematic policies or practices are occurring locally, the state must identify and correct them. Moreover, the problem in many districts is not bad actors per se. It can be a lack of capacity to constructively deal with and understand the causes of misbehavior.

Once plaintiffs establish that school climate and discipline are central to educational outcomes, courts (and the state) have no reason to treat climate and discipline differently than any other core part of the educational program. Just as the state must support and fund teacher training and certification programs and maintain facilities, so too must the state support and improve school climate and discipline. Yet many states have done the opposite by incentivizing and mandating harsh responses to discipline. Other states, at best, delegate so much discretion to local districts that nothing restrains them from making bad decisions or incentivizes them to make good decisions. In short, the state is both vicariously and directly responsible for negative climates that persist in school districts. Thus, the state cannot cast blame on districts.

Sometimes a court may require plaintiffs to establish one last element in their claim and show that the state can actually fix the problem plaintiffs have pointed out. Here, questions of causation can resurface. For instance, even if state policies and practices somehow incentivize student misbehavior, are there tools available to the state to improve climates and reduce student misbehavior? Courts do not want to order states to improve problems that are beyond schools' power to solve.

On this point, plaintiffs must be clear. The state cannot stop student misbehavior altogether, but it can minimize it. Some significant level of misbehavior is a natural part of students growing up. Another portion is a result of the serious emotional, familial, and other challenges that many children face. Schools cannot prevent these misbehaviors (absent far more robust social services and supports than states currently provide to families). What schools can stop—and should be responsible for—is misbehavior that goes beyond the norm. Fortunately, social science has come a long way in helping schools meet this challenge over the past decade. Research on positive behavior supports, restorative justice, mental health services for students, and the like demonstrates that nonpunitive programs improve climates and reduce misbehavior. Thus, the question is not whether states *can* make things better but whether they will. As far as state constitutional duties to deliver adequate and equitable educational opportunities are concerned, the answer is that states must make things better. They must fund and support these programs rather than relying on districts to voluntarily adopt and fund these programs themselves.

Conclusion

The theories laid out in this and the prior chapters beg the question of why the concept of a constitutional right to education that restricts discipline has yet to evolve and be implemented. The answer is threefold. The first reason may be poor execution on the part of litigants. Suspension and expulsion litigation is not nearly as coordinated as school finance litigation. Because the stakes are so obviously high in school finance, the cases are long-term assaults on the state, plotted out well in advance. For the suspended and expelled students, the stakes may be individually high; but the statewide effect is less clear to the litigants, and their cases are not necessarily coordinated or strategized in advance. No one brings a school finance case on the spur of the moment or on their own. But any student with an attorney can bring a discipline case—as they should be able to. For that matter, some have brought cases without attorneys. The downside of individualized litigation, however, is the higher likelihood of random results. Without support from individuals who are more specialized in the field, the exact framing of the legal issues, the exact claims made, and the facts deemed most important are all subject to substantial variance. Sometimes, those variances are problematic. Even putting substance aside, without the attention that outside resources can bring, not all courts will afford well-stated cases the serious attention they deserve. As chapter 2 demonstrates, discipline precedent is replete with judicial opinions that did not appear to fully consider the claims before them.

Second, the effects of precedential game changers can take time to absorb. A constitutional or fundamental right to education completely reframes the way courts should look at discipline. There is every indication that such a right exists. But the idea that school discipline has been reframed, in the absence of a school finance court explicitly indicating as much, may take a while to resonate. School finance litigation went through its own developmental phase from the early 1970s into the 1990s. In some states, it is still developing. Discipline litigation has not gone through this development. A few random courts have been asked to accept a new discipline paradigm on the spot, with almost no guidance from prior courts. Thus, these random courts have understandably been reticent to react. This, however, is not a reason for litigants to shy away from bringing new cases. It is the reason for litigants and advocacy groups to be thoughtful and strategic in planning out the steps by which to translate school finance principles into school discipline success. While they face obvious hurdles, they also face important opportunities for litigants to fully explore the boundaries of school finance principles in ways never considered before.

Third, the theory that school discipline is part of a standard school quality or equality claim calls for reconceptualizing discipline in ways that may not have been possible prior to recent developments in social science. Rather than using the law to block particular suspensions and expulsions, this theory addresses the problem of student misbehavior well before it occurs. The good news is that because this solution is so closely connected to academic outcomes, it fits squarely within existing school finance precedent. It does not require the development of a new doctrine. It only requires doctrine to account for new evidence.

CONCLUSION

Four decades ago, a fundamental shift in the relationship between schools and their students began to occur. In the years and decades that followed, discipline has become increasingly harsh and punitive. Zero tolerance itself has been solidly in place for two decades. This shift now steals millions of students' futures each year, setting many on a path to unemployment, prison, and second-class citizenship. This shift has also undermined the education of those students who try their best to learn and behave. They have seen order and achievement eroded by the toxic environment that harsh and ineffective discipline fosters. School discipline, overall, has been nothing less than a catastrophe in recent decades.

The prospects of interrupting the status quo in discipline have been relatively bleak for some time. For far too long, the battle was simply to slow the spread of harsh discipline. With the fervor surrounding mass shootings at schools and the general get-tough approach to minors, no one imagined it could be reversed. Even today, when the expansion of harsh policies seems to have stopped, old habits and traditions die hard. Many schools cling to them as closely as ever, trusting in the common-sense notion that troublemakers are born, not made, and that they must be dealt with accordingly.

In just the past few years, significant pockets of resistance to the status quo have finally arisen at the federal, state, and local levels. These pockets are part of a full-scale social science and advocacy movement to end punitive discipline and replace it with positive behavioral supports and restorative justice. This movement, while showing important signs of progress, will not unseat the status quo anytime soon. Suspension and expulsion rates have barely budged in most places and continue to increase in others. But even if this movement supplants punitive discipline at some point in the future—and I firmly believe it will—the new discipline policies will have their own flaws. The very best of today's progressive federal- and state-level discipline policies still reveal an unwillingness to fundamentally alter discipline or take the harshest punishments off the board. No matter how much progress is made at the federal, state, and local levels in the coming years, harsh discipline and zero tolerance will almost certainly persist indefinitely in many jurisdictions, just as corporal punishment has. Moreover, it will most likely continue in those states and districts with the most deep-seated racial biases and least sophisticated approaches to discipline. In other words, where reform is needed most, it is also the most unlikely to occur.

Courts are the only institution that can speed reform along and ensure it reaches all students in need. This is not to say that courts know best or are the substantive reformers that discipline needs. School desegregation and school finance litigation have taught far too many hard lessons to the contrary for this book to suggest that. The history of school desegregation, and subsequent resegregation, clearly demonstrates that courts alone lack the power to reform schools. School finance litigation demonstrates the same. Courts can identify the constitutional violation in current policies, but they can neither pass new legislation nor fund it. Throughout school desegregation and school finance litigation, courts have been well aware of this reality, admitting the limits of their authority and expertise in education reform.

But what is equally clear is that without the courts, desegregation would not have happened. Without the courts, extreme inequitable and inadequate school funding would have continued unphased. The politics to support equality and adequacy just do not exist very often. In fact, even when courts prompt states to reform school funding, it is rarely more than a few years before states begin to fall back into their old inequitable habits. Each time, courts, not legislatures, call the system back to order.

The same ideas apply to school discipline. While courts lack the expertise and authority to act alone or even lead the way in discipline, without courts, the movement to reform discipline will be too slow, always incomplete, and subject to retraction. The time is now for litigants to reengage courts—both because a wider social advocacy movement has now formed and because a few signs suggest that courts may be ready. State actors have grown so overzealous in their treatment of minors that some courts have finally begun to say "enough is enough."

At the federal level in particular, the Supreme Court in recent years has struck down the strip search of a student for possessing Tylenol as too invasive, indicated that the police interrogation of a student at school must be informed by the student's age, and found that minors are unsuitable for criminal law's ultimate sanctions.[1] In other words, the state has taken the flexibility previously afforded by the Court and abused it, going further than the Court is any longer willing to tolerate. While none of these cases directly involved due process, they suggest that, under the right circumstances, federal courts are susceptible to positive change.

At the state level, the most promising precedent also happens to be the most recent. Equally important, state courts have never been as hostile to discipline claims as federal courts. State discipline cases are fewer and further between. Thus, the lack of success in state court is more a product of underdeveloped theories and movements than it is hardened resistance by courts. Moreover, now that school finance precedent has matured and the social science case against harsh discipline has solidified, state courts offer a viable venue for discipline reform.

The final questions of this book are where and how to begin this movement. This book has articulated three different legal theories by which to challenge school discipline. All three have distinct strengths and weaknesses. A substantive due process challenge would require the most intellectual and analytic work of courts, asking them to extract guiding principles from the whole of substantive due process precedent. The difficulty of this task has surely played no small role in the poorly reasoned decisions of the past. On the other hand, a substantive due process challenge is grounded in history and logic, rather than policy. Thus, it would not call on courts to make judgment calls, weigh interests, or impose social-science-based remedies. A court would need only strike down irrational and counterproductive discipline practices.

The strength of individual challenges based on the constitutional right to education is the potential to place an absolute limit on almost all harsh discipline, not just irrational discipline. Advocates would not need to identify a prototypical district or plaintiff or challenge the most asinine example of expulsion to succeed. Rather, advocates would need only convince a court that past precedent establishes an individual right or interest in education that triggers heightened scrutiny.

The drawback, however, is that this challenge would potentially require courts, either explicitly or implicitly, to weigh the benefits and burdens of school exclusion and its alternatives. While balancing is not formally part of heightened scrutiny, the weight of a state's asserted interest in excluding students and arguments regarding which discipline practices are sufficiently tailored to the state's interests would often involve value judgments. This reality played a role in the more poorly reasoned opinions discussed in chapter 6. This challenge also implicates the complex distinction between educational rights and duties, with which courts have thus far struggled.

A state constitutional challenge based on the negative effects of harsh discipline on educational environments and academic outcomes may be the doctrinally cleanest of the theories. It fits easily within existing school quality and equity precedent. Plaintiffs, in effect, could simply filter social science literature on school discipline and its effect on academic opportunities through the standard framework of past cases. For that matter, the evidence could just become part of ongoing school finance litigation, negating the need to start a new strategy or movement.

The drawback is that this challenge could not be won based just on the literature. Nor could it proceed as a facial challenge or as a challenge to an individual instance of expulsion, which the other theories could. To make a constitutional claim premised on the negative effects of discipline on school quality, plaintiffs would need to demonstrate particular facts in particular districts that align with the literature and the framework of past precedent. While that evidence can most likely be marshaled, it is far more resource intensive than the other theories.

These strengths and weaknesses, however, are not offered to suggest that advocates pursue one claim over another. To the contrary, each is part of the solution because each addresses a slightly different aspect of our disciplinary problems. The substantive due process claim is not aimed at reforming all discipline. Rather, it would stop the most irrational and harsh discipline. In that respect, it serves as a check on the outer limits of egregious discipline. Addressing egregious discipline is important because when it goes unchecked, it sets a permissive tone for all lesser forms of discipline. But stopping the most egregious discipline would not necessarily stop various other aspects of problematic discipline. Individual challenges based on the constitutional right to education serve that goal. Given the more sweeping nature of the right, it could be used to limit all forms of school exclusion.

But neither of these challenges would necessarily demand that schools reform the toxic educational environments that lead to excessive discipline. The effect of those challenges would primarily be to stop schools from unnecessarily excluding students. In that respect, neither of those challenges would directly protect the interests of the innocent bystanders whose education suffers as a result of negative disciplinary environments. The discipline challenge based on quality and equitable opportunities would address their interests and require schools to address the root of the disciplinary problem—the environment and disciplinary approach to students. In short, each of these theories addresses a distinct and important aspect of school discipline, and thus, each warrants attention before the courts.

Yet that attention will not come without the concerted effort of civil rights advocates. Almost every problematic discipline case decided in the decades following *Goss* and discussed in this book was random and disconnected from the rest. A search of the attorneys in those cases will not reveal involvement by national civil rights advocates. They will rarely reveal representation by local public-interest groups. Typically, those cases have been litigated by small firms and generalist attorneys who happen to have had a suspended or expelled student walk into their offices one day. Even *Seal v. Morgan*—possibly the most progressive of any school discipline decision available—involved a general attorney operating his own firm in Knoxville, Tennessee. His firm litigates personal injury and criminal defense cases.

Each of these attorneys surely did their best to represent their clients, but they lacked the years of particularized training, knowledge, and strategy necessary to consistently secure important precedent. This deficit is best evidenced by the claims that many of them did and did not bring. The complaints and briefs in many of the substantive due process cases noted in chapter 5 sadly reveal attorneys who insufficiently framed the central legal issues and precedent in the cases or buried those claims by including a string of other distracting claims and issues. The point is not to criticize those attorneys but to emphasize that the legal movement this book calls for is not one that the civil rights community has tried and failed. It is a movement waiting to happen.

Civil rights advocates have done it before. They can do it again. With all the flaws and critiques this book has heaped on *Goss v. Lopez*, haphazard litigation is not one of them. On its face, *Goss* presents itself as a random set of suspensions that made their way from a random school district in Ohio all the way to the Supreme Court. This could not be further from the truth.

Various leading civil rights advocates, including the American Civil Liberties Union, the Children's Defense Fund, and the NAACP Legal Defense Fund, built a concerted movement to get school discipline before the Court. They saw the storm coming in discipline, knew its disastrous effects for minority students in particular, and realized that courts were the only institution they could count on to stop it. In the lead-up to *Goss* and in the years immediately following, they carefully developed legal theories and strategically brought cases in particular jurisdictions. The monumental victory in *Goss*, which J. Harvie Wilkinson described as the sequel to *Brown v. Board*, may very well not have occurred without their efforts. At the very least, victory before the Supreme Court would have taken longer to occur and come by a more circuitous route.

Unfortunately, the rights secured in *Goss* were insufficient to protect against future evils. The disciplinary harms students have suffered in the decades following *Goss* demand that the civil rights community once again reconvene around discipline litigation. Surely, this idea has not been lost on advocates. Rather, unfavorable precedent over the past few decades may have dissuaded them (and foundations that would support them) from pursuing litigation strategies. Yet one could just as easily ask if the very reason why precedent has grown unfavorable is because the expertise of the civil rights community has not been leveraged to resist it.

Whatever one may say of the challenges of recent decades, they are behind us now. History is finally on civil rights advocates' side. Harsh treatment of minors and youth is one place where a generally conservative U.S. Supreme Court has been willing to limit the state in recent years, and state supreme courts are a venue where students have been able to seek reprieve from inequitable and inadequate educational opportunities. Equally important, school discipline is one of the areas of research where scholars have reached the most consensus and most conclusive findings regarding the need for change. A meaningful number of policy makers and schools have even been willing to consider these research findings and proposals. The time is now for civil rights advocates to seize the moment and bring a full and final end to zero tolerance, harsh discipline, and basic irrationality in dealing with students.

NOTES

Introduction

1. Ratner v. Loudoun Cty. Pub. Sch., 16 F. App'x 140 (4th Cir. 2001), Appellant Brief at *7.
2. Ibid., 141.
3. 24 Pa. Cons. Stat. § 1317(g).
4. Seal v. Morgan, 229 F.3d 567, 572 (6th Cir. 2000).
5. Ibid.
6. Ibid.
7. Ibid., 576.
8. Connecticut State Department of Education, *Suspensions and Expulsions in Connecticut* (Hartford: Connecticut State Department of Education, 2015), 33, www.sde.ct.gov; see also Daniel J. Losen and Tia Elena Martinez, *Out of School and Off Track: The Overuse of Suspensions in American Middle and High Schools* (Los Angeles: Center for Civil Rights Remedies at UCLA's Civil Rights Project, 2013), 1, 20.
9. See Eric Blumenson and Eva S. Nilsen, "One Strike and You're Out? Constitutional Constraints on Zero Tolerance in Public Education," *Washington University Law Quarterly* 81 (2003): 71; cf. Brent E. Troyan, Note, "The Silent Treatment: Perpetual In-School Suspensions and the Education Rights of Students," *Texas Law Review* 81 (2003): 1641–42 (stating that expulsion and suspension sanctions are not reserved for major infractions).
10. See, e.g., California Educ. Code § 48900 (West 2014) (including "committed an obscene act or engaged in habitual profanity or vulgarity" and "disrupted school activities or otherwise willfully defied the valid authority of supervisors, teachers, administrators, school officials, or other school personnel engaged in the performance of their duties" as expellable offenses); Sandra Tan, "In Buffalo, NY, Students No Longer Suspended for Minor Misbehavior," Breaking the School-to-Prison Pipeline website, April 24, 2013, www.breakingthepipeline.org (site discontinued).
11. "Austin Carroll, Indiana High School Student, Expelled for Tweeting Profanity," *Huffington Post*, March 25, 2012, www.huffingtonpost.com.
12. S.C. Code Ann. § 59-63-210(A) (2013).
13. Miss. Code Ann. § 37-11-18.1 (2014).
14. Daniel J. Losen and Russell Skiba, *Suspended Education: Urban Middle Schools in Crisis* (Montgomery, AL: Southern Poverty Law Center, 2010), 2–3, www.splcenter.org.

15. Eduardo Ferrer, "District Discipline: The Overuse of Suspension and Expulsion in the District of Columbia," DC Lawyers for Youth website, June 20, 2013, http://dcly .org.

16. Every Student Every Day Coalition, *District Discipline: The Overuse of School Suspension and Expulsion in the District of Columbia* (Washington, DC: Every Student Every Day Coalition, n.d.), www.dcly.org.

17. See Massachusetts Advocacy Center, *The Way Out: Student Exclusion Practices in Boston Middle Schools* (Boston: Massachusetts Advocacy Center, 1986), 53 (studying Boston middle school students); see also Christine Bowditch, "Getting Rid of Troublemakers: High School Disciplinary Procedures and the Production of Dropouts," *Social Problems* 40 (1993): 498–99 (showing that 35.2 percent of students suspended were suspended for repeated school violations); Virginia Costenbader and Samia Markson, "School Suspension: A Study with Secondary School Students," *Journal of School Psychology* 36 (1998): 70–71 (showing that 37 percent of students suspended at least once believed that they would be suspended again in the future).

18. Tony Fabelo, Michael D. Thompson, Martha Plotkin, Dottie Carmichael, Miner P. Marchbanks III, and Eric A. Booth, *Breaking Schools' Rules: A Statewide Study of How School Discipline Relates to Students' Success and Juvenile Justice Involvement* (New York: Council of State Government Justice Center, 2011), 37–38, www.csgjusticecenter.org.

19. Linda M. Raffaele Mendez, "Predictors of Suspension and Negative School Outcomes: A Longitudinal Investigation," *New Directions for Youth Development* 99 (Fall 2003): 28–29.

20. Robert Balfanz, Vaughan Byrnes, and Joanna Fox, "Sent Home and Put Off-Track: The Antecedents, Disproportionalities, and Consequences of Being Suspended in the Ninth Grade," paper prepared for the Center for Civil Rights Remedies and the Research-to-Practice Collaborative, National Conference on Race and Gender Disparities in Discipline, Johns Hopkins University, Baltimore, December 21, 2012, http://civilrightsproject.ucla.edu.

21. Coalition for Juvenile Justice, *Abandoned in the Back Row: New Lessons in Education and Delinquency Prevention* (Washington, DC, 2001), 2.

22. See, e.g., Advancement Project, *Test, Punish, and Push Out: How "Zero Tolerance" and High-Stakes Testing Funnel Youth into the School-to-Prison Pipeline* (Washington, DC: Advancement Project, March 2010), 18–19, www.advancementproject. org; Florida Department of Juvenile Justice, *Delinquency in Florida's Schools: A Four Year Study* (Tallahassee: Florida Department of Juvenile Justice, 2009), 5–6, 17–18, www.djj.state.fl.us; Katayoon Majd, "Students of the Mass Incarceration Nation," *Howard Law Journal* 54 (2011): 347–48; Roni R. Reed, Note, "Education and the State Constitutions: Alternatives for Suspended and Expelled Students," *Cornell Law Review* 81 (1996): 606; Terence P. Thornberry, Melanie Moore, and R. L., Christenson, "The Effect of Dropping Out of High School on Subsequent Criminal Behavior," *Criminology* 23, no. 1 (1985): 7; see also Gary Sweeten, "Who

Will Graduate? Disruption of High School Education by Arrest and Court Involvement," *Justice Quarterly* 23 (2006): 471–75 (analyzing the effect of juvenile delinquency referral on a student's graduation).

23. Alyson Klein and Evie Blad, "Discipline Disparities Are Focus of White House Summit," *Rules for Engagement* (blog), *Education Week*, July 22, 2015, http://blogs.edweek.org.

24. Lee v. Macon Cty. Bd. of Educ., 490 F.2d 458, 460 (5th Cir. 1974).

25. Daniel Losen, Cheri Hodson, Michael A. Keith II, Katrina Morrison, and Shakti Belway, *Are We Closing the School Discipline Gap?* (Los Angeles: Center for Civil Rights Remedies, UCLA Civil Right Project, 2015), http://civilrightsproject.ucla.edu.

26. Russell J. Skiba, Robert S. Michael, Abra Carroll Nardo, and Reece Peterson, "The Color of Discipline: Sources of Racial and Gender Disproportionality in School Punishment," *Urban Review* 34 (2002): 330.

27. Losen et al., *Are We Closing the School Discipline Gap?*, 4.

28. David N. Figlio, "Testing, Crime and Punishment," National Bureau of Economic Research, November 2003, 13, www.nber.org.

29. Advancement Project, *Test, Punish, and Push Out*, 4.

30. Ibid., 16.

31. See James Earl Davis and Will J. Jordan, "The Effects of School Context, Structure, and Experiences on African-American Males in Middle and High Schools," *Journal of Negro Education* 63 (1994): 585; Russell J. Skiba and M. Karega Rausch, "Zero Tolerance, Suspension, and Expulsion: Questions of Equity and Effectiveness," in *Handbook of Classroom Management: Research, Practice, and Contemporary Issues*, ed. Carolyn M. Evertson and Carol S. Weinstein (Mahwah, NJ: Lawrence Erlbaum, 2006), 1072.

32. M. Karega Rausch and Russell J. Skiba, "The Academic Cost of Discipline: The Relationship between Suspension/Expulsion and School Achievement," paper presented at the Annual Meeting of the American Educational Research Association, Montreal, Canada, April, 2005, 16.

33. Ibid., 17

34. Brea L. Perry and Edward W. Morris, "Suspending Progress: Collateral Consequences of Exclusionary Punishment in Public Schools," *American Sociological Review* 79 (December 2014): 1082–83.

35. Ibid., 1083.

36. Richard Arum, *Judging School Discipline: The Crisis of Moral Authority* (Cambridge, MA: Harvard University Press, 2003), 34.

37. Perry and Morris, "Suspending Progress," 1071.

38. See generally ibid.; see also Paul M. Bogos, "'Expelled. No Excuses. No Exceptions.'—Michigan's Zero Tolerance Policy in Response to School Violence: M.C.L.A. Section 380.1311," *University of Detroit Mercy Law Review* 74 (1997): 381 (stating that zero tolerance—"and similar measures—often harden delinquent behavior patterns, alienate troubled youths from the schools, and foster distrust" (internal quotation marks omitted)).

39. Alex Nitkin, "Suspensions Down, Schools Feel Safer, but Charter Data Still Absent," Catalyst Chicago, March 19, 2015, http://catalyst-chicago.org.

40. Ricardo Martinez, "Lessons in Racial Justice: How We Are Dismantling the School-to-Prison Pipeline in Denver," *Just Democracy* (blog), Advancement Project, September 15, 2014, www.advancementproject.org/; Padres & Jóvenes Unidos and Advancement Project, *Lessons in Racial Justice and Movement Building: Dismantling the School-to-Prison Pipeline in Colorado and Nationally* (Padres & Jóvenes Unidos and Advancement Project, n.d.), www.advancementprojet.org.

41. Derek Black, "California Limits School Suspensions: Did It Do Enough?," *Education Law Prof Blog*, October 1, 2014, http://lawprofessors.typepad.com/education_law/.

42. 419 U.S. 565 (1975).

43. Erwin Chemerinsky, *The Case against the Supreme Court* (New York: Viking, 2014), 5–6.

44. 430 U.S. 651 (1977).

45. Ibid., 657.

46. Ibid.

47. Global Initiative to End All Corporal Punishment of Children, *Corporal Punishment of Children in the USA* (London: Global Initiative to End All Corporal Punishment of Children, October 2015), www.endcorporalpunishment.org.

48. Human Rights Watch, *A Violent Education: Corporal Punishment of Children in U.S. Public Schools* (New York: Human Rights Watch, 2008), www.hrw.org.

Chapter 1. From Friends to Enemies

1. E. Gordon Gee and David J. Sperry, *Educational Law and the Public Schools: A Compendium* (Boston: Allyn and Bacon, 1978), I-1.

2. State v. Pendergrass, 19 N.C. 365 (1837).

3. Ibid., 365

4. Ibid., 365–66.

5. Ibid., 367.

6. Ibid., 366.

7. Ibid., 366–67.

8. Ibid.

9. Ibid., 367–68.

10. Ingraham v. Wright, 430 U.S. 651, 661 (1977).

11. Green v. Cty. Sch. Bd. of New Kent, 391 U.S. 430, 438, 439 (1968).

12. Douglass S. Reed, *Building the Federal Schoolhouse: Localism and the American Education State* (New York: Oxford University Press, 2014), 66.

13. Quoted in ibid., 68.

14. Ibid.

15. Ibid., 69.

16. Ibid.

17. Ibid. (referencing a *Washington Post* story).

18. Hawkins v. Coleman, 376 F. Supp. 1330, 1335 (1974).

19. Ibid.

20. Ibid., 1336.

21. Ibid.

22. Ibid.

23. Ibid.

24. Ibid., 1338.

25. Children's Defense Fund, *School Suspensions: Are They Helping Children?* (Washington, DC: Washington Research Project, 1975); see also Betsy Levin and Willis D. Hawley eds., *The Courts, Social Science, and School Desegregation* (New Brunswick, NJ: Transaction Books, 1975), 383 (finding that black students were suspended or expelled at twice the rate of their white counterparts); Joe Larkin, "School Desegregation and Student Suspension: A Look at One School System," *Education and Urban Society* 11 (1979): 490–91 (finding that black students were suspended from secondary schools at three times the rate of white students).

26. Children's Defense Fund, *School Suspensions.*

27. Madeleine Cousineau, "Institutional Racism and the School-to-Prison Pipeline," paper submitted for the 105th annual meeting of the American Sociological Association, Atlanta, Georgia, August 14, 2010, 7.

28. 327 F. Supp. 930 (S.D. Fla. 1971).

29. Ibid., 932.

30. 359 F. Supp. 1085 (N.D. Fla. 1973).

31. Ibid., 1091.

32. J. Harvie Wilkinson III, "*Goss v. Lopez*: The Supreme Court as School Superintendent," *Supreme Court Review*, 1975, 30.

33. Ibid., 32.

34. Goss v. Lopez, 419 U.S. 565, 581 (1975) (quoting Joint Anti-Fascist Refugee Comm. v. McGrath, 341 U.S. 123, 170 (1951)).

35. Ibid., 583.

36. Ibid., 592–93.

37. Ibid., 594.

38. Ibid., 591.

39. Ibid., 592.

40. Ibid.; see also Youssef Chouhoud and Perry A. Zirkel, "The *Goss* Progeny: An Empirical Analysis," *San Diego Law Review* 45 (2008): 353 ("Last year, upon the thirtieth anniversary of the Supreme Court's decision in *Goss v. Lopez*, the then-general counsel of the National School Boards Association decried the expansion of *Goss* from a 'three minute give and take' to the 'paralysis' of public school discipline.").

41. See Richard Arum, *Judging School Discipline: The Crisis of Moral Authority* (Cambridge, MA: Harvard University Press, 2003), 30.

42. Ibid.

43. Ibid.; cf. Jessica Falk, "Overcoming a Lawyer's Dogma: Examining Due Process for the 'Disruptive Student,'" *University of Michigan Journal of Law Reform* 36 (2003):

468 (discussing how students perceive traditional due process hearings as adversarial, with school personnel against them).

44. Chouhoud and Zirkel, "*Goss* Progeny," 357 n23.

45. See Betsy Levin, "Educating Youth for Citizenship: The Conflict between Authority and Individual Rights in the Public School," *Yale Law Journal* 95 (1986): 1672 (stating that the legalization of dispute resolution in the schools potentially sets "students and teachers as adversaries rather than as participants in the learning process").

46. See Arum, *Judging School Discipline*, 30 (stating that by the late 1970s, 59 percent of teachers indicated that court decisions had hampered schools). See generally Falk, "Overcoming a Lawyer's Dogma," 468 (discussing the adversarial nature of traditional due process hearings); Levin, "Educating Youth," 1672 (same).

47. See generally Judith Kafka, *The History of "Zero Tolerance" in American Public Schooling* (New York: Palgrave Macmillan, 2011), 6 (discussing the bureaucratization and centralization of discipline in response to *Goss*).

48. Arum, *Judging School Discipline*, 5.

49. Ibid., 4.

50. Pew Center on the States, *One in 100: Behind Bars in America 2008* (Philadelphia: Pew Center, 2008), 5.

51. James C. Howell, "Superpredators and other Myths about Juvenile Delinquency," in *Preventing and Reducing Juvenile Delinquency: A Comprehensive Framework*, 2nd ed. (Thousand Oaks, CA: Sage, 2009), 4 (discussing DiIulio).

52. Quoted in Franklin D. Gilliam, Jr., and Shanto Iyengar, "Super-Predators or Victims of Societal Neglect? Framing Effects in Juvenile Crime Coverage," in *Framing American Politics*, ed. Karen Callaghan and Frauke Schnell (Pittsburgh: University of Pittsburgh Press, 2005), 150.

53. Equal Justice Initiative, "The Superpredator Myth, 20 Years Later," April 7, 2014, www.eji.org.

54. Donna M. Bishop, Charles E. Frazier, Lonn Lanza-Kaduce, and Lawrence Winner, "The Transfer of Juveniles to Criminal Court: Does It Make a Difference?," *Crime & Delinquency* 42, no. 2 (1996): 181–83.

55. Philip Kaufman, Xianglei Chen, Susan P. Choy, Sally A. Ruddy, Amanda K. Miller, Kathryn A. Chandler, Christopher D. Chapman, Michael R. Rand, and Patsy Klaus, *Indicators of School Crime and Safety, 1999* (Washington, DC: U.S. Departments of Education and Justice, 1999), 119 (table A1), www.nces.ed.gov.

56. Advancement Project, *Test, Punish, and Push Out: How "Zero Tolerance" and High-Stakes Testing Funnel Youth into the School-to-Prison Pipeline* (Washington, DC: Advancement Project, March 2010), 10, www.advancementproject.org.

Chapter 2. Judicial Disengagement

1. 393 U.S. 503 (1969).

2. 419 U.S. 565 (1975).

3. Ibid., 574.

4. Ibid., 584.

5. Brooke Grona, "School Discipline: What Process Is Due? What Process Is Deserved?," *American Journal of Criminal Law* 27 (2000): 233.

6. See, e.g., Swann v. Charlotte-Mecklenberg Bd. of Educ., 402 U.S. 1 (1971); Green v. Cty. Sch. Bd. of New Kent, 391 U.S. 430 (1968).

7. 391 U.S. 430 (1971).

8. U.S. Commission on Civil Rights, *Fulfilling the Letter and Spirit of the Law: Desegregation of the Nation's Public Schools* (Washington, DC: Commission on Civil Rights, 1976), 6.

9. 420 U.S. 308 (1975).

10. Ibid., 326.

11. J. Harvie Wilkinson III, "*Goss v. Lopez*: Supreme Court as School Superintendent," *Supreme Court Review*, 1975, 25.

12. *Wood*, 420 U.S. at 326.

13. 430 U.S. 651 (1977).

14. 469 U.S. 325 (1985).

15. Safford Unified Sch. Dist. No. 1 v. Redding, 557 U.S. 364 (2009).

16. Wilkinson, "*Goss v. Lopez*," 40, 42.

17. Ibid., 30.

18. Ibid., 72.

19. David L. Kirp, "Proceduralism and Bureaucracy: Due Process in the School Setting," *Stanford Law Review* 28 (1976): 842.

20. Donald H. Stone, "Crime and Punishment in Public Schools: An Empirical Study of Disciplinary Proceedings," *American Journal of Trial Advocacy* 17 (1993): 351–98.

21. Ibid., 356–57.

22. Ibid., 360.

23. Ibid., 367.

24. 842 F.2d 920 (6th Cir. 1988).

25. Ibid., 922.

26. Ibid., 928.

27. Ibid., 927n5.

28. See, e.g., Jennings v. Wentzville R-IV Sch. Dist., 397 F.3d. 1118, 1124 (8th Cir. 2005); Riggan v. Midland Indep. Sch. Dist., 86 F. Supp. 2d 647, 656 (2000).

29. Gonzales v. McEuen, 435 F. Supp. 460, 464 (D. Cal. 1977); Alex v. Allen, 409 F. Supp. 379, 388 (W.D. Pa. 1976).

30. See Hortonville Joint Sch., Dist. No. 1 v. Hortonville Educ. Ass'n, 426 U.S. 482, 497 (1976) (referring to the "presumption of honesty and integrity" of decision makers in school board hearings); *Jennings*, 397 F.3d at 1124 (same).

31. *Riggan*, 86 F. Supp. 2d at 656–57. See also Murray v. West Baton Rouge Par. Sch. Bd., 472 F.2d 438, 443 (5th Cir.1973); Levitt v. Univ. of Texas at El Paso, 759 F.2d

1224, 1233 (5th Cir. 1985); Brewer by Dreyfus v. Austin Indep. Sch. Dist., 779 F.2d 260, 264 (1985).

32. See Thomas R. Baker, "Construing the Scope of Student Conduct Codes: Recent Federal Rulings Suggest Heightened Court Scrutiny Ahead," *Education Law Reporter* 174 (2003): 575–77.

33. *Goss*, 419 U.S. at 584.

34. Jane Rutherford, "The Myth of Due Process," *Boston University Law Review* 72 (1992): 1–99.

35. Ibid., 6–7.

36. Ibid., 7.

37. Ibid.

38. Ibid.

39. Ibid., 7.

40. 420 U.S. 308, 326 (1975).

41. 16 F. App'x 140, 142 (4th Cir. 2001) (per curiam).

42. Ratner v. Loudon Cty. Pub. Sch., No. 00-944-A, at 5 (July 28, 2000) (slip opinion on file with author).

43. Ibid., 7.

44. Ratner v. Loudoun Cty. Pub. Sch., 16 F. App'x 140, 142 (4th Cir. 2001) (internal citation omitted).

45. Ibid., 143–44 (internal citation omitted).

46. Ibid., 144.

47. Richard Arum, *Judging School Discipline: The Crisis of Moral Authority* (Cambridge, MA: Harvard University Press, 2003), 88.

48. Youssef Chouhoud and Perry A. Zirkel, "The *Goss* Progeny: An Empirical Analysis," *San Diego Law Review* 45 (2008): 372.

49. Ibid., 375.

50. 229 F.3d 567 (6th Cir. 2000).

Chapter 3. The Insufficiency of Policy Reform

1. Brea L. Perry and Edward W. Morris, "Suspending Progress: Collateral Consequences of Exclusionary Punishment in Public Schools," *American Sociological Review* 79 (December 2014): 1067–87.

2. Tracy J. Evans-Whipp, Stephanie M. Plenty, Richard F. Catalano, Todd I. Herrenkohl, and John W. Toumbourou, "Longitudinal Effects of School Drug Policies on Student Marijuana Use in Washington State and Victoria," *American Journal of Public Health* 105 (May 2015): 994.

3. Ibid.

4. Russell J. Skiba, Reece L. Peterson, and Tara Williams, "Office Referrals and Suspension: Disciplinary Intervention in Middle Schools," *Education and Treatment of Children* 20, no. 3 (1997): 295–315; Russell J. Skiba, Robert S. Michael, Abra Carroll Nardo, and Reece Peterson, "The Color of Discipline: Sources of Racial

and Gender Disproportionality in School Punishment," *Urban Review* 34 (2002): 317–42; M. Karega Rausch and Russell J. Skiba, "The Academic Cost of Discipline: The Relationship between Suspension/Expulsion and School Achievement," paper presented at the Annual Meeting of the American Educational Research Association, Montreal, Canada, April 2005.

5. Daniel Losen, Cheri Hodson, Michael A. Keith II, Katrina Morrison, and Shakti Belway, *Are We Closing the School Discipline Gap?* (Los Angeles: Center for Civil Rights Remedies, UCLA Civil Rights Project, 2015), 19, http://civilrightsproject .ucla.edu.

6. Clifton B. Parker, "Teachers More Likely to Label Black Students as Trouble-makers, Stanford Research Shows," *Stanford Report*, April 15, 2015, http://news .stanford.edu.

7. Jason A. Okonofua and Jennifer L. Eberhardt, "Two Strikes: Race and the Disciplining of Young Students," *Psychological Science* 26, no. 5 (2015): 617–24.

8. U.S. Department of Education, "Expansive Survey of America's Public Schools Reveals Troubling Racial Disparities: Lack of Access to Pre-School, Greater Suspensions Cited," press release, March 21, 2014, www.ed.gov.

9. Okonofua and Eberhardt, "Two Strikes," 617.

10. Nolan Rosenkrans, "TPS Implements Preventive Approach to Student Discipline," *Toledo Blade*, May 4, 2014, www.toledoblade.com.

11. Motoko Rich, "Obama to Report Widening of Initiative for Black and Latino Boys: My Brother's Keeper Program Grows to Include More Impoverished Minorities," *New York Times*, July 20, 2014, www.nytimes.com.

12. Teresa Watanabe, "LAUSD to Decriminalize Student Fights, Petty Thefts and Minor Offenses," *Los Angeles Times*, August 19, 2014, www.latimes.com.

13. Tom Mela, "How We Won School Discipline Reform in Massachusetts," *National Opportunity to Learn Campaign Blog*, July 23, 2014, www.otlcampaign.org.

14. Mass. Gen. Laws Ann. chap. 71, § 37H 3/4 (2014), https://malegislature.gov.

15. Sec. 1. Cal. Educ. Code 48900(k)(2).

16. Conn. Gen. Stat. § 10-233c (2012), http://law.justia.com.

17. Connecticut State Department of Education, *Suspensions and Expulsions in Connecticut* (Hartford: Connecticut State Department of Education, 2013), www.sde.ct.gov. Section 10-233c aims to lower the number of students who are suspended from school by setting new standards for sending students home for violating school or district rules. Ibid., 5.

18. Kathleen Megan, "Report: More Students under 7 Suspended; Overall Rate of Expulsion, Suspension Drops," *Hartford Courant*, March 5, 2015, www.courant.com.

19. Southern Poverty Law Center, "North Florida School Discrimination Complaints," August 6, 2012, www.splcenter.org.

20. U.S. Department of Justice and U.S. Department of Education, "Dear Colleague Letter on Nondiscriminatory Administration of School Discipline," January 8, 2014, 11–12, www.ed.gov.

21. Ibid.

22. Andrew J. Coulson, "Administration's Good Intentions Could Hurt Black Students' Achievement," *Cato at Liberty* (blog), Cato Institute, January 8, 2014, www.cato .org.

23. "538: Is This Working?," *This American Life*, October 17, 2014, radio program, www.thisamericanlife.org.

24. Michael Planty, William Hussar, Thomas Snyder, Grace Kena, Angelina Kewal-Ramani, et al., *The Condition of Education 2009* (Washington, DC: National Center for Education Statistics, 2009), 70, http://nces.ed.gov.

25. Losen et al., *Are We Closing the School Discipline Gap?*

26. Tina Jung, "State Schools Chief Tom Torlakson Reports California Sees Significant Drops in Student Suspensions and Expulsions," news release, California Department of Education, January 29, 2014, www.cde.ca.gov.

27. Edward J. Smith and Shaun R. Harper, *Disproportionate Impact of K–12 School Suspension and Expulsion on Black Students in Southern States* (Philadelphia: University of Pennsylvania, Center for the Study of Race and Equity in Education, 2015), www.gse.upenn.edu.

28. Ibid.

29. Joanna Taylor, Matt Cregor, and Priya Lane, *Not Measuring Up: The State of School Discipline in Massachusetts* (Boston: Lawyers' Committee for Civil Rights and Economic Justice, 2014), 2, http://lawyerscom.org.

30. Ibid., 3.

31. Ibid., 4.

32. Kari Harden, "Civil Rights Complaints Filed against Three New Orleans Schools," *Louisiana Weekly*, April 24, 2014, http://newamericamedia.org.

33. "Administrative Complaint Requesting Investigations into Three New Orleans Charter Schools Operated by Collegiate Academies—George Washington Carver Preparatory," letter to Secretary Arne Duncan, U.S. Department of Education, April 14, 2014 (on file with author).

34. Ibid.

35. 158 Cal. Rptr. 3d 173 (Ct. App. Cal. 2013).

36. Ibid., 179.

37. Taylor, Cregor, and Lane, *Not Measuring Up*, 9.

38. Ibid., 8, table 2.

39. Ibid.

40. Ibid.

41. J.W. v. Birmingham Bd. of Educ., 2:10-CV-03314-AKK, 2015 WL 6945118, 1–2 (N.D. Ala. September 30, 2015).

42. U.S. Department of Justice, Civil Rights Division, *Investigation of the Ferguson Police Department* (Washington, DC: U.S. Department of Justice, March 4, 2015), 37, www.justice.gov.

43. Ibid., 37–38.

44. Susan Ferriss, "Virginia Tops Nation in Sending Students to Cops, Courts: Where Does Your State Rank?," Center for Public Integrity, April 10, 2015, www.public integrity.org.

Chapter 4. Making Discipline Rational

1. 420 U.S. 308, 326 (1975).
2. Ibid., 311.
3. Strickland v. Inlow, 348 F. Supp. 244, 248 (W.D. Ark. 1972).
4. Strickland v. Inlow, 485 F.2d 186, 191 (8th Cir. 1973), vacated and remanded sub nom. *Wood*, 420 U.S. 308.
5. *Wood*, 420 U.S. at 322.
6. Ibid., 325.
7. Ibid., 326.
8. Ibid.
9. 521 U.S. 702, 719–21 (1997).
10. Collins v. Harker Heights, 503 U.S. 115, 125 (1992) (quoting Daniels v. Williams, 474 U.S. 327, 331 (1986)).
11. 411 U.S. 1 (1973).
12. 347 U.S. 497 (1954).
13. Ibid., 499.
14. Laurence H. Tribe, "*Lawrence v. Texas*: The 'Fundamental Right' that Dare Not Speak Its Name," *Harvard Law Review* 117 (2004): 1897–98.
15. Kenji Yoshino, "The New Equal Protection," *Harvard Law Review* 124 (2011): 749–50.
16. Plyler v. Doe, 457 U.S. 202, 216 (1982) (quoting F. S. Royster Guano Co. v. Virginia, 253 U.S. 412, 415 (1920); Tigner v. Texas, 310 U.S. 141, 147 (1940)).
17. See, e.g., D.C. Code § 48-904.01 (2014); see also Aaron C. Davis, "D.C. Poised for Giant Leap toward Legalizing Marijuana," *Washington Post*, October 24, 2013, www.washingtonpost.com.
18. See, e.g., Ariz. Rev. Stat. Ann. § 13-3411 (2009); see also D.C. Code § 48-904.07a (2014).
19. See, e.g., Tenn. Code Ann. § 49-6-3401 (2014) (giving principals the power to suspend students for being charged with a felony off school grounds).
20. See, e.g., Greenville County School, Policies § JCDAA (2008), www.boarddocs .com.
21. 542 U.S. 507 (2004).
22. Ibid., 534.
23. S.C. Code Ann. § 59-63-210(A) (2013).
24. Ibid., § 59-63-210(B).
25. Ibid., § 59-150-250(B).
26. Blakely v. Washington, 542 U.S. 296, 301–2 (2004).
27. Ibid., 302.

28. Ibid., 306–7.
29. Richard H. Fallon, Jr., "Some Confusions about Due Process, Judicial Review, and Constitutional Remedies," *Columbia Law Review* 93 (1993): 310.
30. 110 U.S. 516, 527–28 (1884) (internal citations omitted).
31. Zinermon v. Burch, 494 U.S. 113, 125 (1990).
32. BMW of N. Am. v. Gore, 517 U.S. 559, 568 (1996). See also State Farm Mut. Auto Ins. v. Campbell, 538 U.S. 408 (2003).
33. Christine N. Cimini, "Principles of Non-arbitrariness: Lawlessness in the Administration of Welfare," *Rutgers Law Review* 57 (2005): 484–85.
34. Furman v. Georgia, 408 U.S. 238, 309–10 (1972).
35. Seal v. Morgan, 229 F.3d 567, 578 (6th Cir. 2000).
36. See, e.g., People v. Washington, 665 N.E.2d 1330, 1336–37 (Ill. 1996); State *ex rel.* Holmes v. Court of Appeals, 885 S.W.2d 389, 397–98 (Tex. Crim. App. 1994). See generally Ursula Bentele, "Does the Death Penalty, by Risking Execution of the Innocent, Violate Substantive Due Process?," *Houston Law Review* 40 (2004): 1359 (analyzing innocence in the context of substantive due process). In *Herrera v. Collins*, Justice Blackmun, joined by Justices Souter and Stevens, stated definitively, "Nothing could be more contrary to contemporary standards of decency or more shocking to the conscience than to execute a person who is actually innocent." 506 U.S. 390, 430 (1993) (Blackmun, J., dissenting) (internal citations omitted). The three dissenting justices agreed with Justice O'Connor's concurring opinion on this point. See *Herrera*, 506 U.S. at 419 (O'Connor, J., concurring).
37. See, e.g., *Seal*, 229 F.3d at 578; see also Susan Bandes, "Simple Murder: A Comment on the Legality of Executing the Innocent," *Buffalo Law Review* 44 (1996): 503.
38. See Bentele, "Does the Death Penalty," 1368.
39. See Joseph E. Kennedy, "Making the Crime Fit the Punishment," *Emory Law Journal* 51 (2002): 853–54 (discussing how sentencing should take into account those who are morally innocent and further discussing a theory that those who act immorally should still be punished, even if they believed their behavior was legal).
40. See, e.g., Goss v. Lopez, 419 U.S. 565, 574 (1975); Tinker v. Des Moines Indep. Cmty. Sch. Dist., 393 U.S. 503, 511 (1968).
41. *Goss*, 419 U.S. at 574; *Tinker*, 393 U.S. at 511; T.L.O. v. New Jersey, 469 U.S. 325 (1985).
42. *Tinker*, 393 U.S. at 511.
43. *Seal*, 229 F.3d at 575.
44. *Hamdi*, 542 U.S. at 530 (plurality opinion).
45. E.g., Osteen v. Henley, 13 F.3d 221, 225 (7th Cir. 1993); Newsome v. Batavia Local Sch. Dist., 842 F.2d 920, 925–26 (6th Cir. 1988); Gorman v. Univ. of Rhode Island, 837 F.2d 7, 16 (1st Cir. 1988).
46. Recognizing the state's legitimate interest in preserving its finite resources, the Court has acceded to balancing the risk of error against the burden of more process, but the Court has not suggested that avoiding the question of guilt and

innocence is a legitimate means of achieving that end. See generally Mathews v. Eldridge, 424 U.S. 319, 348 (1976).
47. *Goss*, 419 U.S. at 579.

Chapter 5. Individualizing Discipline

1. 229 F.3d 567 (6th Cir. 2000).
2. Ibid., 575.
3. Ibid., 575–76.
4. Ibid.
5. Ibid., 576.
6. Ibid.
7. Langley *ex rel.* Langley v. Monroe Cty. Sch. Dist., No. 1:05CV40, 2006 WL 2850349, at *4 (N.D. Miss. Oct. 2, 2006).
8. Tarkington Indep. Sch. Dist. v. Ellis, 200 S.W.3d 794, 803–4 (Tex. Ct. App. 2006).
9. 341 F.3d 1197 (10th Cir. 2003).
10. 342 U.S. 246, 255 (1952).
11. Ibid., 256.
12. Tenement House Dep't v. McDevitt, 215 N.Y. 160, 168 (1915).
13. See King *ex rel.* Harvey-Barrow v. Beaufort Cty. Bd. of Educ., 704 S.E.2d 259, 260–61 (N.C. 2010); Phillip Leon M. *ex rel.* J.P.M. v. Greenbrier Cty. Bd. of Educ., 484 S.E.2d 909, 911 (W. Va. 1996).
14. Lee v. Macon Cty. Bd. of Educ., 490 F.2d 458, 460 (5th Cir. 1974).
15. *Seal*, 229 F.3d at 582 (Suhrheinrich, J., dissenting).
16. Ibid.
17. 543 U.S. 551 (2005).
18. Ibid., 569 (citing Johnson v. Texas, 509 U.S. 305, 367 (1993)); see also Eddings v. Oklahoma, 455 U.S. 104, 116 (1982) ("Even the normal 16-year-old customarily lacks the maturity of an adult.").
19. *Roper*, 543 U.S. at 569.
20. Ibid., 569 (majority opinion).
21. Ibid., 570 (internal citations omitted).
22. 132 S. Ct. 2455 (2012).
23. People v. Siackasorn, 149 Cal. Rptr. 3d 918, 922 (Dist. Ct. App. 2012).
24. State v. Bennett, 820 N.W.2d 769, 2012 WL 2816806, at *4 (Iowa Ct. App. 2012).
25. Josie Foehrenbach Brown, "Developmental Due Process: Waging a Constitutional Campaign to Align School Discipline with Developmental Knowledge," *Temple Law Review* 82 (2009): 970–71.
26. American Psychological Association Zero Tolerance Task Force, "Are Zero Tolerance Policies Effective in Schools? An Evidentiary Review and Recommendations," adopted by APA Council of Representatives, August 9, 2006, 8.
27. BMW of N. Am., Inc. v. Gore, 517 U.S. 559, 568 (1996); see also State Farm Mut. Auto. Ins. Co. v. Campbell, 538 U.S. 408, 416 (2003).

28. *BMW*, 517 U.S. at 575, 580, 583.

29. Ibid., 575.

30. See, e.g., *State Farm*, 538 U.S. 408.

31. Tracy A. Thomas, "Proportionality and the Supreme Court's Jurisprudence of Remedies," *Hastings Law Journal* 59 (2007): 134–35; see also Wood v. Strickland, 420 U.S. 308, 326 (1975).

32. Ratner v. Loudon Cty. Pub. Sch., 16 F. App'x 140, 143 (4th Cir. 2001) (Hamilton, J., concurring) (per curiam).

33. Ibid., 144.

34. 20 U.S.C. §§ 1412(a)(1)(A), 1415(k)(1) (2012).

35. Richard Arum, *Judging School Discipline: The Crisis of Moral Authority* (Cambridge, MA: Harvard University Press, 2003), 181–82 (discussing students' perception of overly strict discipline and how it can exacerbate students' misbehavior rather than deter it).

36. Dona M. Kagan, "How Schools Alienate Students at Risk: A Model for Examining Proximal Classroom Variables," *Educational Psychologist* 25 (1990): 107 (citing Porter W. Sexton, "Trying to Make It Real Compared to What? Implications of High School Dropout Statistics," *Journal of Education Equity and Leadership* 5 (1985): 92).

37. Ibid.

38. Ellen Jane Hollingsworth, Henry S. Lufler, and William H. Clune, *School Discipline: Order and Autonomy* (New York: Praeger, 1984), 19.

39. Bethel Sch. Dist. No. 403 v. Fraser, 478 U.S. 675, 681 (1986) (quoting Charles A. Beard and Mary R. Beard, *New Basic History of the United States* (1968), 228; Ambach v. Norwick, 441 U.S. 68, 76–77 (1979)).

40. *BMW*, 517 U.S. at 584.

41. 114 F. Supp. 2d 504, 512 (N.D. Miss. 1999) (internal citation omitted).

42. 414 U.S. 632 (1974).

43. Ibid., 644.

44. Ibid.

45. Ibid. (quoting Vlandis v. Kline, 412 U.S. 441, 446 (1973)).

46. Stanley v. Illinois, 405 U.S. 645 (1972).

47. See, e.g., Patterson v. New York, 432 U.S. 197, 210, 215 (1977) (prohibiting the "shifting of the burden of persuasion with respect to [an important] fact").

48. Hamdi v. Rumsfeld, 542 U.S. 507, 534 (2004) (plurality opinion).

49. John J. Garman and Ray Walker, "The Zero-Tolerance Discipline Plan and Due Process: Elements of a Model Resolving Conflicts between Discipline and Fairness," *Faulkner Law Review* 1 (2010): 298.

50. Brent E. Troyan, Note, "The Silent Treatment: Perpetual In-School Suspensions and the Education Rights of Students," *Texas Law Review* 81 (2003): 1640; see also *Wood*, 420 U.S. at 319.

51. Colvin *ex rel.* Colvin v. Lowndes Cty. Miss. Sch. Dist., 114 F. Supp. 2d 504, 512 (N.D. Miss. 1999).

52. *Cleveland Bd. of Educ.*, 414 U.S. at 647–48 (quoting Stanley v. Illinois, 405 U.S. 645, 656 (1972)).
53. Ibid.

Chapter 6. The Constitutional Right to Education

1. 347 U.S. 483, 493 (1954).
2. Dennis J. Hutchinson, "Unanimity and Desegregation: Decisionmaking in the Supreme Court, 1948–1958," *Georgetown Law Journal* 68 (1979): 45–46 (quoting Warren, C.J., Memorandum on the District of Columbia Case, n.d., Box 263, HHB(LC), 3–4).
3. Hans J. Hacker and William D. Blake, "The Neutrality Principle: The Hidden yet Powerful Legal Axiom at Work in *Brown versus Board of Education*," *Berkeley Journal of African-American Law and Policy* 8 (2006): 47.
4. Bolling v. Sharpe, 347 U.S. 497, 500 (1955).
5. Hutchinson, "Unanimity and Desegregation," 47.
6. 411 U.S. 1 (1973).
7. Okla. Const. art. XIII, § 1.
8. Pa. Const. art. III, § 14.
9. Gershon M. Ratner, "A New Legal Duty for Urban Public Schools: Effective Education in Basic Skills," *Texas Law Review* 63 (1985): 815.
10. William E. Thro, "To Render Them Safe: The Analysis of State Constitutional Provisions in Public School Finance Reform Litigation," *Virginia Law Review* 75 (1989): 1666.
11. Cal. Const. art. IX, § 1.
12. Ill. Const. art. X, § 1; Ga. Const. art. VIII, § 1, ¶ 1.
13. Robinson v. Cahill, 303 A.2d 273, 295 (N.J. 1973).
14. Serrano v. Priest (Serrano II), 557 P.2d 929, 951 (Cal. 1976).
15. See Dupree v. Alma Sch. Dist., 651 S.W.2d 90, 93 (Ark. 1983); Horton v. Meskill, 376 A.2d 359, 373 (Conn. 1977); Seattle Sch. Dist. v. State, 585 P.2d 71, 71 (Wash. 1978); Washakie Cty. Sch. Dist. v. Herschler, 606 P.2d 310, 333 (Wyo. 1980).
16. 790 S.W.2d 186 (Ky. 1989).
17. Ibid., 212.
18. See, e.g., Alabama Opinion of the Justice, 624 So. 2d 107, 165–66 (Ala. 1993); Idaho Sch. for Equal Educ. Opportunity v. Evans, 850 P.2d 724, 734 (Idaho 1993); McDuffy v. Secretary, 615 N.E.2d 516, 554 (Mass. 1993); Claremont Sch. Dist. v. Governor, 703 A.2d 1353, 1359 (N.H. 1997); Leandro v. State, 488 S.E.2d 249, 255 (N.C. 1997); Abbeville Cty. Sch. Dist. v. State, 515 S.E.2d 535, 540 (S.C. 1999); Lake View Sch. Dist. No. 25 v. Huckabee, 91 S.W.3d 472, 485 (Ark. 2002); Carrollton-Farmers Branch Indep. Sch. Dist. v. Edgewood Indep. Sch. Dist., 826 S.W.2d 489, 527–28 (Tex. 1992).
19. Michael A. Rebell, "Poverty, 'Meaningful' Educational Opportunity, and the Necessary Role of the Courts," *North Carolina Law Review* 85 (2007): 1527.

20. These cases include Doe v. Superintendent of Sch., 653 N.E.2d 1088, 1096 (Mass. 1995); Kolesnick *ex rel.* Shaw v. Omaha Pub. Sch. Dist., 558 N.W.2d 807, 813 (Neb. 1997); Phillip Leon M. v. Greenbrier Cty. Bd. of Educ., 484 S.E.2d 909, 914, 916n12 (W.Va. 1996); State *ex rel.* G.S., 749 A.2d 902, 908 (N.J. Super. Ct. Ch. Div. 2000); *In re* R.M., 102 P.3d 868, 876 (Wyo. 2004); Clinton Municipal Separate Sch. Dist. v. Byrd, 477 So. 2d 237, 240 (Miss. 1985); Bd. of Trustees v. T.H., III, 681 So. 2d 110, 115–17 (Miss. 1996); King v. Beaufort Cty. Bd. of Educ., 704 S.E.2d 259 (2010). For a full discussion of these cases, see Derek W. Black, "Reforming School Discipline," *Northwestern University Law Review* 111 (2016).
21. For a full discussion, see Black, "Reforming School Discipline."
22. Ibid.
23. Daniel J. Losen and Russell Skiba, *Suspended Education: Urban Middle Schools in Crisis* (Montgomery, AL: Southern Poverty Law Center, 2010), 9, www.splcenter .org.

Chapter 7. Ensuring Quality Education through Discipline

1. Russell J. Skiba, Ada Simmons, Lori Staudinger, Marcus Rausch, Gayle Dow, and Renae Feggins, "Consistent Removal: Contributions of School Discipline to the School-Prison Pipeline," paper presented at the Harvard Civil Rights Conference School to Prison Pipeline Conference, Cambridge, MA, 2003.
2. M. Karega Rausch and Russell J. Skiba, "The Academic Cost of Discipline: The Relationship between Suspension/Expulsion and School Achievement," paper presented at the Annual Meeting of the American Educational Research Association, Montreal, Canada, April 2005, 16–18.
3. Ibid., 16.
4. Ibid., 20.
5. Linda M. Raffaele Mendez, Howard M. Knoff, and John M. Ferron, "School Demographic Variables and Out-of-School Suspension Rates: A Quantitative and Qualitative Analysis of a Large, Ethnically Diverse School District," *Psychology in the Schools* 39 (2002): 259–77.
6. Ibid., 273.
7. Amalia G. Cuervo, Joan Lees, and Richard Lacey, *Toward Better and Safer Schools* (Washington DC: National School Boards Association, 1984), 9.
8. Richard Arum, *Judging School Discipline: The Crisis of Moral Authority* (Cambridge, MA: Harvard University Press, 2003), 156.
9. Ibid., 182. In fairness to Arum, his conclusions about the initial causal problems and final solutions in discipline are, in some respects, far different from those in this book. Arum argues that courts themselves made discipline worse. Court intervention made the process more adversarial and deprived school administrators of the moral authority necessary to run effective discipline systems.
10. See, e.g., Xin Ma and J. Douglas Willms, "School Disciplinary Climate: Characteristics and Effects on Eighth Grade Achievement," *Alberta Journal of Educational*

Research 50, no. 2 (2004): 180–82 (finding that students' perceptions of their school's disciplinary climate were significantly correlated to student achievement across subjects).

11. James Earl Davis and Will J. Jordan, "The Effects of School Context, Structure, and Experiences on African American Males in Middle and High School," *Journal of Negro Education* 63, no. 4 (1994): 581 ("teacher absences had the strongest association with Black male achievement").

12. Rausch and Skiba, "Academic Cost of Discipline," 22.

13. Russell J. Skiba, Reece L. Peterson, and Tara Williams, "Office Referrals and Suspension: Disciplinary Intervention in Middle Schools," *Education and Treatment of Children* 20, no. 3 (1997): 295–315.

14. Ibid.

15. Dona M. Kagan, "How Schools Alienate Students at Risk: A Model for Examining Proximal Classroom Variables," *Education Psychologist* 25 (1990): 107.

16. These calculations are based on the Office for Civil Rights' 2011 Civil Rights Data Collection, ocrdata.ed.gov.

17. For further analysis of this data, see Derek W. Black, "Reforming School Discipline," *Northwestern University Law Review* 111 (2016).

18. Ibid.

19. Shi-Chang Wu, William Pink, Robert Crain, and Oliver Moles, "Student Suspension: A Critical Reappraisal," *Urban Review* 14, no. 4 (1982): 245–303.

20. Ibid., 255–56.

21. Mendez, Knoff, and Ferron, "School Demographic Variables," 273–74.

22. Jason P. Nance, "Dismantling the School-to-Prison Pipeline: Tools for Change," *Arizona State Law Journal* 48 (2016).

23. Robert B. Cairns and Beverley D. Cairns, "The Natural History and Developmental Functions of Aggression," in *Handbook of Developmental Psychopathology*, 2nd ed., ed. Arnold J. Sameroff, Michael Lewis, and Suzanne M. Miller (New York: Kluwer Academic / Plenum, 2000), 403–29; J. Ron Nelson, Gregory J. Benner, Kathleen Lane, and Benjamin W. Smith, "Academic Achievement of K–12 Students with Emotional and Behavioral Disorders," *Exceptional Children* 71 (2004): 59–73; Robert W. Roeser and Jacquelynne S. Eccles, "Schooling and Mental Health," in Sameroff, Lewis, and Miller, *Handbook of Developmental Psychopathology*, 135–56; João Lopes, "Intervention with Students with Learning, Emotional, and Behavior Disorders: Why Do We Take So Long to Do It?" *Education and Treatment of Children* 28 (2005): 345–60; Vern Jones and Louise Jones, *Comprehensive Classroom Management: Creating Communities of Support and Solving Problems*, 7th ed. (New York: Pearson Education, 2004); James K. Luiselli, "Focus, Scope, and Practice of Behavioral Consultation to Public Schools," *Child and Family Behavior Therapy* 24 (2002): 5–21; Heather E. Sterling-Turner, Sheri L. Robinson, and Susan M. Wilczynski, "Functional Assessment of Distracting and Disruptive Behaviors in the School Setting," *School Psychology Review* 30 (2001): 211–26.

24. Valerie E. Lee and Anthony S. Bryk, "A Multilevel Model of the Social Distribution of High School Achievement," *Sociology of Education* 62, no. 3 (1989): 172.

25. Ibid., 185 (abbreviation deleted).

26. Xin and Willms, "School Disciplinary Climate," 185.

27. Richard Arum and Melissa Velez, "Class and Racial Differences in U.S. School Disciplinary Environments," in *Improving Learning Environments: School Discipline and Student Achievement in Comparative Perspective,* ed. Richard Arum and Melissa Velez (Stanford, CA: Stanford University Press, 2012), 298.

28. Ibid., 302.

29. Gary Orfield, *Reviving the Goal of an Integrated Society: A 21st Century Challenge* (Los Angeles: Civil Rights Project / Proyecto Derechos Civiles, 2009), 14, http://civilrightsproject.ucla.edu.

30. Arum and Velez, "Class and Racial Differences," 302.

31. Ibid.

32. Ibid., 317.

33. 678 A.2d 1267 (Conn. 1996).

34. Vergara v. State, No. BC484642, 2014 WL 6478415 (Cal. Super. Aug. 27, 2014), *rev'd* No. 8258589, 2016 WL 1503698 (Cal. Ct. App. 2016).

35. Derek W. Black, "The Constitutional Challenge to Teacher Tenure," *California Law Review* 104 (2016).

36. Rose v. Council for Better Educ., Inc., 790 S.W.2d 186, 211 (Ky. 1989).

37. 119 N.J. 287, 375 (1990).

38. Ibid., 373

39. Abbott v. Burke, 495 A.2d 376, 388 (N.J. 1985).

40. See also Black, "Reforming School Discipline."

Conclusion

1. J.D.B. v. North Carolina, 564 U.S. 261 (2011); Safford Unified Sch. Dist. No. 1 v. Redding, 557 U.S. 364 (2009); Roper v. Simmons, 543 U.S. 551 (2005).

INDEX

Abbott by Abbott v. Burke, 194
Aberrant behavior, 42
Academic failure, 152, 167, 193
Academic performance, 10, 16
Achievement, 10, 14, 15, 16, 19, 78, 79,
    89, 167, 180, 182, 183, 184, 195, 228n24;
    academic, 15, 16, 19, 78, 79, 89, 167,
    181, 183, 184, 187, 189, 191, 193, 194, 195,
    198, 199, 203, 220n22, 227n23; gap,
    13, 14, 89, 187–91, 195, 197; school's
    discipline rate, 14, 15, 167, 180, 181, 182,
    184, 187, 195, 196, 197, 213n32, 226n10,
    228n27
Achievement gap, 13, 14, 89, 183, 187–91,
    195–97
Adequacy lawsuits, 174, 196, 204
Administrators, 6, 40, 41, 54, 69, 83, 88,
    91, 102, 107, 165, 198, 211n10, 226n9;
    benevolent, 49, 53, 56
Advancement Project, 14, 44, 212n22,
    214n40
Adversarial, 38, 40, 41, 42, 49, 56, 215n43,
    216n46, 226n9
Affirmative duty, 53, 141, 142, 144
African American students, 12, 13, 17,
    32, 33, 35, 36, 37, 45, 53, 81, 96, 183,
    185, 186, 187, 188, 189, 190, 197, 213n31;
    arrests, 36; discipline rates, 13, 32, 34,
    35, 37, 190; law enforcement referrals,
    96; out-of-school suspension, 36, 90;
    school misconduct criminalization,
    33, 34, 83, 84; suspension rates, 12, 13,
    17, 35, 36, 89, 90, 187, 188
Alcohol, 4, 5, 44, 54, 103, 104, 105, 106, 107,
    108, 116, 117, 129, 177

Alternative schools/programs, 84, 175,
    176, 179
American Civil Liberties Union, 208
American Psychological Association, 150,
    223n26
Arrests, 11, 43, 46, 82, 95, 97, 212n22
Arum, Richard, 16, 41, 73, 75, 182–83,
    189–90, 195, 197, 213n36, 228n27
Assessment, 10, 35, 60, 131, 149, 153,
    227n23
Automatic/mandatory penalties, 8, 13,
    46, 60, 148; meaningful hearing, 60;
    procedural due process, 19, 62, 66, 68,
    69, 70, 71, 73, 101, 107, 161, 176

Bad faith, 64, 106, 111
Benevolent administrators/disciplinar-
    ians, 29–32, 38, 40, 45, 46, 49, 52, 53, 56
Bias, 13, 18, 21, 36, 37, 45, 53, 63, 64, 65, 127;
    racial, 12, 13, 17, 23, 35, 36, 80, 81, 83, 84,
    85, 86, 97, 204
Blakely v. Washington, 123–25, 221n26
BMW v. Gore, 150–55, 159, 222n32
Bolling v. Sharpe, 113–14, 169–70, 225n4
"Broken windows" theory of policing, 42
Brown, Josie, ix, x, 149, 223n25
Brown, Michael, 95
Brown v. Board of Education, 32, 37, 38, 52,
    53, 168, 169, 170, 209, 225n3
Bryk, Anthony, 188, 228n24
Bush, President George H. W., 172
*Butler v. Rio Rancho Public School Board
    of Education*, 139
"Bystanders, innocent," 78, 129–35, 198,
    207

189, 206; courts' involvement in, 23, 24, 25, 38, 176, 178, 200, 201, 204, 205 207, 208; crisis, 18, 23, 29, 85, 98; discriminatory, 12, 36, 37, 45; disparities, 12, 13, 35, 37, 83, 85, 87, 90, 97, 187, 188; effective, 167; egregious, 207; excessive, 207; fair, 51, 67, 68; guidance, 87; harsh/draconian, 4, 6, 7, 14, 15, 16, 17, 19, 20, 22, 23, 33, 47, 26, 49, 58, 75, 77, 78, 80, 85, 86, 89, 90, 92, 94, 96, 97, 101, 102, 111, 112, 114, 120, 121, 122, 128, 129, 130, 136, 139, 142, 143, 149, 152, 154, 155, 156, 157, 175, 182, 183, 199, 203, 204, 205, 206, 207, 209; illegitimate, 66; improve, 191, 195; intent in, 137; irrational and biased, 18, 21, 46, 68, 76, 84, 116, 206, 207; as management tool, 38; no-nonsense, 90, 92; parents' right to, 29; permissible, 98; policy, 16, 17, 20, 26, 48, 51, 58, 68, 81, 82, 84, 85, 86, 91, 96, 101, 109, 115, 116, 125, 129, 160, 164, 167, 177, 199; practices, 59, 109, 149, 206; proactive and preventive approach to, 81–82; problems, 18, 98, 101, 183, 189, 197; process, 60, 69, 71; punitive, 17, 18, 23, 78, 87, 88, 198, 203, 204; rational, 101, 108, 109, 122, 150; reform, 20, 81, 82, 85, 86, 88, 97, 102, 166, 177, 191, 195, 201, 204, 205, 207; as resistance to desegregation, 32–42, 45; and school climate, 182, 183, 189, 191, 193, 195, 197, 199; as teaching tool, 29, 31, 38, 39, 40, 41, 45, 46, 49, 50, 87; unwarranted, 51; used to exclude undesirables, 46, 52, 79; zero tolerance as a general operating principle in, 43, 44, 163

Discriminatory discipline, 12, 36, 37, 45
Disorder, 183
Disorderly conduct, 43, 44, 45; environment, 180, 183
Disparate impact, 84

Disrespect, 7, 34, 37, 44, 86, 89, 91, 94, 112, 119, 155, 177, 178
Disruption, 7, 8, 65, 83, 86, 129, 136, 137, 155, 156, 159; disruptive students, 34, 75, 82, 129, 136, 155, 156, 159, 215n43; "habitually disruptive," 8, 40
Dress-code violations, 7, 89
Dropouts, 11, 78, 97, 212n17, 212n21, 224n36; rates, 10, 157
Drugs, 3, 6, 7, 8, 42, 44, 75, 116, 118, 119, 124, 128, 132, 142, 143, 144, 145, 177, 178, 218n2; counseling, 61; meaning of, 3, 117; offenders, 112; policies, 79; possession, 43; test, 61; use, 79
Due process, 18, 19, 21, 23, 24, 38, 40, 41, 45, 48, 49, 50, 52, 53, 54, 55, 56, 57, 58, 59, 62, 63, 64, 65, 66, 67, 68, 69, 70, 71, 72, 73, 74, 76, 77, 92, 98, 101, 105, 106, 107, 108, 109, 110, 111, 112, 113, 114, 115, 116, 118, 120,123, 125, 126, 130, 131, 134, 136, 137, 138, 139, 140, 142, 144, 145, 146, 147, 149, 150, 153, 155, 157, 158, 161, 163, 164, 170, 176, 205, 206, 207, 208, 215n43, 217n19, 218n34, 222n29, 222n36, 223n25, 224n49; analysis, 77, 108, 149; charades, 101; hearings, 46, 59, 64, 76, 101, 162; principles, 111, 138, 153; protections, 48, 49, 56, 93, 106, 160; rational, 101; requirements, 66; review, 69, 73, 101, 102, 108, 111; rights, 66, 74, 98, 105, 108, 113; traditions, 140; violations, 53, 115. *See also* Procedural due process rights; Substantive due process
Due Process Clause, 69, 109, 111, 114, 126–27, 150, 162, 164
Duncan, Arne (Secretary of Education), 11, 220n33

Eberhardt, Jennifer, 80–81, 219n7
Educational death penalty, 11, 23, 113, 143, 152

ABOUT THE AUTHOR

Derek W. Black is Professor of Law at the University of South Carolina School of Law, where his teaching and scholarship focus on educational equality and opportunity, civil rights, and constitutional law. His work is regularly published in leading law reviews and cited by litigants and courts. He offers daily commentary and analysis on the *Education Law Prof Blog*.